C000050817

FREDERICK WHIRLPOOL VC

FREDERICK WHIRLPOOL VC

THE HIDDEN VICTORIA CROSS

ALAN LEEK

Pen & Sword
MILITARY

First published in Australia in 2018 by Big Sky Publishing Pty Ltd

First published in Great Britain in 2019 by
Pen & Sword Military
An imprint of
Pen & Sword Books Ltd
Yorkshire - Philadelphia

ISBN 978 1 52675 910 8

A CIP catalogue record for this book is available from the British Library.

Printed and bound in England by TJ International

Pen & Sword Books Ltd incorporates the Imprints of Pen & Sword Books Archaeology, Atlas, Aviation, Battleground, Discovery, Family History, History, Maritime, Military, Naval, Politics, Railways, Select, Transport, True Crime, Fiction, Frontline Books, Leo Cooper, Praetorian Press, Seaforth Publishing, Wharncliffe and White Owl.

For a complete list of Pen & Sword titles please contact

PEN & SWORD BOOKS LIMITED
47 Church Street, Barnsley, South Yorkshire, S70 2AS, England
E-mail: enquiries@pen-and-sword.co.uk
Website: www.pen-and-sword.co.uk

or

PEN AND SWORD BOOKS
1950 Lawrence Rd, Havertown, PA 19083, USA
E-mail: Uspen-and-sword@casematepublishers.com
Website: www.penandswordbooks.com

Contents

For my grandchildren, Coen, Liam, April, Chloe, Rhys,
Millie and Evie. May they ever know peace.

Foreword

Frederick Whirlpool, The Hidden Victoria Cross is a detailed look at an intriguing man. Whirlpool has long been known as the first soldier in Australian uniform to be presented with the Victoria Cross. It was also known that he was fighting for the British East India Company's army when he earned the medal during the Indian Mutiny of 1857-58, and that Whirlpool was not his real name. Myth and error have surrounded almost all other aspects of his life.

In this book, Alan Leek attempts to set the record straight. He uses letters from the family, as well as official records and newspapers, to determine more about the man's early life under his original name of Humphrey James. As the author points out, the story has been difficult to put together, in large part because Whirlpool himself worked hard to obscure his origins and distance himself from his Victoria Cross. The medal was a burden to him, as were the lifelong injuries from the battle in which he earned it. The man behind that medal has remained in the shadows—until now.

Having migrated to Victoria in 1859 or 1860, Frederick Whirlpool joined the Hawthorn and Kew Volunteer Rifles. It was while wearing the uniform of this unit that he was invested with the Victoria Cross for his brave actions in India. Presented to him by Lady Barkly, the Victorian governor's wife, it was the first Victoria Cross presented publicly in Australia, and the first presented to a man in an Australian uniform.

To place the story of any individual soldier into the context of his time is a great challenge for military historians. This is even more true when researching the soldiers of the British Empire. Whirlpool's world-spanning career was not unusual—British soldiers were sent to all parts of the Empire. These soldiers left fragmented records in each place they visited, records that often pose as many questions as they answer. Leek, a former policeman, has brought his considerable detective skills to bear in writing this book.

Today, the Australian War Memorial is the custodian of Frederick Whirlpool's Victoria Cross. It is displayed proudly in our Hall of Valour, beneath the Tomb of the Unknown Australian Soldier. There, the Memorial also commemorates the actions of the 100 Australian Victoria Cross recipients. Whirlpool's story is distinct from those other recipients, and yet it too is a quintessentially Australian story. We witness in his story the same self-effacing bravery, the struggle to adapt to civilian life, and the burden of fame.

Frederick Whirlpool, The Hidden Victoria Cross shows the strength of the connections between the nineteenth-century Australian colonies and the rest of the British Empire. It places Whirlpool into the broader context of his family, his service, and the world in which he lived. It is an admirable contribution to Australian military history.

The Honourable Dr Brendan Nelson AO
Director
Australian War Memorial

PREFACE

From the deep recesses of my earliest memories, two things are clear. First, the discomforting itch of clothing salvaged from surplus army uniforms; rough woollen cloth made to be durable in tough times, woven from the fleece of crossbred sheep, which at other times might have been used for carpets. In the immediate aftermath of the Second World War, nothing went to waste and my brothers and I were kitted like mini soldiers. Though I did not understand the reasoning behind the need to wear this discomforting rig, it seems that I always knew what khaki was and there was plenty of it to be had from burgeoning army surplus stores.

The second enduring memory is of visits to my paternal grandparent's well ordered and modest home, and the splayed oak framed photograph of a young soldier, open faced and smiling slightly at the camera. The faux timber-grained mount, sepia toned and set against a gilt sleeve, lent gravitas to the image as it stared down from its prime position overlooking the dining table.

In front of the tiled hearth of the living room, I lay on the soft sheepskin rug and examined the 'dead man's penny', a British Commonwealth Memorial Plaque to the fallen, set in a honey coloured oak shield. I would later learn to read its inscription; 'Thomas Henry Markham', my grandmother's eldest brother. I don't recall my grandmother ever speaking of him, but he was always present. His memory had been charged to the women of the family and his mother had his photograph enlarged and framed, in a masculine manner, without mawkishness. She also had the 'penny' mounted for timeless display, and sadly maintained his medals and the badges she wore, to show that she had sons serving at the front. Prominent among the campaign medals was the Military Medal for bravery, earned several months before he was blown to pieces at Ypres, in 1917, and *passed out of the sight of men'*. Also safely lodged was the letter from his chaplain, advising of his death. These items were eventually passed to me, though I was never told of the actions that earned him his bravery award or those that led to his death. Nor did I understand the significance of the medals, apart from the Military Medal, which spoke for itself.

Somehow I knew they were important, for these treasures instilled in me the need to ensure that his memory was maintained.

Growing up in the post Second World War period with crisp black and white films, some of them overt propaganda, cemented in a young mind some understanding of conflict, sacrifice and heroism. Overriding all of this was the understanding of and reverence for the Victoria Cross and its recipients. I grew up knowing the name of Frank Partridge VC and I mourned with the rest of Australia, his tragic death, almost twenty years after the end of hostilities. Albert Chowne VC, Edward Kenna VC and John Edmondson VC, were also household names. Who could not have known of Sir Arthur Roden Cutler VC, who would become Governor of New South Wales? It was also a time when Second World War servicemen were still reintegrating into their old lives, some with great difficulty, and even World War I veterans were plentiful. I wondered what might have been the story of my mathematics teacher, part of whose jaw had been shot away. He smelt strongly of liquor and cigarettes and had little patience with children, or perhaps, life. His challenges, already huge, must have been exacerbated by my inability at algebra and maths generally. We fought our own battles — he winning by gruffly forcing my retreat into the corridor for each lesson, which in no way assisted my struggle. My early life was filled with the wonder and mystery of those who had served.

After stumbling over the name Whirlpool VC in pursuit of other material, I was intrigued by it and what I deemed to be his initials. Searching further, I discovered that this man, Frederick Whirlpool, had indeed earned the Victoria Cross almost 160 years earlier, in India, during the suppression of the Sepoy Mutiny. I learnt that his Victoria Cross had been presented to him in Melbourne in 1861, and that he had been a schoolteacher and an unsuccessful applicant for the police force there. After that, the trail grew thinner, fading into decades of guesswork and falsehoods as researchers failed to find the truth. This is precisely what Whirlpool wanted. He would not have wanted his story told.

One glaring omission was that he lacked a monument, which might commemorate this member of an elite band of brothers, whose deeds earned him the highest recognition for valour. I knew his resting ground well, though it seemed to be just another repository of those whose varied lives had been lived. I must have passed it thousands of times, without a second thought of what might be hidden there. Little did I know that of all the stories that might reside there, this one had fallen to me to reveal.

My initial fear was that a headstone had once settled above his grave in the small Presbyterian cemetery in South Windsor, but had been destroyed by natural forces or wanton vandalism. Experience of vandalism of the monuments and grave markers of police who had died gallantly at the hands of murderers came to mind. These men were remembered for a time, but lesser beings had seen fit to desecrate memorials to their courage. I feared the worst for Frederick Whirlpool's memory and began my search for answers. Answers I was never intended to find.

INTRODUCTION

Born more than 185 years ago and having deliberately and assiduously hidden his life, Frederick Whirlpool, whose VC was the first pinned to the breast of a man in an Australian uniform, has piqued wide interest since. Guesswork and supposition have been fruits of those attempts, not least because Whirlpool laid a trail to confuse. That, combined with the passage of time, lost records, mistaken recollection and wrong assumptions, provided only a sketch of his life; an outline built on falsehoods, which have flowed into myth. Recent claims that he was born in Liverpool, (he had claimed it himself) are without basis. He was said to be an only child, crippled by migraine, which affected his mood and afflicted his relationships. A thin account of how he earned the Victoria Cross was known. Its presentation in Victoria was well recorded, but more detail has been overlooked. His life in New South Wales was reclusive after his teaching career faltered, and it has been claimed that his only friend was a Scottish swagman who called on him occasionally. One claim that he was an alcoholic was based on one instance of his falling from grace while a teacher. That his father was a major in the British army is still asserted. He's been given the name Conker and it is said he lived off charity. Yet all these claims, and more, are false. His mysterious life can now be revealed.

Frederick Whirlpool was born, Humphrey James, in County Carlow, in 1831, one of the eight children of Humphrey and Lavinia James. He and his family were firmly embedded in Ireland, particularly the County Louth township of Dundalk. The precise actions, for which he was awarded the VC — previously obscured and concealed by his reticence and low social rank — can now be fully revealed thanks to extant records and letters. Arriving in Australia and subsequently exposed to the glare of fame when his cross was invested, he withdrew more, and covered his tracks to avoid the limelight. Nothing was known of his movements between his teaching in Victoria, his attempt to join the police force there and his failed teaching positions in New South Wales and their aftermath. Hitherto unknown sources have revealed much about these movements and their outcomes. The reason for him declining a position in the Victoria police is explained. Rich veins have revealed his life in New South Wales, filling gaps including his time in the New South Wales police and subsequent imprisonment.

On joining the Honourable East India Company army in 1854, Humphrey James claimed to have been born in Liverpool. It is here the subterfuge began. He was born in Ireland to a liberal Quaker-Catholic family. Existing letters from his siblings, his own letters and other records were located in the State archives of New South Wales and Victoria, and helped unravel his past. Previously untapped letters of fellow soldiers provided insight into the murderous mutiny campaign.

The Indian Mutiny was horrific and bloody with abuses on both sides. British retribution was as severe as it was extreme, obdurate and cruel. For the most part the Central India campaign under Major-General Sir Hugh Rose, seems to have been restrained, but only when measured against actions elsewhere, including the retaking of Delhi. Rose's revenge, too, was swift and unforgiving and no less horrific because it was worse elsewhere. During the rebellion prisoners mostly were tried and savagely executed, or summarily slaughtered. Only towards the end of the campaign were excesses more subdued. Where I have looked at possible abuses, I have not attempted to sheet home blame, but to try and fathom what might have turned the mind of an ordinary soldier.

The Whirlpool VC was purchased from A.H. Baldwin & Sons, London, in 1963 for £550, by Denys Croll, a New South Wales teacher, medal enthusiast and numismatist, who believed it to be the first presented in Australia. This work traces the passage of his Victoria Cross from the time it was invested, its return to England, on to South Africa, back to England and finally back to Australia.

The VC was won by Whirlpool, a private of the Honourable East India Company's 3rd Bombay European Regiment, for his actions in 1858, at the siege and taking of the city, fort and palace of Jhansi and a month later at the fort of Lohari, where he was near-fatally wounded.

This book tells the previously unknown story of an enigmatic man whose life of heroism, suffering, sadness and loss was concealed by his own reticence and by his having no descendant to keep his memory alive. Given his time again, he might take some comfort that this lifting of the veil is no hagiography, or panegyric. He might also be pleased that his cross takes its rightful place among others in the Hall of Valour at the Australian War Memorial, Canberra. As Private Frederick Whirlpool VC, he remains in the Victoria Cross Register. As Humphrey James, Irish born Australian, soldier, teacher, militiaman, policeman and recluse, he now takes *his* place too, in the rich mosaic of history.

CHAPTER ONE

———

EVENING SHADOWS

'Our sins, like to our shadowes,
When our day is in its glorie scarce appear:
Towards our evening how great and monstrous they are!'

Sir John Suckling
'Aglaura' 1638

The old man lived alone; by preference, not necessity or circumstance. He had withdrawn from the world 30 years earlier, kept his own counsel and mostly shunned society. Neighbours considered his behaviour as simply eccentric, and accommodated his foibles, knowing he had contributed as a soldier and schoolteacher. Most were unaware he had once known fame, across the colonies, in India and in Britain, or that he had found public adulation abhorrent and had run from its bitter taste.

A hand hewn slab hut at McGrath's Hill on the outskirts of Windsor, served as his home. Part of the third European settlement on mainland Australia, it nestled in the abundantly fertile Hawkesbury Valley, at the foot of the Great Australian Divide. Two rooms of slab, some wattle and daub and a shingle roof were adequate and familiar to the times, one of many such settler huts in the area. One room was partitioned to take his cot and palliasse, which he called his charpoy, though his use of bat, or Indian soldier's slang, would be restrained to deter the inquisitive. The remaining space housed the warming fireplace, which also served as cooking hearth. A small vernacular table, which he had fashioned from packing cases, a rough bodger chair, a table he used for sewing and the detritus of everyday living were his only adornments. The floor was of packed earth, gathered from ant nests and rammed home. It provided an earthy glow to the interior, which was yellowed by smoke from the hearth and his pipe. He was not a man in need of easy comfort. His rudimentary, but comfortable early life in Ireland, the hardship of the great famine and years in the East India Company Army had taught him not to be self-indulgent or wasteful. The 'lean-to' clinging precariously to the rear of the structure and held upright by the stacked woodheap, served as a wash room where he could ensure that he and his limited clothing could be cleaned, in keeping with his proud appearance. Beyond that was his rich loam plot for vegetables. He had plenty of time to garden and there was not a weed to be found. He enjoyed his patch and its bounty, but he did not own the land on which he lived. Years earlier, he had lived in nearby Pitt Town, at a place then known as North Rocks, on land belonging to John Dick Smith, a local merchant, who had allowed him use of it *quid pro quo* or at least at a peppercorn rent. He would never live in the shadow of charity. But he had moved closer to the more populated McGrath's Hill at the urging of Smith, who saw his ageing friend in need of ready amenity, including regular deliveries of goods he was no longer able to gather for himself.

It was clear life and his past disappointed him, no matter in what guise he lived it. But his time in India as Frederick Whirlpool had been the most agonising, both physically and mentally. He had told his sister, Deborah, in a recent letter, that he was damned and destined to roast, believing that there was no alternative to his descent into Hell.

His letters, the first in sixteen years to his family in England and America, were an attempt to right his abandonment of those who loved him. Deborah's reply scolded him as only sisters can and beseeched him not to be so reckless with his words. Reckless. Not silly or overstated, but reckless, in case he might be right. Raised in a solid though not pious family, Deborah nonetheless feared an omnipotent Almighty. The old man would never read the letter.

He had taken to his bed early as was his wont. Frugality had no need for candles or lamps, when daylight could facilitate reading. But he was an avid reader and considered well-read by the few who knew him.

As Whirlpool slept, Windsor, not much more than a mile away, was alive with anticipation of a total eclipse of the moon. Nearer still, John Tebbutt, a respected Fellow of the Royal Astronomical Society, was at his telescope, making notes. It was to be the first total eclipse in 19 years and if the weather permitted, valuable observations would be made. Tebbutt had advised the community of the imminent event and gave details of its expected timing on 24 June, 1899. It had been raining for days but the sky gave every appearance that the cloud cover was thinning and the spectacle would be enjoyed.

This was a timely diversion from the clamorous and sometimes rancorous debate, which had divided the community and the colonies ahead of federation. It had come to a head just two days before with the referendum on the Commonwealth Constitution Bill. Supporters of the bill — 'billites' — and opponents — 'anti-billites' — were among more than 300 people gathered outside the newspaper office of the *Windsor and Richmond Gazette*, blocking the street to watch the referendum tallies conveyed by telegraph from Sydney, then displayed on blackboards and calico screens.[1] The 'billites' won an overwhelming victory clearing the way for Australia to be declared a nation 18 months later — January 1, 1901, the start of a new century ushering in a new nation. This was the first time a nation's constitution had been decided by its people by way of referendum, or at least by some of its people. Women had been enfranchised in South Australia and Western Australia, but would not gain the vote in New South Wales for another three years. Of the 116 electoral rights issued in the country town of Lismore, six were granted to aboriginal men in a foretaste of what would take their people another 60 or more years to fully achieve.[2] How sweet the irony, had the referendum been carried by six votes. But it was not to be a close result. A Sydney Morning Herald correspondent reported from the Hawkesbury that, 'The voting passed off quietly here and very little enthusiasm was displayed. The anti-billites were very demonstrative, but as the Sydney returns continued to give a large majority for the bill they became somewhat silent. Federalist's were jubilant when it became known that victory was assured.'[3]

With the vote of the people emphatically in favour of the bill, a new focus was welcome and the community prepared to take in the astronomical event. As the moon slowly melted into Earth's shadow the town was thrown into total darkness to the wonderment of most and confusion to others who had lost their way in their own gardens, as the *Gazette* gleefully reported. Tebbutt's prediction proved sound that the eclipse would allow a beautiful and spectacular view of the Milky Way, not normally visible when the moon was full. The transit of the moon into the shadow of Earth was not a quick affair. It would take hours for the light to return; to those to whom it would return.

* * *

The delivery man from Dick Brothers store in Windsor, had called in his dray that morning with provisions and to take a new order, as he had done two days earlier and would do so again the following day. The deliveries mostly were made twice weekly with forward orders given to the delivery man as required. It was an unhurried arrangement and the purchases rarely exceeded three or four shillings, and varied little, although Whirlpool had indulged in a new sixpenny pipe several weeks earlier. His needs were meagre and delivery days were his main contact with the outside world, though he didn't dally and had little time for small talk. His account would be settled quarterly in line with his pensions and when he visited his bank in Windsor. The delivery man would be the last person to see him alive.

Despite his isolation, he maintained a friendship with John Dick Smith, his landlord and proprietor of Dick Brothers' Windsor store. Smith was a native of Glasgow, many years younger than the old man and a devout and active member of the Presbyterian Church. Part of the great 19th century Scottish diaspora, he had come to New South Wales to work for his uncles, eventually buying their store from them. He took an active interest in the old recluse and knew more than anyone about him, but still only what the old man allowed him to know. Smith's interest would provide the thread that prevented the old man's story from fading into oblivion. He knew the old man as Humphrey James and knew he had once been known as Frederick Whirlpool. He knew Whirlpool had been awarded the Victoria Cross, but not the manner in which it had been earned. James told him he had lodged it and his Indian Mutiny medal with the pensions office in Sydney. Smith later provided information to the *Windsor and Richmond Gazette* to enable the observation that he was, '...an educated and well-informed man, having been, when in the service, an Army schoolmaster for a portion of his military career. During the Indian Mutiny, he distinguished himself by his valour, and he obtained the highest prize a soldier strives for — the "Victoria Cross". Different to most old soldiers, it was difficult to get him to talk of his achievements — so says one who knew him well.'[4] Not about to let the old man's achievements go unnoticed, Smith would provide further information to the local newspaper as if to ensure the community appreciated that this reclusive eccentric's life had been worthwhile, indeed substantial.

The cold night drew in and could not be kept from the hut. The old man rugged himself as the fire burnt down, and slumbered, drifting in and out of insomnious sleep. Insomnia had been his burden for many years. He knew sleep shone a light on the immensity and monstrousness of his experiences. He hadn't felt well for days and had not been up to the walks and calisthenics that he regularly undertook to maintain fitness. He was proud of his straight carriage and ready gait, despite being just over three weeks short of his sixty-eighth birthday. But time was catching up.

No-one can know the memories that visited him, in sleep or awake, but it is clear that Whirlpool was a troubled man. His belief in a fiery eternity might have been influenced by the heat of battle, rough justice and personal sacrifices he had not expected to offer when joining the Honourable East India Company Army, and being immersed in the suppression in what would become known as the Indian Mutiny. He had played a major part in that conflict as a lowly ranked private of the 3rd Bombay European Regiment, under the command of Major-General Sir Hugh Rose and his Central India Field Force.

This night was to be his last. His belief that he was damned and destined for eternal torment was strong; as strong as 19th century religious teachings could make it. Gehenna had been calling him for more than 40 years. He fell back into unconsciousness and as life ebbed from his frail and damaged body, his extremities began to discolour and darken, as if in concert with this darkest of nights when the moon dipped and was lost.

Dick Brothers' delivery dray arrived the next morning. The driver hammered on the flimsy door but failing to rouse the old man, called his name. When no answer broke the chill silence, he feared the worst and ran for help to the nearby Killarney Inn, known as Carey's Hotel after its popular licensee. With Carey, he returned to the hut, forcing the door to find the old man dead in his bed. There was no sign of trauma and his lifeless skin now highlighted the elongated weals of old scar tissue on his face, neck and head, where they were not hidden by the wisp of his mutton-chop whiskers. What couldn't be seen was the silver plate, which had clasped his shattered and trepanned skull in place since he was a young man.[5]

Police were summoned and Constable James Kell Tate rode out to the hut. He briefly interviewed the delivery man and Carey then entered the hut where experience told him the dark discolouration to the old man's ears, throat and fingertips were telltale signs of heart failure. Tate arranged for the local undertaker to collect the body. Undertaker Richard Dunstan's enterprise was displayed in his advertising, providing a glimpse at the balance between dying and the day to day needs of the living in the 19th century colony as he juggled the roles of, 'Builder and Undertaker. Wall-papering and House-painting done.'[6]

An inquest was held at Carey's hotel four days later, with coroner, James Bligh Johnston finding that Humphrey James, also known as Frederick Whirlpool, had died as a result of 'a failure of the heart to action ...' Dr. Gibson had certified death, obviating a post-mortem examination and sparing the old man a final indignity. James was also found to have clothing, a bed of little value and £160.5.8. deposited in the savings bank at Windsor.[7]

Constable Tate interviewed John Dick Smith, who had been distressed to learn from his cart-man of his old friend's death. His information assisted Tate in completing his report to the Curator of the Estate of Deceased Persons, as James had died intestate. The report informed the curator that Humphrey James was otherwise known as Frederick Whirlpool and that he was an Imperial Army pensioner. It indicated that he was born in Ireland and had not married. A letter found in the hut indicated that he had brothers, Josiah James in Leeds, and Samuel James in Pennsylvania. Other contents of the hut were assiduously listed and a small iron boiler, saucepan, frying pan, bucket, bottles of salad oil, tins of milk, a billy can and six dozen of bottles were deemed worthy of mention. They would later be sold by the curator for ten shillings. Seven shillings and sixpence in cash and a Bank of New South Wales passbook were also found. The report noted briefly that the deceased was said to have left a Victoria Cross Medal at the Pension Office in Sydney.[8]

In the absence of anyone else, John Dick Smith assumed the role of executor, planning the funeral and seeking to notify James' known family. His serious approach and Scottish tenacity were called to the fore when dealing with the office of the Curator of Intestate Estates in Sydney. He wrote to the curator on 2 August, 1899 and was refused information, which would enable him to write to James' relatives. Letters passed back and forth, the curator ceding, enabling Smith to write to Samuel James in Pittsburgh, Pennsylvania.[9]

In late November 1899, Samuel James replied, thanking Smith for his many kindnesses and for attending to the obsequies of his late brother. He advised that James was survived by brother Josiah in Bradford, England, a sister, Mrs. W Prescott of Dublin [Dinah]; a sister, Mrs. Samuel Manifold of Liverpool [Deborah]; a brother Benjamin 'who was out in the Indian Mutiny with Humphrey, after which they never met again.' Benjamin had returned to England before leaving for the United States, serving two terms there in the army and was now a pensioner in Patton, California. He advised that their father had died in 1875 and their mother some years later. He continued. 'I have not the slightest recollection of his personal appearance, he having joined the army and left home when I was only a baby, or little more. Another brother (Tom) did the same thing almost, only he went to sea and died in Rio de Janeiro, Brazil, and I have practically never seen him either. I have in my pocket Humphrey's last letter to his relations, written to my brother Josiah; it is on two leaves ... He began it on the 31st January last and finished it on the 4th May, so you see he took his time about it, and he has given us a pen picture of himself, as well as he could, and told us all about his habits and about your man bringing him his weekly supply of groceries; what exercise he took, calisthenics, and moderate walking; said he was as straight in carriage as he ever had been, and we were congratulating ourselves on the fact that he was going to be a regular correspondent and more sociable, when now it is all over and that was the last flare up of the expiring embers and he is gone.

I do not know why he would not go back to England and live within reach of his friends and relatives; why he should choose such a lonesome life is a mystery to me. I know I could not stand it. But then I am married and have a family, and (as far as I know) he was a bachelor. I hope that I shall meet him in the sweet bye and bye, and if I do we certainly will have to be introduced.'

Sadly, Samuel then asked, 'Had Humphrey no intimate friends; did no-one call at his lonely shanty to talk to him; what did he do when he wanted company; did he ever go to church; was he profane, pleasant or irritable? ... I will send the newspaper to England so that my brother Josiah and sister Deborah, can read how he died, all alone, without a friend near to say a cheering word, or even help him to his couch to die. I wonder if he was in bed when he died, or did he fall to the floor? It is a foolish question to ask.'[10]

He concluded expressing a desire to have some little trinket of Humphrey's. The propitious Smith would have answered Samuel's questions but the only thing he had had of Humphrey's was a bank passbook, and that had gone to the curator.

James had agonised over his letters to his brother Josiah and sister Deborah. He started them stiltedly and worked on them over the ensuing months. It was not easy to take up the threads after sixteen years and he laboured over their form and content, setting them aside, often wondering if they were worth sending at all. Yet the familial call was strong and he persevered, despite his misgivings, to reattach himself to his siblings. He would not have known that his brother William had died in England on 27 February, less than a month after he began to write his letter of denouement. But his brother Josiah had written later, informing him of it. This news urged James to continue his efforts. He knew that time was running out for all of them. He enclosed his letter to Deborah with the one to Josiah. Deborah wasted no time in replying to him on 29 June, having no way of knowing that James had died five days earlier. Her letter reveals much about her, Humphrey, and the James family.

'70 Harlow St
Toxteth Park
Liverpool
29 June 1899

My dear Brother Humphrey

'Josiah enclosed your letter to me and I was very glad to see you are becoming more sociable and not holding aloof so much as you have done. Really when I think of it 16 years without writing to your brothers and sisters and we all so anxious to hear of your welfare. I can hardly forgive you and then when you did write you never asked how long was your Mother dead or was she dead. I thought it so strange of you, you see you were estranged from us and forgot all about us.

'I expect, and as my husband says you living out in the Bush and don't often see Men and Women like us, you have got into that careless way that you don't care for writing, and yet you are such a splendid writer and speller — in all that long letter I don't detect a single word spelled wrong. I had bad spelling. Humphrey you write strange, Don't be so reckless, don't write so reckless, don't talk about being damned and being roasted etc. etc. We all love you. Poor William used to cry when he spoke of you and he was always talking of you and doating and telling me the same old tales over and over again. I suppose Josiah has told you that he is gone to rest, died on 27th February this year. Josiah came down and was present at his funeral. I often go and see his grave. Poor William he was very stout, about 14 stone.

'Poor Mother died 7th March, 1890. She lived here with me 11 years and was bedridden nearly 12 months. She went so thin and worn and when she died I missed her awfully. I thought it a terrible trouble, but oh I had a worse one in store for me when my dear boy Humphrey 21 years old went to South America and died there in Ocos de Guatemala. You might ask, perhaps, what was he doing there. Well his fathers brother James Manifold was there and he went to him, thought he would make a little money and stay two years or so. He was there only two months when he died, it nearly finished me when I got the news. He was such a good boy and so thoughtful for me. Ah well it was a terrible blow for us. We have not got over it yet and it was two years last January 3rd. ... I am in this house 13 years so I am not fond of moving. I took Mother to Dundalk to bury her in Father's grave and Uncle Josiah's. Also Josiah helped me pay the expenses; it wasn't a great deal and it was her wish to be buried there. My dear Mother, if I was well off I would go and see it this summer but I can't. ... I spent a fortnight with Josiah and his wife in Leeds last summer they have a very lovely house and she is a very kind hearted woman. Their 2 sons fine young men were home on furlough from Gibraltar, they both came to L'pool and spent a week with us.

'Humphrey I wish you would come home and live amongst us, you who has enough to keep you comfortable would you be afraid of the sea trip. Tell me what you think of it, think it over. I think it would be nice to end your days in your own land. I would love to see brother Sams' wife and family and home. I was told he had a house fit for any gentleman to go into. He is a good fellow is Sam. ... I hope to hear how Ben is doing. Sam generally sends Ben his letters to Jos or me ... and now I think I have told you all the news but I would like to have a proper photo of you, not that likeness you drew in your letter.

'I remember what you were like, you were good looking. I am sorry you are a Mormon Humphrey. I am a Wesleyan Methodist. The Church is going to the dogs indeed ... and now I will close with love from your Affectionate Sister
Deborah Manifold'[11]

The letter remained at the Mulgrave Post Office near McGrath's Hill and James was never to learn of his extended family, or to bear his sister's mild wrath. Deborah's words hint at a close family and confirm the strong relationship she had with her mother, Lavinia. Lavinia's brother, Josiah Murphy, was buried in the Dundalk grave with her husband Humphrey and it was her wish to be buried there also. Theirs had been a happy marriage. That Deborah, her husband Samuel Manifold, and brother Josiah James, ensured that she was returned to Dundalk, in County Louth, also shows deep love, warmth and fidelity to family. How William showed a somewhat moribund affection towards the memory of his brother Humphrey, revealed old sorrows, which could not be consoled. Deborah maintained contact with her brothers, Samuel and Benjamin, in the United States and Josiah nearer to home. Her entreaties to Humphrey to return to the fold showed that time, distance and silence had not weakened her resolve to unite her siblings once again and the deep love and affection she had, and had always had for what was obviously a robust and happy family.

Shortly after, another letter to James arrived at the Mulgrave Post Office. It was from his brother Samuel, the youngest of the James children, who was about six years old when he last saw Humphrey, 45 years earlier. Writing on 15 July, 1899, three weeks after Humphrey's death, he said, 'My dear far distant Brother Humphrey. I had the pleasure, the great pleasure, this afternoon, of receiving a letter from Debby, a little one, enclosing a double sheet of foolscap from the Antipodes, closely written and containing one of the most wonderful uninspired dogma of religion and creed that I ever perused. Plague on it man, you ought to be here in Utah, in Salt Lake City; Australia is no place for you, who knows but you might succeed Joseph Smith or whoever is the president of that polygamous community, which is at the present time occupying a very prominent place in the eyes of the American people on account of the seat of the Senator elect from that State having been contested because he is a too much married man according to Christian ideas or at least the ideas of the would be decent people of this glorious republic.'

James had professed faith in the Church of Jesus Christ of the Latter Day Saints — the Mormons, a church founded by their prophet Joseph Smith — and Samuel was having none of it. He didn't hold back in his mildly jocular denunciation of the church. Moving on to their brother Benjamin, he said, '... so you noticed Ben's (what will I call it?) enthusiastic endorsement and acceptation of all that Swedenborg raved about, I sent Debby one of his letters in which he had embodied one of Swedenborg's books I guess and it scared her, and no wonder, and the next thing we knew he was in the military asylum, in a straight [sic] jacket and they are very suspicious of him yet, though he tells me he is as sane as any of his keepers or officers — now — yes my dear elder brother, you be careful of too much Swedenborg, or too much of the book of Mormon. Why Humphrey! You are real mean! You know that I was only a kid when you were a grown man and I have no more idea of what you and Tom looked like than I have of what the prophet Daniel did. I have Bill's picture taken alongside of myself — I have

Josiah's, lots of them and Ben's too and if you knew how I would like to have one of yours I think you would make an effort and try and squander the little sum that the photographer would demand please do I implore you ...'[12]

This letter too, expressed warmth and embraced the family. Samuel, in this and another letter written to authorities later, showed a gentle warmth for his siblings, particularly Benjamin, who had been committed to the military asylum, 'Patton', in California. He had served in India during the mutiny, and made his way back to England, when the Indian Army was disbanded. After emigrating to America he enlisted in the Union Army for five years on 2 July, 1860, and was attached to the 5th U.S. Infantry.[13] Though receiving a back injury at Fort Craig, New Mexico during an action against the Confederate Army, in February 1862, he was discharged at the expiry of his full term.[14] He re-enlisted on 13 November, 1866, giving his birthplace as Louth, Ireland. Attached to the 14th Infantry Regiment, he was subsequently engaged in the American Indian Wars.[15]

Samuel kept in touch with him and on at least one occasion travelled to California to bring him back to Pennsylvania 'for a change of air'. Whilst Samuel also gently chided Humphrey for his assertion that he had joined the Mormons, he wasn't to know that Humphrey had also claimed to have been a Quaker and a member of the Church of England. He seems to have eschewed his parents adherence to the Church of Ireland, or perhaps the church was represented in Australia through its tenuous affiliation with the Church of England. As will be seen later, James came under the influence of an evangelical preacher in Victoria who himself waxed and waned over creed. It seems that he was searching for something; perhaps absolution. It is certain that he was troubled by his past and sought comfort *Dei gratia*; by the grace of God, if not wholly, then by hedging his bets.

None of the James children were transfixed by religious dogma, leaving them able to bend to their individual leanings. This stemmed from their being products of mixed marriages of some complexity. Firstly, of their maternal grandparent's Catholic and Quaker union and later, their parent's Church of Ireland and Quaker mix.

On joining the Carlow Constabulary in 1822, Humphrey James, senior, patriarch of the family, was just 23 years old and 'native county' on his service record was unambiguously given as Carlow. Lavinia, also a native of Carlow, was born Lavinia Murphy to a Catholic father and a Quaker mother, whose name was Lecky. She adopted her place in the congregation of the Church of Ireland, in deference to her husband, when they married in Carlow in March 1826. What resulted was a loving and relaxed family, educated and free to question their faith. This was very much at odds with the accepted order of the day, which demanded that the children born to the union of a Catholic and a non-Catholic must be raised Catholic. The Murphy's ignored this edict and at least one daughter used her mother's maiden name to avoid the association of the Murphy name to Catholicism.[16] The James family was close knit, warm and imbued with a nurturing spirit, not unlike any family of its type at the time, but stronger and more liberal than most. The stuff that bound them was understood. Even Benjamin in one of his more lucid moments was to write to Samuel on 7 May, 1899, 'Deborah is a great sister to have. I tell you she is the jewel of the family ...'[17]

Deborah had become the glue of the family well prior to their mother's death. She maintained contact and gathered them in wherever she could. In this she followed her mother's lead when she had nursed her paralysed and invalided brother Josiah Murphy for three years before his death. Deborah nursed her mother and her eldest brother, William. She had taken in their sister Dinah too, and did what she could to support her in her fragile marriage. But what of this family? Where was it formed? How was it sustained and why did Humphrey James not only leave its fold, but change his name, his identity and obfuscate for the rest of his life?

CHAPTER TWO

———

CARLOW & DUNDALK

'His own parents,
He that father'd him, and she that had conceived
him in her womb, and birth'd him,
They gave of this child more of themselves than that;
They gave him afterward everyday - they became part of him.'

Walt Whitman 1819-1892
'There was a child went forth'
'Leaves of Grass' 1855

Humphrey James senior had been a Carlow county policeman for 14 years when the Irish Constabulary was formed in 1836, and county forces were amalgamated. He was posted to Dundalk with his wife and three surviving children. Their first child was William, who was born in County Carlow in October 1827. Thomas followed in 1829 and Humphrey two years later, again in County Carlow, on 17 July 1831. Susanna, born 1833 and Elizabeth, born 1835 did not survive infancy. Benjamin was born on 28 February 1838, after the move to Dundalk. Dinah followed in 1840 and Deborah in 1842. Josiah was born in 1845 and the last child, Samuel, in 1848. All but the first three surviving children were born in or near Dundalk. Josiah's birthplace is recorded as Mullacrew, several miles from Dundalk and it is possible that Humphrey senior had been posted there or that he and Lavinia were in Mullacrew for a major fair which followed Josiah's birth by a few days.

It was in Dundalk — at 28 Jocelyn Street — that the family took root and where the parents would spend their lives until Humphrey senior's death there on 15 September 1875, after nearly 50 years of marriage. Lavinia moved to Liverpool, into the care of Deborah and her husband Samuel Manifold for 11 years, but requested that upon her death she be returned to Dundalk to be buried with her husband and her brother Josiah Murphy,[1] in the grounds of St. Nicholas' Church of Ireland in Dundalk, known locally as the 'green church' due to its patinated spire.

Once a major market town, Dundalk in County Louth, is about 50 miles north of Dublin on a bay at the mouth of the Castletown River. For nearly twenty years, this picturesque seaport, garrison town was the home of the young Humphrey James who would, for a time, metamorphose into Frederick Whirlpool.

Pigot's 1824 'Directory of Ireland' describes Dundalk in great detail and paints a picture of a prosperous and busy port servicing the county. It noted that the town was 'pleasantly situated in a valley surrounded by rich enclosures, and backed by a bold outline of mountains … The houses are of stone or brick … The church is a fine ancient building and the inhabitants are much indebted to the present rector, the Rev. Elias Thackeray … The other public buildings are the charter school; the courts of justice and the new sessions house … The barracks are large enough to contain several troops of horse. The town also possesses a literary society of some eminence and the general fever hospital of the County of Louth. The principal manufactures here are those of salt, soap, candles and tanned leather … '[2]

By 1852, Thom's Irish Almanac claimed that Dundalk had a population of just under 11,000 people. The figure was 11 years old, but did indicate the population, allowing for some boundary changes, had declined by 3,500 in the four years from 1837 to 1841, and this, some years before the worst of the looming famine.[3]

Humphrey senior was well educated. His copperplate signature as a witness to Dinah's marriage on 8 May 1870, at St. Nicholas', attests to this. Membership of the established church provided him ample scholastic opportunity and, in turn, he ensured his children — girls and boys — got the best possible education. Later in life, Dinah and Deborah wrote haltingly and without style, perhaps the result of advancing age or the then commonplace practice of girls ending their studies earlier in life. The boys however, wrote well and stylishly with a steady hand and handsome copperplate. Education, it seems, was taken seriously in County Louth. Dundalk, in particular, was blessed with abundant schools, some of them accessible to the poor.

Humphrey junior claimed in later life he was schooled for four years at the Dundalk Institute, where the Incorporated Society, the school's administrator, covered his tuition costs. Humphrey senior could almost certainly not have afforded the fees for day scholarship (which his son undertook) let alone the £12 annual fee charged for boarders.[4] This, particularly so, given it is likely that sons William and Thomas were already enrolled. Benjamin also attended the Dundalk Institute, although much later than Humphrey who, most likely, showed sufficient promise at junior school to be offered one of the 30 free places at the Institute through the mid-1840's. This would have seen him learning there until 1847 or 1848.

The Dundalk Institute has a long history, beginning as a Charter School in 1739, funded by the Incorporated Society for Promoting Protestant Schools in Ireland. It still holds to the Protestant tradition, as the Dundalk Grammar School, to the present day. In 1835 the school was reorganised as the Dundalk Educational Institution, largely due to the efforts of the Reverend Elias Thackeray. It ceased operation during Word War 1 when the buildings were used to billet troops, who used the unsecured records of the school to start their fires, thus depriving us of any reference to Humphrey James or his brothers.[5]

A vignette of the Dundalk Institute is provided by the celebrated author and journalist, William Makepeace Thackeray in 'The Irish Sketchbook 1842' which he published in 1843 under the *nom de plume*, 'Mr. M. A. Titmarch.'[6] Thackeray appears to be in an agreeable frame of mind despite his personal travails, not least of which was the ruinous disability of his wife through post-natal depression that was to see her permanently confined. He was introduced to the Vicar of Dundalk, Elias Thackeray, to whom he was related and whose virtues he was to extol at length. (Another cousin, Edward Thackeray, would win the Victoria Cross as a lieutenant at the siege of Delhi in 1857). With the vicar, he visited the church with the green spire and sagely commented, 'The building being much injured by flame and time, some hundred years back was repaired, enlarged, and ornamented — as churches in those days were ornamented — and consequently lost a good deal of its Gothic character. There is a great mixture, therefore of old style and new style and no style: but, with all this the church is one of the most commodious and best appointed I have seen in Ireland.'

He noted that the vicar was responsible for repairs and had spent a considerable sum on them, tauntingly observing that from the income of the church, '... he has merely to maintain a couple of curates and a clerk and sexton, to contribute largely towards schools and hospitals, and relieve a few scores of pensioners of his own, who are fitting objects of private bounty.'

This evidence of support by the church for the Dundalk Educational Institution, adds to the impression that the school prospered under the directorship of Elias Thackeray, who ensured its success in educating many of the children of the county.

They then ' ... went from the church to a school, which has been long a favourite resort of the good vicar's; indeed to judge from the schoolmaster's books, his attendance there is almost daily, and the number of the scholars some two hundred. The number was considerably greater until the schools of the Educational Board were established, when the Roman Catholic clergymen withdrew many of their young people from Mr. Thackeray's establishment.'

At about the same time Humphrey James was a student at the school, his enrolment made easier by Catholic children being disbursed to other schools. Thackeray made no mention of free education, but outlined various costs of enrolment and enlarged upon the means of entry to the Institution, noting, 'Nor is there anything in the establishment savouring of the Dotheboys Hall ...[7] The Incorporated Society have abundant cause for believing that the introduction of Boarders into their Establishments has produced far more advantageous results to the public than they could, at so early a period, have anticipated; and that the election of boys to their Foundations only after a fair competition with others of a given district, has had the effect of stimulating masters and scholars to exertion and study, and promises to operate most beneficially for the advancement of religious and general knowledge ... Dundalk Institution embraces the counties of Louth and Down, because the properties which support it lie in this district.'

Once enrolled, the boys (in this case) were ordered by an 'Arrangement of School Business'. From Monday to Saturday the boys rose at 6am, washed and prepared themselves until 7am, then undertook scripture by the Master, and prayer until 7.30am. Then followed Reading, History etc. until 8.30am when a half hour breakfast was taken. 9am to 10am was set aside for play. Further lessons followed, depending upon the day. They included English Grammar, Algebra, Geography, Euclid, Mensuration, Writing, Book-keeping, Spelling, Catechism and Scripture. Dinner was taken between 2pm and 2.30pm and Supper from 7.30pm to 8pm. Scripture and prayers completed the day at 9pm when the boys retired to bed. A note in the 'Arrangements' indicates that the sciences of navigation and practical surveying were taught, as was drawing for students who had a taste for it.

Breakfast was 'stirabout', (oatmeal porridge) and milk. Dinner on Sunday and Wednesday comprised potatoes and 10 oz. of beef. On Monday and Thursday 1/2 pound of bread and broth. On Tuesday, Friday and Saturday, two pounds of potatoes and milk. Supper comprised 1/2 pound of bread and milk, except on Monday and Thursdays when potatoes and milk were provided, presumably for variety. No mention is made of vegetables or fruit, but as the meals clearly focused on boarders, it is certain that Humphrey James and his brothers fared better at home. The diet was contrived in 1842, only a few years before the onslaught of the potato famine. But for its time the school diet was far superior to what was available to the vast majority of the population, which relied entirely and exclusively upon the potato.[8]

Thackeray would return with enthusiasm later in his 'sketchbook,' his endorsement genuine and vigorous.

'I never saw, in any public school in England, 60 cleaner, smarter, more gentle manlike boys than were here at work. The upper class had been at work on Euclid as we came in, and were set, by way of amusing the stranger, to perform a sum of compound interest of diabolical complication, which, with its algebraic and arithmetic solution, was handed up to me by three or four of the pupils, and I strove to look as wise as I possibly could. Then they went through questions of mental arithmetic with astonishing correctness and facility; and finding from the master that classics were not taught in the school, I took occasion to lament this circumstance, saying, with a knowing air, that I would like to have examined the lads in a Greek play. Classics, then, these young fellows do not get. Meat they get but twice a week. Let English parents bear this fact in mind; but that the lads are healthy and happy, anybody who sees them can have no question; furthermore, they are well instructed in a sound practical education — history, geography, mathematics, religion.'

His final remarks called on newspaper editors to lobby for similar schools in England, 'to show how, and with what small means, boys may be well, soundly and humanely educated,' reinforcing his comments by comparing against his well documented brutal schooling, '... under the bitter fagging and the shameful rod.' He concluded by citing a practical example of acceptance of the Dundalk model of education,

'It was a proud day for Dundalk, Mr. Thackeray well said, when at the end of one of the vacations there, fourteen English boys, and an Englishman with his little son in his hand, landed from the Liverpool packet, and, walking through the streets of the town, went into the school-house quite happy. That was a proud day in truth for a distant Irish town, and I can't help saying that I grudge them the cause of their pride somewhat. Why should there not be schools in England as good, and as cheap, and as happy?'[9]

Thackeray's description of the school, was glowing and no doubt correct at the time of his visit and well intended, but his casual observations clouded an undercurrent of unsanctioned cruelty and bullying. The school was of its time and older boys were sometimes able to assert themselves over the younger boys by bullying and cruelty. Thomas Hunter, who was born in 1831, the same year as Humphrey James, suffered not only bullying from one particularly oafish boy, but vindictive and cruel treatment from the 'second teacher' who delighted in savage punishments. Hunter entered the Dundalk Institution in about 1842 at age 12 and like James, studied there until the age of 16 or 17. He left Ireland for America at 19 and became a teacher, eschewing administrative roles in favour of a lifelong passion for teaching. He rose to be one of the foremost educators of his time as Dr. Thomas Hunter for whom the prestigious Hunter College, which now forms part of the City University of New York, is named.

In his autobiography, which was published many years after his death, Hunter provides an engaging picture of the times, the school and the friendship he had with Humphrey James. 'I had a companion in my misery, a boy of my own set named Humphrey James. He was also from a little seaport town like myself. We both loved the ocean and talked of ships and sailors as a relief from the nostalgia from which we keenly suffered. ... I met Humphrey at the bottom of the campus. At this time we were studying the history of Great Britain and Ireland written of course by a High Church Tory, or we would not have been allowed to read it at all ... in this text book were five words which clung to me, and I found myself repeating them over and over again. They were "The Solemn League and Covenant."

In studying the Chapter we learned what these words meant. When Humphrey and I were lying in the long grass at the bottom of the campus, I suddenly exclaimed, "Humphrey I want to enter into 'a Solemn League and Covenant' with you for the purpose of breaking up the bullying brutality of the big boys over the little boys." No two nations could have more precise and particular rules about their treaty than we were making about our league and covenant. "Our plan is this; - when a big bully abuses you strike him and I shall rush to assist you; when I am abused you must rush to my aid. So that two will beat one, if we only have the courage to stick at it. While one attack the bully in front the other must attack him from behind. Then frequently changing positions the big fellow will be discouraged and beaten." There was a big cowardly bully named Pack ... who without rhyme or reason, - for the mere fun of the thing - struck me a hard blow on the chest, causing me to fall and hurt my back. ... so anxious was I to pay him back that I could not wait for a natural quarrel with him, but I was resolved to provoke one. It was the season of marbles. Humphrey and I entered the ball court, where Pack was playing. I though the bully deserved a thrashing and I was determined that the two boys who had formed the "Solemn League and Covenant" should administer it. Accordingly I walked up to the ring and deliberately kicked the marbles out of it. If an earthquake had opened at his feet, he could not have been more astonished. But with the craft that sometimes accompanies cowardice, he failed to strike me. He simply said," If you do that again I'll break every bone in your body." I made no reply, I simply waited until the marbles were replaced and I kicked them out the second time. For very shame's sake, he must strike me or be forever disgraced among his schoolmates. Humphrey jumped on his back and held his arms while I pommeled at his face; then Humphrey attacked his face while I held his arms; and so on alternately until the big bully was compelled to cry out for quarter. Pack was completely cowed. If he bullied any more it must have been where neither Humphrey nor I saw him. The reduction of Pack became known. Other small boys formed "Solemn Leagues and Covenants" for mutual protection, and soon there was an end to the cruel brutality of the older boys. At that time while boxing was forbidden, it was winked at, on the ground, it was said, that it made the boys courageous and manly.'i

This touching account provides a rare window into the early life and tenacity of Humphrey James. It survives from the affectionate memory of a man who rose to great heights as an educator. Humphrey James also keenly sought to educate children and others throughout his life, which speaks volumes for the Dundalk Institute, a school that also produced three Victoria Cross recipients.

Later in life, James claimed he had worked as a clerk, seafaring man, surveyor's labourer and a school-teacher. In his claim to clerical experience, we find some truth. The other work roles will be examined in due course. He was employed as a clerk after leaving school at 16 or 17 years of age. The name Humphrey James appears in Court Records in Dundalk in 1854, the first being 4 March, when he was listed as a witness in a case of neglecting to pay poor rates. The complainant in the matter, which was finalised, was John McArdill. Again, on 24 March, Humphrey James was called as a witness in two matters of neglecting to pay poor rates. From this we can be certain that James worked as a clerk at the Dundalk Poor-Law Union, rising to a responsible position, that required him to assist in prosecutions.[10] Slater's 1846 Commercial Directory of Ireland informs us that the Dundalk facility ranked as the 48th of such unions in Ireland and was declared in June 1839, about a year after the Poor Law Act was introduced.

The Dundalk Poor Law Union concerned itself chiefly with the County of Louth, but included parts of the counties of Monaghan and Armagh. The Union was responsible for the collection of the Poor Tax which was levied on landowners and split between them and tenants equally, unless the value of the property was below £4, in which case the landowner paid the whole amount. The taxes raised were used to support the local workhouse, where the poor were urged to resort, to not be a burden to a charitable community. The Poor Tax was based on the English model and the young James was a bookkeeper who appeared as a witness in Court to prove non-payment of the tax. John McArdill appears as a complainant in many of these matters over a number of years and was the responsible party for such prosecutions. As many of the tenants could not pay the tax, defaulters were plentiful and the non-appearance of the majority of them indicated that they either stalled as long as they could, or simply left their allotments.

This was galling work for James, which could not give to other than the most black hearted, any satisfaction. He was employed at the Poor Law Union long enough to have seen the mass evictions of the poor, starving and distressed at the latter part of the great famine and at a time when the Quaker Central Relief Committee, though performing laudable charitable work, refused to work through the Poor Law Act. Prosecutions involving James' testimony ceased after 24 March 1854, and later that year he enlisted in the Honourable East India Company Army for service in India. John Dick Smith, his friend and protector, possibly his only friend in the latter part of his life in Australia, related part of this episode as recounted to him by James. Smith had supplied the information to the editor of the *Windsor and Richmond Gazette* for the 1 July edition, about a week after James' death.[11] It appeared as an obituary and read in part, 'The following interesting facts concerning an old resident, who died suddenly early this week at his residence, McGrath's Hill, may prove interesting to our readers. The late Mr. Humphrey James was a native of the North of Ireland. When quite a lad he enlisted in the British Army, assuming the name of Frederick Humphrey James Whirlpool. His reason for doing this, he used to tell his friends, was owing to his being a youth of violent passions, and becoming estranged from his father, owing to a quarrel, he left his home, his father telling him he had a temper like a "whirlpool". "And henceforth that shall be my name", said the hasty young fellow, as the vessel left his seaport home, and this name he ever afterwards was known by.'

Some incorrect assumptions were included in the obituary. James had not joined the British Army, but the Honourable East India Company Army. He did not join under the name stated, but simply as Frederick Whirlpool and he did not use that name ever afterwards. One sliver of truth, which must have come from James, was that his hometown was a seaport in the north of Ireland.

The reason for the quarrel with his father is lost to time, but some clues survive. In 1854, when James enlisted, he was barely 23, having spent all of those years with his parents and seven surviving siblings. At the time of his leaving, assuming that William had already left, as had Thomas, his remaining five siblings were aged six to 16, light company for a young man, and straitening for him. After the 1845 — 1849 famine, the population of Ireland collapsed by more than 2 million, from a population of about 8 million, through either death or emigration. Departures were still running apace, with young women sponsored to all parts of the world to take up domestic positions. Vere Henry Lewis Foster, benefactor, philanthropist and organiser, alone estimated that between 1847 and November 1889, he had assisted 22,615 women to leave Ireland and planned to send thousands more.[12]

Prospects for partnership at home were diminishing rapidly. Indeed like Humphrey, his brothers William, Thomas and Benjamin, would never marry. His brother Samuel married in America and Josiah, in England. Overriding this was the realisation that it was time for him to break loose and to experience the world outside Dundalk. He lived in a seaport garrison town, where the comings and goings of those who had seen exotic places would not have been unknown to him. His imagination was fed by ships and cargo arriving from other ports and the departure of soldiers from the barracks. His uncle Josiah Murphy had been a Troop Sergeant Major in the 12th Royal Lancers and had seen overseas service. By 1851 he was a pensioner, living with his sister Jane in London prior to joining the James' in Dundalk. Perhaps he was the catalyst. The Crimean War was at its height, but it is clear that fighting was not James' main focus. In any event, indications were that the conflict was winding down and should he choose to join the British Army, he may well find himself back in a Irish garrison. The Honourable East India Company Army was recruiting and had recently formed the 3rd Bombay European Regiment to send to India to bolster the Bombay Presidency and its garrison. India was as foreign as imagination allowed and would be an adventure. Peter Stanley, provides solid insight into what may have motivated James and many young men like him. Apart from questioning the long held view that recruits were of an inferior class, he found, 'The Company's recruiting parties ... could afford to be relatively selective. During the mid 1850's (when the force expanded) recruiting parties still needed to find only twenty men each month in each of its seven recruiting districts to meet the beating orders specifying their quotas. It is therefore arguable — especially as [became] apparent, from their careers in India — that the Company accepted and was sought by men who saw it not simply a refuge from poverty but a route to prosperity and even respectability ... The appeal of India itself should not be underestimated, both as a destination for adventurous young men and as an exotic country where humble men acquired fabulous riches. Recruiting sergeants naturally retailed stories of the "splendours" of India, an impression evidently widely current.'[13]

A likely explanation for disagreement with his father is that Humphrey's brother Thomas — two years older and having left home to become a sailor — had died near Rio de Janeiro. A loving father might understandably not want another son to venture overseas, particularly when that son had a secure and respectable occupation at home; a job the father might well have facilitated. Stanley again provides a window, 'In surveying the reasons for which those whose letters, diaries or reminiscences have survived, however, it is striking how many were prompted to enlist by an emotional rather than economic crisis, particularly with their families ... many men ... enlisted under assumed names, a sign that they wished not to be traced. They included Joshua Grierson, one of the stormers of the Kashmir gate, and Frederick Whirlpool, awarded the Victoria Cross in 1858. That the Company's army served as a refuge of the kind which the French Foreign Legion was later romantically portrayed is suggested by the number of black-coated men who enlisted as privates, in much greater numbers than the Queen's force. They included law students, opticians and accountants ... '[14]

There is ample evidence that James left his family not because of his quarrelling with his father, but in spite of it. His later life indicated that he was not interested in wealth and certainly not fame. There is nothing to suggest that his father was domineering or overbearing. Indeed, the picture emerges of an enlightened man who educated his children, including his daughters, and was devoid of religious dogma. Unlike his son, no mention is made of his temper or violent passions. This was a loving family led by a loving father who simply did not want to lose his son.

Similarly, James Bodell, who was born in the same year as Humphrey James, recorded his joining on impulse, the 59th or 2nd Nottingham Regiment in 1847, aged 16. Bedecked with regimental ribbons and drinking with his companions on his way home, he was able to tell his mother what he had done. He recalls his father coming home and his mother recounting his actions. He buried himself in his bedclothes pretending to be asleep. 'He came and sat on a Chair alongside and called me twice and I threw the Blankets off me and sat up in bed, and said Yes Father. He commenced, is this true that your mother tells me about you enlisting for a soldier. I said Yes Father it is true, and if you buy me off I will enlist again, because I am determined to see foreign Countries. He sat there several Seconds and said foolish boy. I had made up my mind to start you in a business. I said it is no use Father I certainly intend to see other Parts of the World ... When I looked at Father again, I saw the tears on his Cheek and recollect no more.'[15]

John Brown, also 16, recalled enlisting in 1853 and parting from his father at Leith in July of that year. 'With his father sobbing inconsolably Brown was unable to offer comfort, standing "motionless gazing on the blank and vacant spot untill my eyes became dim" '.[16]

Like Bodell, Brown and countless others, Humphrey James had made up his mind. In the latter part of 1854, he sailed by packet steamer from Dundalk to Liverpool.

'But pride congealed the drop within his e'e:
Apart he stalked in joyless reverie,
And from his native land resolved to go,

And visit scorching climes beyond the sea;
With pleasure drugged, he almost longed for woe,
And e'en for change of scene would seek the shades below.' [17]

CHAPTER THREE

ENGLAND AND THE 3ʳᵈ BOMBAY EUROPEAN REGIMENT

'White handkerchiefs wave from the short black pier
- as we glide to the grand old sea —
But the song of my heart is for none to hear
If one of them waves for me.'

Henry Lawson
'The Vagabond' 1895

It was his new beginning. As the packet left the pier at Warrens Point, on Dundalk Harbour, beginning its 16-hour passage to Liverpool, Humphrey James must have been exhilarated by the mystery ahead. For many young men — Bodell and Brown included — it was their coming of age moment. It is hardly possible that some of his family did not stand at the pier to see him off. His father would have been there, as tearful as father's Bodell and Brown, in their turn. For Humphrey James, his home and the watchers on the pier grew smaller with each turn of the steamer's screws. Soon there would be nothing of Ireland but the sea that bore its name. Like so many, he would never return. But James was not thinking that far ahead. Anything was possible. From Liverpool he would travel to Glasgow and the Honourable East India Army Recruiting District Office at the address he had noted, carefully folded and placed in his coat pocket.

The journey to Liverpool was uneventful, dulled by the torporific throb of the engine and the motion of the ship. But as the mouth of the Mersey came into view, the immensity of the city — one of the world's largest and busiest seaports — would awaken the senses and overwhelm the likes of James and those who had not ventured here before.

He would have marvelled at its miles and miles of warehouses, wet docks and the imposing customs house, their grandeur tempered on disembarkation by the scene of a dirty, bustling place of industry; the bi-product of successful enterprise. He was quickly swallowed by the swarm of sudorific activity. James gawped at the immensity and strangeness of what he saw. He and the other newcomers tried to gain their bearings in this heaving mass, the likes of which they could not have known. Nothing in his experience could prepare him to take in the huge and multi-storied Albert Dock building and its massive neighbours, whose sweep seemed to have no end. The port was noisy and acrid, overpowered by the rancid smells of stock, tar, coal fires and the din of industry mixing with the ever present and thick miasma, which enveloped the behemoth. The shipbuilders, foundries, tallow soaked soap manufactories, chandler's shops, inns, bawdy houses and brothels were noisily conducting trade, and the giggling, painted doxies were doing their enticing best to attract custom. For those with just a few pennies left from their other excesses there was a warren of lanes and alleys for the furtive 'twopenny standup'.

His sister Deborah would not marry and move to Liverpool for another 15 years, but James knew people here among the more than 300,000 Irish expatriates in Liverpool, who made up an estimated 25% of the city population and for the most part, bent their backs to hard labour.[1] He would not have time to reacquaint himself with old friends. Soaking up what he saw; the newness of it, the strange smells and even stranger accents would have heightened his excitement and anticipation of adventure. Every day from hereon would be new and wondrous, in stark contrast to his days as a clerk in Dundalk, where monotony wove its pallid pattern. His lodgings were mean and overcrowded, sordid and far from clean, but for the tariff, better than sleeping over the rope at a twopenny hangover, or worse. It was all that he needed while waiting to get to Glasgow as soon as he could, and that would entail 3rd class passage on the first available train.

Beyond the slums that housed many of his compatriots, Irishmen were not welcomed by the English. They were seen as a drain on their resources, including jobs and medical care, such as it was and mental health issues amongst the Irish were causing overcrowding in the city asylums, and crime in its gaols.[2] The greatest influx had occurred during the great famine, but it had continued since and political agitation was afoot to curb it. The *Liverpool Mail* newspaper carried regular accounts of Irish immigration, disease and crime, during the famine years and afterwards in a seemingly endless account of how the influx could not be curbed. The following account from 1847 provides some sense of the numbers of desperate people arriving in Liverpool.

'From returns exhibited on Wednesday by Lord Sandon and the Reverend Augustus Campbell, rector of Liverpool, it appears that about 50,000 Irish came into the port in the month of March and 24,709 in the first 14 days of April. No less than 6,470 arrived last Saturday and Sunday, some of them in a state of actual fever, and multitudes, so predisposed to fever from exhaustion that they fell sick shortly after their arrival. Smallpox, diarrhœa, dysentery, and fever prevail, and there are 40 about deaths a-day.'[3]

Despite the wretched state of these people, in 1849, the *Liverpool Mail,* warned its readership. 'It is neither just nor charitable to the peaceable and industrious inhabitants of this orderly and well-regulated town (even if it were consistent with sound policy), to make fit an Irish poorhouse and an Irish gaol; a pest-house for the reception of Irish fever, and a prison-house for the correction of Irish crime.'[4]

The following year, the *Liverpool Mail* reported, 'Mr. Hodson called attention to the immense number of poor Irish who were daily being brought over from Ireland at 4d a head. He inquired if the vestry had not some power over the steam-boat proprietors ... to prevent the evil of which he complained.'[5]

It was as well that James' stay was to be brief. He may have been a wide-eyed traveller, but he was focused enough to avoid the pitfalls of the jug and over friendly ladies. His lean belongings would not have attracted the attention of the notorious 'runners'; thieves and fraudsters who would seize luggage in the hope of extracting payment for its return. Nor would confidence tricksters and touts mulct his hard-earned meagre savings. And there were other dangers. This ancient port had quickly grown beyond its infrastructure needs and although private companies had provided piped water to the wealthy, the poor still made do with barrels and questionable wells, ensuring that sanitation was scant and the ever present threat of disease and contagion hung over them. Housing provided to workers on the docks and built by their employers, provided relief to some, but a vast number still lived in squalor. This was no place in which to tarry. James made quickly to Glasgow and again found mean lodgings.

On 23 October 1854, he presented at the Honourable East India Company Recruiting District Office at 132 Mains Street. His literacy was superior to most applicants and he had no trouble answering questions of him, or completing the required forms for enlistment, avoiding the traps that might have uncovered his real identity, for he had now become Frederick Whirlpool, born in Liverpool, Lancaster. Little did he know that this would become his *nom de guerre,* nor was it his intention. Despite his new name, he would never see himself as a destructive Charybdis, nor was fighting anticipated. Described as being 23 years of age, 5'7" tall, with brown hair, grey eyes and a fresh complexion, he gave his occupation as 'clerk'. It was noted that the nape of his neck was marked by cupping. This dubious treatment, still used today, may have left permanent scars if the process of 'wet cupping' had been applied to his neck to align the 'humours'. This process involved a small incision made to the area with a knife or scarifier and the cup applied over the wound to release blood in the manner of artificial leeching. Whilst the 'cupping' raised comment, it was no impediment to his entry into the Indian Army. What it does imply however, is that James was financially able to seek medical attention, giving a hint of his above average standing in Ireland where the vast majority of the population were impoverished and barely able to subsist. Similarly, when applying for a police position in Australia years later, he offered himself for either the foot or mounted sections, indicating that he could ride. This, and a later position at the Sydney Riding School, suggests a somewhat comfortable position in Dundalk, which must have enabled him to learn this skill, when so many would not have had the same opportunity.

After compearance before a magistrate for attestation, and undergoing a medical examination, he had materialised as Frederick Whirlpool, No. 2200, and would be trained at the Company's Warley Depot in Essex, with hundreds of other new recruits. There was, however, one more hurdle to leap at Warley before his acceptance. There, Lieutenant Colonel Thomas Leslie imposed a system which did much to maintain the quality of the recruits shipped to India each summer. The depot letter books show how Leslie and his staff enquired into many recruits' circumstances, weeding out deserters from the Queen's service, truant apprentices, and other undesirables, often undoing the recruiting sergeants' best efforts.'[6]

If questioned in this way, James must have brazened it through, taking the hurdles in his stride. Change of name may have aroused suspicion, but would not draw censure in itself. Sir Hugh Rose, commander of the Central India Field Force, observed that he had always thought the name Whirlpool had been assumed, yet he did not trouble himself with it.

Major-General Sir Owen Tudor Burne provides an anecdote in his 'Clyde and Strathnairn'. Lord Clyde, as Sir Colin Campbell (itself an assumed name, for he was born Colin Macliver), was appointed Commander-in-Chief of India on 12 July 1857. Lord Strathnairn, as Major-General Sir Hugh Rose, led the Central India Field Force, which included the 3rd Bombay European Regiment. Rose succeeded Campbell as Commander-in-Chief of India on 4 June 1860. In 1865 he returned to England and was appointed Commander-in-Chief of Ireland, a position he held until 1870, when he entered retirement at the age of seventy. Burne had married Sir Hugh Rose's niece, Agnes Douglas, and although he claimed to have been a 'sometime military secretary to the Commander-in-Chief of India', (from 1861) his family connection provided more access to Rose than the latter position would enable. The role of Sir Hugh Rose and its impact on Humphrey James will be examined later, but it is necessary here to address the suggestion raised by Burne. 'Sir Hugh Rose always thought that the name Whirlpool was assumed, and afterwards learnt that the man was a son of Mr. Conker, the postmaster of Dundalk. When the General was in command in Ireland the parents came to thank him for his kindness to their son, who was then in New South Wales.'[7]

This anecdote, retold to Burne by Rose, many years after the event is at best, a mixed bag of fact and error. Rose was in Ireland between 1865 and 1870, and the period resides in part of James' time in New South Wales, from 1862 until his death in 1899. The name Whirlpool certainly was assumed and does not appear in common genealogical lists of surnames. It may be that James' parents called on the commander-in-chief to thank him for his kindness to their son, who had been severely wounded and had recovered, against all odds. They would have been eager to hear word of him from someone who had seen him in India. No person by the name of Conker is listed as ever having been the postmaster of Dundalk, in Rose's time, or before. Humphrey James, senior, was born with that name, was a native of Carlow who joined the constabulary in 1822 as Humphrey James. He married in 1826 as Humphrey James and all of his children bore the surname 'James'. The name seems to have emanated from Monmouthshire in Wales and Humphrey James senior's forebears were part of an early 'plantation' of Welsh, Scots and English into Ireland. Humphrey senior received a constabulary pension in the name James and he and Lavinia are buried in that name. It makes no sense that he and Lavinia would have used an assumed name when meeting Rose. It is clear that Burne's mention of the name Conker in his 1895 edition, is the first time time it was raised. The information was related many years after the event and is retold by a second party. Rose, who died at 84 in 1885, just ten years before publication of the story, was recorded as becoming frail and could be excused an error. The whole account is therefore unreliable and clearly an error of recall. How easily these things occur can be seen by the next recorded mention of the meeting by Forrest,[8] by which time (1904), Mr. Conker had become Major Conker. The mistake became writ and is, unfortunately, perpetuated.

James was fully aware that he had enlisted for ten years and that he would be actively discouraged from marrying. This seemed to be no barrier to him or his fellow recruits and as time proved, he had no intention of marrying or returning home under any circumstances. Marriage could wait and at this time would be considered an impediment. Entitlements and a pension, which came with longer service were far from the considerations of this young man. If many of his cohort joined the Company's army with the intention of then taking up civil positions at greater advantage, this was not in James' mind. He had left clerking for its mundaneness and to re-enter it now would be an anathema to him and dull his new found release. A seed had germinated in his mind and he aspired to teach. He would make several attempts at it, both in India and later in Australia. His removal from his family was now complete. There was no going back, even had he wanted it. He would never see his parents again, or his siblings, with the exception of Ben, who would follow him to India.

Stanley encapsulates James' position neatly. Describing the Bengal Army intake, which was similar to that of the Bombay Army, he notes, 'They appear to have come from the broad strata of Anglo-Irish society which provided the rank and file of the Queen's army. Most observers agreed, however, that the Company's service attracted a "superior" grade of recruit, with higher proportions of artisans and clerks and a smaller proportion of simple labourers.'[9]

Reminiscing in 1911, perhaps with timeworn resignation and polished recall, Lieutenant General Sir William Butler, bemoans the falling standards of recruits from fifty and more years earlier.

'… no soldiers equalled ours in strength, courage, and endurance. That day is gone … men are now taken who would have been rejected with scorn a few years ago; we get recruits no longer from the rural districts, but from the slums of the big cities, … I shall never forget the sorry contrast that presented itself … where one draft of a hundred and twenty men of the new model formed up on the high shore from the boats. The old soldiers had come down … to see the new arrivals. The contrast between the two sets of men was not flattering to the newcomers. The men were … of the old type, … of splendid physique and well-chiselled feature. I often look now as soldiers pass and marvel what has become of those old Greek gods, for not only are the figures gone, but the faces have also vanished — those straight, clean-cut foreheads, the straight or aquiline noses, the keen, steady eyes, the resolute lower jaws and shapely turned chins. What subtle change has come upon the race?'[10]

He seems to have forgotten the overweight, flabby-faced soldier who, with others, had broken into the liquor store on board their transport ship in 1860 and was too drunk and too fat to be extricated by his colleagues.

This Greek god spent most of the rest of the voyage in leg irons.[11]

This is not to say his recollections were altogether flawed. Like others closer to events, Butler held early recruits in higher regard than have later commentators who took the easier path of generalisation. His were comments, which added weight to the argument, that the recruits of the mid 19th century were not a 'rag tag' lot. His 'new type' though, stepped up three years later, when millions of young men served with distinction, several hundred thousand of them to be slaughtered on the battlefields of the Great War.

James' change of name has been explained, but not the reason for it. He was 23 and not being in his minority, was fully capable of making the decision to join the army, and doing it without subterfuge. Certainly, he was angry at the attempts to keep him in the desperate confines of his family and the crushing limitations this would impose on his searching intelligence. His alias was not adopted to avoid detection from those who might seek him. It was not to hide some malfeasance in Ireland, but it would define who he was and who he would become on his own terms. Yes, the name had been born of his father's invective, but henceforth it would be worn as a mark of his coming of age as an independent and free spirit, unshackled from the expectations of others and the country, which could offer him but little. Almost fifty years later, his remaining siblings would attest to the fact that he corresponded with them and more importantly, with his father, indicating that some sort of reconciliation had occurred, or that the rift was never as serious as has previously been assumed. His letters stopped inexplicably in 1883, about eight years after his father's death and seven years before his mother's. He would write once more, but only letters to his brother Josiah and sister, Deborah and in the months before his death.

* * *

Upon his attestation, Frederick Whirlpool was ordered to present himself, at an appointed hour, at the recruiting office in preparation for travel to the Warley Depot near Brentwood, in Essex. With fellow recruits, the march to the Glasgow railhead began with jollity and pride and little concern for what lay ahead. The rail link between Glasgow and London had been well established for some years, as had the link between London and Brentwood/Warley, from where a short march saw the new recruits arrive at the depot.

A little bedraggled, the recruits marched into the depot on 31 October, where they were met by the weekly orderly staff sergeant, who took account of them and their needs, or 'necessaries'. Required to wash their feet and legs, they were marched to the hospital for a medical inspection. Once passed by the surgeon and the searching enquiries of the commandant, they were taken to the bathing room and washed with soap and warm water. Their uniforms were then issued, '... one flannel jacket, one pair of flannel drawers, one forage cap, one pair of stockings, one shirt, one towel, one pair of grey trowsers, one stock and clasps, and two ounces of soft soap.'[12] To ensure that the flannel jacket and drawers were not 'made away with', the men were required to produce them on parade each Sunday morning. It seems that everything had a value in the mid 19th century. The new recruits dressed, handing over their soiled clothes to be washed, before being posted to various companies. Whirlpool was posted to No 5 Company, 3rd Bombay European Regiment.

At 12 noon on the Thursday following their arrival, the new men were present when their laundered belongings, bundled individually, were taken to the barrack gate for sale to the general public. Their embrace by the military was complete.

Each recruit was entitled to a bounty for joining the service and the Warley Depot standing orders provide a salutary account of how this money might, by past experience, be wasted. Recruits were encouraged to remit some to their families, with facilities provided to this end.

Recruits were introduced to the serious business of fighting with weapon training, particularly the use of the India Pattern Standard Infantry Musket or 'Brown Bess', a weapon that had been in use since the late 18th century and was nearing the end of its service. Weighing a little more than nine and a half pounds (4.39kg) it added to the knapsack, greatcoat, cartridge box and water bottle, ensuring that travel would not be easy.[13]

Only the year earlier, the Enfield Pattern or the Pattern 1853 Enfield rifle musket had been developed and would soon be introduced into the Indian Army. In 1857, attempts to introduce it to Indian sepoys would be one catalyst for a large scale mutiny against the British overlords, based on real, imagined or contrived objections to the use of cartridges greased by lard or beef tallow, abhorred by the vast majority of Muslims or Hindus. This was the weapon carried by Whirlpool into Central India. By strange coincidence, this weapon, or a variant of it, when adopted by the Irish Constabulary, also caused consternation amongst the Irish citizenry who determined it as proof of the resented militarisation of the police.[14]

Writing to Brigadier C.S. Stuart on 18 March 1858, Sir Hugh Rose outlined the benefits of the upgraded weapon in the field ... 'I found the greatest good at Rathgur from placing the men with Enfield Rifles in Rifle Pits, in advance of the attack in order to pick off the men on the Enemy's defences, and keep down their fire ... I have observed that our Enfield's frighten the rebels as much as artillery.'[15]

Unlike many generals of the time, Rose was quick to discern the value of the new weapon and it's Minié-type bullet. He had experience of it in the Crimea and had advised the French commanders there of its benefits in protecting infantry from anticipated Russian cavalry assaults, should a field campaign be undertaken.[16]

Still at Warley Depot, Whirlpool settled into his new life and accepted the parades, roll calls, drill parades and fatigue duties. Standing orders demanded daily parades and roll calls, with full regimental dress required on Saturdays when necessaries were inspected, and medical inspection parades on the first and third Tuesdays of each month. From May to September drill was conducted at 6am to 7.30am and on afternoons as ordered. For the remainder of the year, morning drill was held from 10am to 11.30am and afternoons from 2pm to 3.30pm. Punishment drills were conducted when necessary, but were not to exceed four hours daily, exclusive of normal parades and drills. Standing orders made clear ... 'As it is at the drill that the young soldier receives his first impressions of the service, it is of the utmost consequence that his treatment should be such as not to intimidate or disgust him — the utmost coolness, and patience are therefore requisite on the part of the Drill Serjeants.'[17] Instructions to sergeant's major conducting drill went further and ensured that they were to ' ... see that they are conducted with temper, and that the recruits are not harshly spoken to.'[18]

Every effort was made to maintain the services of the new recruits. Much effort had gone into recruiting, grading, attesting, delivering and outfitting men of worth for the Honourable East India Company service and their loss through desertion as the result of harsh treatment was seen as failure.

The company had endowed the depot with a number of valuable books as the foundation of an extensive library, '… from a desire to provide amusement and instruction to the men … and to afford them the opportunity, whilst in England, of spending their leisure hours in a manner that would prove advantageous to them hereafter.'[19]

Company army education was valued and promoted as early as the 1820's, by the provision of books in Indian Stations, as well as at depots and on voyages. 'Men schooled each other, but the Company also provided educational opportunities within its European corps without parallel in the Queen's army. Not only were recruits encouraged to attend school at the depot and on board troopships, but also the establishments of European regiments, which included in the 1820s, a schoolmaster, a reading master and writing master, later joined by two assistant schoolmasters, a librarian and (for soldiers' children) a school mistress.'[20]

This system carried into the 1850s, when the Queen's army followed suit. The well-read Whirlpool, would have felt quite at home in the library and gladly paid his tuppence a week to be there. Another tuppence a week would allow him entry to the Depot school, which had been established by the Commandant and was conducted for two hours each evening by the schoolmaster. Although Whirlpool's education was superior to the basic competencies in reading, writing and arithmetic offered at the school, his interest in teaching was nurtured in the depot, on his way to India, and once settled there. He may have engaged in informally teaching his fellow recruits, which probably brought him to the notice of his superiors and to an assistant schoolmaster's position. He claimed to have been a schoolmaster in the army, according to his friend John Dick Smith, in New South Wales, but he was mistaken only in style, as he was in assuming that Whirlpool had joined the British army. It is certain that Whirlpool was not a braggart. He did not claim to have been an army schoolmaster in his application to become a teacher in New South Wales in 1865.

Indeed, he did not mention his army service at all. His reasons for omitting this will be examined later. Teaching was, however, a passion that he carried and nurtured years later in Victoria and New South Wales. Without knowing why, he had developed didactically, a leaning which would never leave him.

Now fully-fledged soldiers, though still referred to as recruits, Whirlpool and his cohort were inspected by the surgeon the day prior to their anticipated embarkation. Officers were directed to make great exertions to keep the men 'in a state of regularity' and to ensure good order on the march to the embarkation point. They were urged to '… use every exertion in their power to prevent the men getting liquor'. Staff Sergeants were ordered to march '… on the Pivot, and the acting Non-commissioned Officers on the reverse flank of their divisions, and will be held responsible that no straggling or irregularity takes place, and that none of the men fall out without permission, on the march.'[21] Bitter experience had obviously taught officers that some of the men might suffer a change of heart and think better of their decision to go to India.

'Second Issue' or 'Sea Clothing' was issued in a haversack for the upcoming journey on the day of departure. It comprised '… two check shirts, canvas trowsers, canvas frock, canvas cap, a set of combs, one pair of boots, paper, thread and needles, three boxes of blacking, and one tin pot and cover.' Orders added that, 'It being essential for the health and comfort of the men during the voyage, that their equipment, and necessaries should be kept as complete as possible, Colonel Hay begs to call your particular attention to the necessity of guarding against any of these articles being made away with, more especially in the river, where there are not only great facilities and temptations to dispose of them, than at sea, but the men are liable to be plundered immediately on their going aboard … To guard against this evil, Colonel Hay would recommend that you give orders, as soon as the detachment has got on board, for all the knapsacks and haversacks to be placed together, in the portion of the ship appointed to the troops, with sentries posted, to prevent any person but the men having access to them, until the ship gets to sea.'[22] A weekly inspection ensured that all equipment was kept complete and in order.

Whirlpool's regiment boarded the *Salamanca*, on 29 November 1854, as it readied for departure. It had been built in Sunderland, Durham, and was completed in 1853. Being relatively new, its passengers were spared the privations of those suffered in older, unwholesome vessels. She was about 927 tons and able to carry approximately 350 passengers and crew, of whom, in this instance, 157 were infantry bound for the Bombay Presidency. The voyage proceeded smoothly and a speedy passage of nearly four months was achieved, arriving in Bombay on 26 March 1855. It was a continuous and unbroken journey, as many were, although the only priority for a speedy passage would have been the commercial considerations of the Honourable East India Company and the private business of the captain. If the ship made a speedy passage and was first into port, premium prices could be achieved for the captain's and to a lesser extent, the senior officer's private merchandise. 'The picture of the East Indiaman sailing along at a moderate speed and making snug for the night must be recognised as erroneous when it is remembered that the commander had paid £5,000 for his command — a sum equivalent to the cost of his ship — for the purpose of making his fortune: and that he was carrying an investment of upwards of £5,000 for sale in the East. He was hardly likely to hang about unnecessarily, especially as the first man to arrive obtained the best price for his goods.'[23]

CHAPTER FOUR

———

INDIA

'Take up the White Man's burden -
Send forth the best ye breed -
Go — bind your sons to exile
To serve your captives' needs;
To wait, in heavy harness,
On fluttered folk and wild —
Your new caught sullen peoples,
Half devil and half child.'

Rudyard Kipling
'The White Man's Burden' 1899

The *Salamanca* arrived in Bombay when the Crimean war and the siege of Sebastapol were at their height. Signs that peace was imminent, albeit more than a year after the populace had generally guessed the conflict would run its course, created some optimism, although it would not end for another year. But that was a world away. Whirlpool and his compatriots disembarked at Bombay and did their best, still on unsteady legs, to appear as soldiers. They had arrived and would mockingly be known as 'griffs' or 'griffins', a mildly derogatory term for newcomers to India, usually applied for their first year of duty. They would not be considered 'old soldiers' for several years,[1] but it would not be long before circumstances would dictate otherwise. Many would not see out five years, or even three, and no-one would think to call the survivors 'griffs'.

Disease was a serious reality in India, as was the intolerable heat. But what would follow in 1857-58, would test their resolve, stamina and every fibre of their being, as they fought in a conflict that would change India, its overlords and the course of history. The Honourable East India Company and its army would be dissolved and the administration of its Indian territories subsumed by the Crown.

Bombay (Mumbai) was first sighted from the *Salamanca* as the ship approached its rendezvous with the pilot, who would guide them to anchor. The prominent tree lined shore, promised exotic encounters. The lighthouse was more familiar to new arrivals because of its European form, but the nearby town was certainly strange in parts. As they passed the local fishing fleets, the boats of native traders approached bearing various fruits for sale to eager, malnourished passengers. So too, the Parsees came offering goods and among them were many servants bearing testimonials, who vied for employment. Trade was conducted as the pilot readied to guide the *Salamanca* to a safe berth. Once secured, the anchor was dropped and the 'recruits' awaited orders to disembark. No time was wasted in the longboats ferrying passengers and troops ashore. Tents were erected near the esplanade, where many Europeans camped during the hottest period of the year, and soldiers slept on solid ground for the first time in four months. There would be no time for the bazaar and, in the following days, they would begin to make their way to the much favoured Poona (Pune) cantonment, adjacent to the city of Poona, where the seat of the Bombay Presidency operated during the monsoon season of June to October.[2]

Fully kitted and dressed in their regimental red and blue, the new soldiers of the 3rd Bombay European Regiment (3rd Europeans) commenced their march to the Bori Bunder railway terminus, near the storehouses of Bombay, from where the recently built railway had advanced to the town of Callian (Kalyan), a distance of about 50 kilometres. The railway allowed for a speedy passage, as the three locomotives, 'Sahib', 'Sindh' and 'Sultan' rattled along new ribbons of steel with fourteen fully laden carriages in tow.

From Callian, the troops began the 100-kilometre or so march to their base at Poona. Predecessors had trodden the same road for nearly fifty years and this trek would help rid them of their sea legs. It took them to Campoolie (Khopoli) at the base of the Bhor Ghat, through the pass and on to Poona. Three years later, engineering feats would extended the railway to Poona, with viaducts and tunnels, over and under the Bhor Ghat range.

The Campoolie encampment had long been established, with bungalows for officers and civilians on the higher ground of the Ghat. In the village itself soldiers were accommodated in open sheds forming three sides of a square, known as pendalls, (pandal) and were, '... erected along the principal roads for the accommodation of troops on the line of March.'[3] It was here that Whirlpool's regiment camped for the evening, before setting off again, at 5am, a pattern followed on each of the five days of marching to Poona. In December 1857, just two years later, Mrs. Leopold Paget made the journey, albeit in more comfort. She described the route as '... a beautiful drive to Poona through a much more wooded and cultivated country with a line of fine hills in front of us: and as we neared the old metropolis of the Deccan, roads multiplied and pretty little bungalows with luxuriant gardens sprung up, and before entering the cantonment we passed by a fine bridge over the Moola-Mutra river. I overtook the troops just before reaching the lines, and with some difficulty found my way to a bungalow which had been prepared for us in the 3rd European lines by the kindness of a friend ... '[4]

Life at the Poona Cantonment was close to idyllic and it was here that drill and exercises honed this new regiment. Use of the new Enfield rifle musket was taught and competitions in marksmanship were eagerly contested. Meanwhile Whirlpool found time to share his knowledge with his fellows, and his keenness for teaching was not lost on his superiors. Appointment to schoolmaster was reserved for sergeants, so Private Whirlpool was made an assistant schoolmaster.

Poona City was headquarters of the Poona District, Bombay, and would, before Whirlpool left India, be a terminus of the Southern Mahratta Railway. It stands 1,800 feet (approximately 849 metres) above sea level and is a little over 60 miles (96.5 kms) from the coast. Built at the confluence of the Mutha and Mula rivers, its 1850's population exceeded 73,000 and was made up of Hindus, Muslims, Christians, Parsi's and Jains, in order. The climate was considered agreeable. After 1818, a British military victory established the city as headquarters of a British District and the principal cantonment in the Deccan. The Imperial Gazetteer of India noted, 'East of the city is the military station, with an area of 4½ square miles ... Within cantonment limits, northwards to the Mutha-Mula river and for two miles along the road leading west to the cantonment of Kirkee, are the houses of the greater part of the European population ...'[5]

Poona was a major learning centre and home to many education institutions, including the Army School of Education, then known as the Normal School, Bombay Army. The 3rd Europeans made full use of the school and a latter day army educator, Archie White VC, MC, believed Whirlpool undertook training there.[6]

Between the city and cantonment was the Sadr Bazaar, which provided Europeans with familiar comforts and necessaries, as noted by Mrs. Paget. '... and in the evening we drove through the Sudder Bazaar (or shops for Europeans), a picturesque street of low houses, planted with rows of trees like a boulevard, to a piece of water called the Bund, a favourite resort of an evening, where carriage and riding parties meet and converse, and return home by lamp or moonlight.'[7]

The genteel evening pastimes did not include the private soldier, although he would not be excluded from daytime shopping when on leave, although the pursuits of some were often further afield. Throughout the city the huts of prostitutes were plentiful, each containing several women and later in the 19th century they would be regulated into a 'lal bazaar', for the use of soldiers. The 'lal', or red bazaars were controlled, '... by an Old Bawd, an experienced procuress, who was paid a salary by the canteen fund, with their occupants subject to regular medical inspection.'[8]

Control of the spread of venereal diseases was attempted, by the establishment of 'Lock Hospitals', for the enforced isolation and treatment of female prostitutes. But in the mid nineteenth century, prostitution continued to wreak havoc on regiments, and no doubt, regiments on prostitutes. Holmes observed. 'There were always wide regimental variations in VD statistics: one RHA (Royal Horse Artillery) battery in Poona had 41 per cent of its men infected, and another had only 13.5 per cent.'[9] 'During the 1830s the rate of venereal disease ran between 32 and 45 per cent in British regiments in India.'[10]

The fact that larger numbers of the men did not contract venereal diseases, indicates that, as in the wider community, morality, religion and personal preference would certainly have played a role. Some men simply would not engage with prostitutes.

Poona was a city of variety; theatres, churches, public institutions, parks, entertainments and other pleasurable pursuits, as well as the base needs of the soldiery. Life here was comfortable and routine. The citizenry and administration flocked to the city for the monsoon season and naturally, merchants and traders followed. The imposed presence of soldiers was not a burden to bear for the 3rd Europeans.

The Honourable East India Company had its beginnings at a time of European expansion when Spanish, Portuguese, Dutch, French and belatedly, the English, vied for supremacy. Once peace negotiations between England and Spain failed, Queen Elizabeth granted a charter to the Governor and Company of Merchants of London, on 31 December 1600, for a period of 15 years.[11] After setbacks in the East Indies, in moves against the Dutch and battles against the Portuguese, the Honourable East India Company traded only with India and their headquarters were established at Surat.

This arrangement applied after Bombay was ceded to England, as part of the wedding dowry of Portugal's Catherine of Braganza, upon her marriage to Charles II in 1662. In 1668, Charles gifted Bombay to the company. The East India Company's interest in Bombay advanced as Surat declined, but it prospered, despite some early setbacks and Cromwell continued to support it, although engaged in political upheaval at home. In effect, the Honourable East India Company became the body which governed important parts of India, establishing presidencies and protectorates and working closely with independent states.

Nearly bankrupt, assistance was afforded by the home government, but at the cost of a dual control mechanism, which was to last until 1858. The Regulating Act of 1773, provided for a Governor-General and a small council, which supervised Madras and Bombay, from Bengal. Expansion led to the India Act of 1784, which enabled virtual control of India by the government in Britain. That, and various conflicts, ensured that the company took possession of previously held Dutch and French territories. Jean Sutton draws attention to the fact of this strange arrangement caused comment in the British parliament. 'During his term in office [Lord William Bentinck, Governor General] the company's charter again came up for renewal and its position was hotly debated. Parliament eventually agreed, in Macaulays words, 'that the strangest of all governments ... designed for the strangest of all empires' should be allowed to continue its stewardship for a further twenty years ...'[12]

That the strangeness of the arrangements were apparent in the closing years of its existence, to those in power, gives relief to the modern viewer who is more than likely perplexed that a private company could rule a disparate continent, or parts of it, raise its own army and navy, fight insurrections and hold almost all of the powers of government. I can think of no modern parallel and perhaps it is just as well. Capitalism weaves its magic more subtly in the modern era.

In this sphere, Frederick Whirlpool found his niche. He would not question the status quo. What the 'higher ups' did was not his concern, nor that of his fellow soldiers. He had joined the Indian Army and understood that it was different from that of the Queen's in some particulars, and that each had its merits and disadvantages. Indian Army soldiers were better paid, but enlistment was for a longer period; so long that the British army referred to them as, 'East India Convicts', a reference to the EIC on their shako plates, as indeed did the soldiers themselves.[13] Rapidly changing events and the lack of a vacancy prevented Whirlpool from pursuing his teaching dream before the outbreak of what was to become known as the Indian Mutiny, ostensibly on 10 May 1857, at Meerut.

CHAPTER FIVE

———

MUTINY

mū'tĭnȳ n., &v.i. 1. n. open revolt against constituted
authority, esp. by soldiers etc. against officers;
the (Indian or Sepoy) M~, revolt of Bengal native troops, 1857-58.

OED

Earlier instances of mutinous unrest occurred among the Bengal
Native Infantry in the months before the rising at Meerut. Indiscipline
and the collision of caste and rank were seen as root causes, and the
dissatisfaction had been apparent for a number of years. Discipline
could not be maintained while rank was usurped by caste transcendence.
Their British Officers did little to address it, believing that their rule
was inviolate.

There has been much debate about the causes of the mutiny
over the past century and a half and opinions still vary. How the
British dealt with the insurrection and its horrors, was bound to
have ramifications for their soldiers and the Indian people. It must
be remembered that the conflict began as a mutiny of sepoys in
the service of the Indian army, particularly the Bengal army, who
had in many cases murdered their European officers, their wives
and children, as well as European and Anglo Indian civilians, and
their native servants. The mutiny spread to revolt, as prisoners were
released and others used the opportunity to settle old scores, or
to merely gain from the confusion. It is necessary when trying to
fathom Frederick Whirlpool's part in the Central India Campaign
as a member of the 3rd Bombay European Regiment, which saw
a great deal of fighting, to examine those sparsely recorded series

of actions in some detail. It is also helpful to understand how he earned the Victoria Cross and to see what he and many of his cohort experienced, impacting on post-war life.

Some latter-day Indian historians would have us accept that the events of 1857-58 were India's first war of independence. Their inventions and embellishments are no different from the sorts of tools other countries have used to craft their own epochal histories and mythologies. Mid-19th century India was not a nation, but a conglomerate of seized and independent states, varied in customs, language and religions. Parts of the sub-continent were annexed by traders and invaders, by treaty, permission of state rulers, or force, but it was England, through the offices of the Honourable East India Company, which would prevail and establish herself as ruler, protector and possessor of immense territories, for 350 years. Their charter, granted by Queen Elizabeth, would see Britain, her government and the company of merchants as strange bedfellows, who, in peculiar circumstances, imposed themselves on a people who were weakened by their lack of cohesion. The proud nation states within the sub-continent have a long tradition of sophistication, advanced learning, highly developed arts and societal structure. Cultural and religious differences saw them engaged in ongoing conflict with each other, not unlike the city states of Europe, and beyond, some of which would meld to become nations. Unification of India would be a long time coming, but the sub-continent itself remains divided, particularly by the uneasy partition of India and Pakistan. The divisions within the sub-continent were evident until the mid 20th century and though undoubtedly nation states, schisms remain. 'It is easy for Westerners to think of themselves as belonging to this or that nation, but it was ... a comparatively new idea in the countries of Africa and Asia. For most of the teeming millions of Gandhi's India it was by no means natural to think of themselves as members of the Indian nation. We have to remember that most could not ... read: that most rarely moved outside the little world of their own villages; that they were divided from each other, not only by the fact that they lived in fairly static groups, but also by caste, by religion, by enormous differences in wealth and education.'[1]

This portrayal of India in the early 20th century was no less relevant than in earlier times, and despite it, common threads did exist. It is not difficult to imagine there being a deep-seated resentment underlying the European presence in the various Indian states, even if there was no strong sense of nationalism prevailing at the time. The people of India both resented and welcomed the presence of the English, as they had the Portuguese, French, Dutch and others, depending upon what individual gains and benefits they might reap. Still, they feared for the existence of their religions, culture and societal structure. The English initially went to great pains to ensure that the religious rites of the people were respected and allowed to flourish without hindrance. In the early days this was understood by the people, despite some modifications to cultural mores, such as the abolition of the practice of *'suttee'*: the burning alive of widows on their husband's funeral pyres. Sacrifices of *Meriah*, victims purchased for the purpose, or infanticide, either by killing off unwanted females or sacrificing first born children to crocodiles, or sharks as an offering to the gods for more children. In one area the sacrifice of a male child every Friday, was abolished by the English and great efforts over many years expunged the vile death cult of the *Thuggie*, who preyed on travellers to destroy them and steal their belongings, in the first instance for heavenly and the second, earthly reward.[2] 'It had been the first maxim of the English that there should be no interference with religion, but that was overridden where homicide was involved: they had interfered even with customs sanctioned by religion — to save widows from the pyre, traveller's from the noose, and infant daughters from suffocation.'[3]

Sanctioned by religion *suttee* may have been, but it was not a requisite of the Hindu faith. The late 18th and early 19th century French missionary and chronicler of Hindu custom, Abbé Dubois observed that the practice was never tolerated by Mohammedan rulers and that it was practised by fanatics. The theologian noted, 'Nobody is a greater admirer than myself of the wise spirit that animates this enlightened and liberal Government in manifesting to its Hindu subjects such a full and perfect tolerance in the practice of their civil and religious usages; and nobody is more fully alive than I am to the dangers and difficulties that an open defiance of these prejudices, which are looked upon as sacred and inviolable, would give rise to. But does the abominable custom in question form part of Hindu Institutions? Are there any rules which prescribe its observance by certain castes?

All the information which I have been able to gather on the subject tends to make me believe that there are no such rules. The infamous practice, although encouraged by the impostors who regulate religious worship, is nowhere prescribed in an imperative manner in the Hindu books.'[4]

Despite official policy not to engage in religious propaganda amongst Indians, Christian missionaries did their best to garner converts, although with limited success. Over a hundred missionaries were proselytising in India by 1824, and only a year before, had claimed at Serampore, converts numbering 1000, but others believed the number was nearer to 300. Whatever the actual number, proselytising reinforced the belief amongst sepoys that the Company was intent upon altering their religion.[5]

Some English commanders too, found irresistible the urge and opportunity to proselytise. 'Nor was it any longer just the missionaries who dreamt of converting India ...The Commissioner of Peshawar, Herbert Edwardes, firmly believed an empire had been given to Britain because of the virtues of English Protestantism. ... the district judge of Fatehpur, Robert Tucker, had recently set up large stone columns inscribed with the Ten Commandments in Persian, Urdu, Hindi and English and used "two or three times a week to read the Bible in Hindoostanee to large numbers of natives who were assembled in the compound to hear him". Such Evangelical enthusiasm had even spread to the British Army in India. According to one trooper of the Dragoon Guards, '... a religious mania sprang up and reigned supreme ...' It was a similar case in the Company's own army, where officers like Colonel Steven Wheler ... were in the habit of reading the Bible to ... sepoys as well as proselytising to ' natives of all classes ... in the highways, cities, bazaars and villages ...'[6]

Technologies, such as telegraph, railways and western medicine aroused deep suspicions. Each inroad was seen as a potential threat to the Indian way of life and particularly, the omnipresent fear of conversion to Christianity. Had not the English *firinghee* already interfered? The proposal to secure agreement from Brahmins to serve across the seas upon enlistment was unacceptable to them, as it would involve a breach of caste. 'Most Indians would agree that there had been progress ... but no Indian, surely, could fail to be aware of something a little chill and clammy near his heart when he regarded the conquerors who were bringing his countrymen so marked a progress in things they would hardly have chosen for themselves.'[7]

Measures to annex princely states, activated by Governor General Dalhousie, were extremely unpopular. His interpretation of the 'doctrine of lapse', which saw annexation of states where the ruler had died without a natural heir, was seen as unfair, even by some British leaders. Custom provided for adopted heirs to be recognised, but Dalhousie would not concede. Malleson claimed, '... he laid fast hold of the one abstract truth that English government, English laws, English learning, English customs, and English manners, are better than the government, the laws, the learning, the customs, and the manners of India; and with all the earnestness of his nature and all the strength of his understanding he wrought out this great theory in practice.'[8]

From 1848 to 1852, Dalhousie annexed five states and was to add three more before returning to England. Of the latter were Jhansi and Oudh (Awadh) and of those, Oudh, was to play a very serious role in the causes of the mutiny, as many of the sepoys in the three Indian armies of Bengal, Madras (Chennai) and Bombay (Mumbai), had been drawn from that state. The annexation of Oudh by Dalhousie did not involve 'lapse', but the ruler, the seventh Nawab Nasir-ud-din, was deemed unsuitable, as was his successor, and efforts were made to have him agree to surrender his state whilst retaining his title. Upon his refusal to accede, Oudh was annexed. That manoeuvre and its attendant taxation measures, caused widespread dissatisfaction amongst the native sons of Oudh.

Jhansi, the battle for which, will feature in Whirlpool's story, was annexed by Dalhousie, upon the death of the childless Maharaja Gungadhur Rao in November, 1853, despite his entreaties to Dalhousie that his adopted son, Damodar (Anand) Rao, should succeed him and that his widow should act as regent. His widow, the Rani of Jhansi, Lakshmibai, would be drawn into the mutiny four years later, either willingly or vicariously, and would be likened, by contemporary commentators, to Joan of Arc. The soldiers of Sir Hugh Rose called her 'Jezebel', an appellation reserved for a deceitful woman, given her perceived role in the massacre of Europeans.[9] A more likely comparison might have been Boudicca (Boadicea), whose husband was ruler of the Celtic Iceni people in Britain. He sought to bequeath his kingdom to his two daughters and jointly to Rome. Disdainfully, the Romans annexed the kingdom, flogged Boudicca and raped her daughters. She rose up and led an uncompromising war, inflicting great losses upon them. Eventually defeated, she is thought to have died by her own hand, or through sickness.

The Rani of Jhansi joined the mutiny and led her forces against the British, still harbouring disaffection over her treatment, and died in battle against them. It is probable that the Rani was forced to join the mutiny, as it became obvious that her perceived hand in the murder of British inhabitants at Jhansi could not be adequately defended. Far from leading her troops into battle against the British armies, the Rani defended her fort and palace by leading her defenders and inspiring them to stand firm. After the battle of Betwa, where a relieving army, under the command of Tantia Tope, was defeated and her defences were breached, she fled. Many of her escort were killed and the Rani also died, though bravely, in retreat. The Rani's foray was short and reactive, rather than proactive and therefore the parallels, though of course not exact, do seem to go deeper into personal circumstance rather than in Joan of Arc's visitations which urged her to fight for a godly purpose and for the greater good of her nation. The comparisons stemmed from the fact that the combatant in each case was a woman, battle leader and a martyr, rather than the actions they undertook.

Also fomenting mutiny, was the changed attitude of the British towards the Indians. Early accounts show that despite the inability of sepoys to achieve comparative rank, their relationship with their 'brothers-in-arms' was firm, cordial and one of fidelity. This began to deteriorate, some say because of proselytising, others due to the influence of more *memsahibs* arriving in India. 'The great Englishmen of the last century had taken the country, its people and their ways with noble openness of mind; Warren Hastings had been content 'to leave their religious creed to the Being who has so long endured it and who will in his own time reform it'. That would not be the attitude of Honoria Lawrence, a woman whose human love was deep, whose religion was warm, ever-present and living, who spoke for the best men of her generation when she wrote, 'There is something very oppressive in being surrounded by heathen and Mahommedan darkness, in seeing idolworship all around.'[10]

European women were arriving in increasing numbers as the rules limiting marriage and the quotas of wives allowed in cantonments were being relaxed. One anonymous observer noted in 1853, 'Every youth, who is able to maintain a wife, marries. The conjugal pair become a bundle of English prejudices and hate the country, the natives and everything belonging to them. If the man has, by chance, a share of philosophy and reflection, the woman is sure to have none. The 'odious blacks' the 'nasty heathen wretches' the 'filthy creatures' are the shrill echoes of the 'black brutes' the 'black vermin' of the husband. The children catch up the strain. I have heard one, five years old, call the man who was taking care of him a 'black brute'. Not that the English generally behave with cruelty, but they make no scruple of expressing their anger and contempt by the most opprobrious epithets that the language affords.'[11]

Other examples of racist invective abound and must be considered amongst the causes of disaffection. 'And if there seems a coldness in the attitude to Indians even of men ... whose lives were literally given up to service and who fervently believed that all they did was for the good of Indians — it is not surprising that something worse should have arisen among lesser men, that there should have been people who talked about niggers and danced quadrilles on the platform before the Taj Mahal.'[12]

It is no accident that a sense of superiority had developed among Europeans at this time, as the questions of race, the origins of species and their traits were being examined and discussed, particularly amongst those who identified with the 'superior' types. It was the time of Darwin and his distant cousin Francis Galton, the father of eugenics. It was also the beginning of the fading period of British imperialism.

This potent mix caused a fragmented unease, which was given impetus by rumour, gossip, active insurrection and sedition. Apparently unaware of its implications, those who should have known better, allowed the port-fire to be ignited when the question of greased cartridges for the new Enfield musket rifle was raised. The dangers implicit in this move seem not to have been considered. Requiring a lubricant of lard or fat, or a mixture of both, to ensure ease of placement into the barrel of the musket, the screwed top of the paper cartridge needed to be bitten off, powder poured into the barrel and the projectile seated home by ramming. Cattle being sacred to Hindus and pigs, unclean to Muslims, claims were made that this process was unacceptable to followers of both faiths. This issue, and perhaps all of the others, came to a head on 9 May 1857 at Meerut when the skirmishers of the 3rd Light Cavalry refused to handle the new cartridges. Meerut was the site of a factory producing the cartridges, which may have added to the sepoy's disquiet. Eighty-five men were sentenced to ten years imprisonment with hard labour for disobeying orders. They were marched out in front of their units and European troops, who formed three sides of a square. The prisoners were assembled on the fourth side where their sentences were read out. They were stripped of their insignia of rank, made to remove their boots, and were shackled by leg irons. Some accepted their punishment quietly, but others remonstrated with their overlords and accused their fellow sepoys of inaction. A young officer of the 3rd Light Cavalry reported that, as the prisoners filed past their regiment, some threw their boots at their Colonel, G.C. Smyth — cursing him loudly.[13] Another officer of the 3rd had warned Smyth and Hewitt that he had been told of the impending revolt by a loyal sepoy, but was laughed off. Smyth at least warned the Commander in Chief of it, but his actions on this day caused its outbreak.[14] 'Smyth spent the rest of his days arguing that his punishment parade had saved India for the British because it had caused the Mutineers to act prematurely, and had prevented a single rising all over the country on the agreed date.'[15] No-one could dispute his assertion and it probably allowed him to sleep soundly, but his actions and the inaction of his commander, General Hewitt, 'a muddled old man of 50 years service',[16] ensured that the mutiny had begun and would rapidly spread, without challenge from the European contingent at Meerut.

Lord Dalhousie whose own decisions played no small part in the uprisings was to warn in 1856, just prior to his departure from India, '... cruel violence might be suddenly committed by men who up to the last moment had been regarded as harmless, even by those who knew them best.'[17]

When Lord Canning addressed a function marking his departure to take up the Governor-Generalship he warned, 'I wish for a peaceful term in office. But I cannot forget that in the sky of India, serene as it is, a small cloud may arise no larger than a man's hand, but which growing larger may at last threaten to burst and overwhelm us with ruin.'[18]

About 5pm the day after the punishment parade, fires broke out and all of the sepoy battalions rose in revolt. After opening the gaol and releasing their comrades and other prisoners, they murdered their European officers, their wives and children, estimated to be fifty Europeans and Eurasians and their families. They plundered all they could lay hands on and drove on towards Delhi, some thirty miles away.

From this spark, the conflagration grew and the overthrow of European strongholds, the murder of Europeans, Eurasians, soldiers and civilians and their families continued apace. Though the number of European troops at Meerut numbered some 2,200 and their sepoy force slightly more numerous at about 3,000, poor leadership and indecision allowed the escape of the mutineers towards Delhi where they knew that no British contingents were in place. British officers in Delhi, vastly outnumbered by their own sepoys who joined the mutiny, could offer but little resistance. Some escaped, but many were killed. The arsenal was defended for a while, but eventually was blown up by its nine defenders, to prevent it falling to the mutineers, killing six of them.[19] To add to the confusion and poor leadership, Meerut had failed to warn Delhi of the approach of the mutineers. Brigadier Wilson, in a letter to his wife, was damning of the 67 year old general, Hewitt, describing him as '... a dreadful old fool, a sad stumbling block. He thinks of nothing but preserving his old carcass from harm.'[20]

Jerosch concludes, as if to highlight the failings of Hewitt and his ilk, 'This is indeed one of the most peculiar things about the Mutiny of 1857: while in the latter phases of the insurrection the British fought with almost inconceivable determination, perseverance and stubborn resolve, at the outbreak of the rebellion both the British military and civilians were, with very few exceptions confused, bewildered and incapacitated. ... the British ... had a sense of superiority which included the belief that their military and political invincibility could be taken for granted.'[21]

Officers, their wives and children were murdered in scenes, which were to be repeated in other parts of the country, notably in Lucknow (Lakhnao), Cawnpore (Kanpur) and Jhansi, where insurrection, treachery and maniacal criminality, sometimes unrestrained by mind altering *bhang*, added to the profligacy and daring of the mutineers and spurred them on. Not a single European was left alive in Delhi, and at Cawnpore the treachery was at its height as the Europeans had been offered safe passage, only to be ambushed and shot down at the point of their departure, at the river. The surviving men were executed and later, 200 women and their children were murdered by butchers from the bazaar after the mutinous sepoys refused to shoot them. Hundreds of men, women and children died here.

Word of the outbreak at Meerut did not reach England until 26 June 1857, some six weeks after the event. Once the situation became clearer in England, and the press made the tragedy widely known to the population, public agitation for vengeance was widespread. Vengeance was the catch-cry and justice was never a consideration. Revanchism was afoot. 'It was partly the suddenness of the treachery, partly the murder of English women that roused such a frenzy of hatred. Men of any race would wish to punish the slaughter of their women, but the English were roused to a special pitch of passion. The Victorian Englishman had raised for himself an ideal picture of womanhood, based in part on poetic convention and no doubt often sentimental, but it was held with all the force that could be banked up by sternly repressed instinct ... To hear that the women of his own race, to whom he himself gave so chivalrous a precedence, had been treacherously slaughtered reached the centre of the English officer's being, the very heart of his emotions.'[22]

Thomas Lowe, Medical Officer to the Madras Sappers and Miners, arrived in Bombay from the Crimea on 31 May 1857, to be met with the news of the mutiny. B Company of the detachment, en route to their base in Madras, were offered to the Bombay government and received orders to march to Aurungabad to join the moveable column of the Deccan, under the command of Major-General Woodburn. Lowe's 1860 account of the Central India Campaign,[23] though a personal one, provides vivid detail of some of the operations that were undertaken to re-establish control of the region. Lowe prefaces his recollections, which in part seek to elucidate some of the actions taken by the army. 'At this rather remote period, since the thrilling interest felt in the course of the events has naturally died away in the self-satisfying knowledge of safety, since murder is no longer feared, and the voice of mourning hushed, the reader may, perhaps, wonder that our vengeance was so great. It was necessary. Nothing less could have answered the ends; and though a drum-head court martial is a short affair, and soldiers long accustomed to scenes of blood sit in judgement, yet justice is done. The people were drunk with the blood of our countrymen, mad with excesses, blind to everything but fatalism, and desirous of nothing but rapine and political chaos, and for such a state of affairs an active and potent remedy was needed.'[24] Lowe's views are of their time and consequently, while self-serving, tend to give voice to the feelings of those whose duty it was to suppress the uprising, restore order and wreak vengeance. Others, like the Governor General, Lord Canning, took a softer line and earned the sobriquet 'Clemency Canning' from the soldiers and the English press. Nobody, it appears, saw the perversity in the British outlawing religious homicide, whilst pursuing their own form with such fervour. Canning wrote to Queen Victoria in September 1857, advising her of his misgivings at the treatment of Indians in Delhi, '... violent rancour of a very large proportion of the English Community against every native Indian of every class. There is a rabid and indiscriminate vindictiveness abroad, even amongst many who ought to set a better example, which is impossible to contemplate without something like a feeling of shame for one's fellow countrymen. Not one man in ten seems to think that the hanging and shooting of 40 or 50,000 Mutineers beside other rebels, can be otherwise than practicable and right...'[25]

Soon after, Canning issued a proclamation which was sure to further his claim to his sobriquet, though for the most part, his order seemed to have been ignored. 'The Governor-General has perused with a loathing to which he finds it impossible to give adequate utterance, the accounts of some of the means by which misguided natives have been compelled to depart this life. He expressly orders that no native shall in future be hanged, shot, or blown from a gun ...'[26]

In a perplexing move, he added a strange order, which seemed to ensure that those deserving of execution by blowing from the gun, should have their suffering reduced. The result — and there is no record of the means having been adopted — seems to have given the appearance of the victim having been executed twice over. '... but that in the very few cases in which it can be necessary, for the sake of example, to inflict the last penalty, the native's head shall be removed while he is under the influence of chloroform, or of opiates, to be administered as kindly as possible by the regimental surgeon.'[27] The victim's remains were then to be blown from the gun. Strange as this order seems, it would have been seen by Canning's critics as 'soft'.

Reinforcements were sent from the Crimea, diverted from China and recalled from Burma. Forces were sent from England, the foremost in early July, when some 30,000 men of all arms were sailing to India.[28] The government and company were aware that the outbreak could loosen their grip on India, if not release it for all time. For the most part, mutiny had been confined to the Bengal army. The Madras and Bombay armies had largely remained loyal. Afghanistan remained true to its alliance and the Indian princes, with notable exceptions, remained loyal. 'In short, everywhere in the Punjab an example was set, which can never be forgotten, of courage, energy and far-sightedness in time of peril. The Chiefs of Patiala, Nabha, Kapurthala, and other Sikh States came forward, moreover, with offers of military assistance; and not only provided guards for English ladies in out-stations, but assisted materially in the siege of Delhi and in the subsequent re-occupation of the disturbed territory surrounding that city.'[29]

Had they turned, India would have been lost, as the native armies greatly outnumbered the English. In 1857 the Indian Army comprised 45,522 Europeans and 232,224 natives.[30] For more than 200 years India had been ruled by bluff, bolstered by the belief that English strength was omnipotent. But weaknesses had been detected through reports from the Crimea and massive setbacks in Afghanistan, where English invincibility was shown for its basis in myth and mysticism, rather than fact.

Telegram from the magistrate at Meerut advising that 85 prisoners were detained. The line was cut the following day. Source: blog.chaukhat.com

CHAPTER SIX

THE RESPONSE

'Oh, wherefore come ye forth in triumph from the north,
With your hands, and your feet, and your raiment all red?'

Thomas Babbington Macaulay
'The Battle of Naseby' 1824

Days of inactivity following the fall of Meerut had allowed the fall of many other stations before General Anson, the Commander-in-Chief, prepared to march on Delhi, regarded at this time as the centre of the rebellion. Two days later, on 27 May, Anson died of cholera. He was succeeded by General Sir Henry Barnard who had been accused by his staff of indecisiveness at Delhi. By 1 June, Barnard had advanced towards the rebels. Brigadier Archdale Wilson, after what was described as a disastrous delay,[1] marched out of Meerut and joining Barnard with 3,000 Europeans and one battalion of Gurkhas, reached the outskirts of Delhi on 8 June. By 5 July, Barnard too was dead from cholera, as were many other ranks. General Reed assumed command and was said to be in poor health. Within two weeks he had handed the command to Brigadier Archdale Wilson who expressed his own doubts as to his ability to lead. Burne describes Wilson as,

'… an officer who, possessing no special force of character, did little more than secure the safe defence of the position until the arrival of Brigadier Nicholson from the Punjab, August 14th, 1857, with a moveable column of 2500 men, Europeans and Sikhs.'[2]

The rebels were also badly led, particularly by the son of the newly installed King, who was described as incompetent, and the King's grandson, who, though given high command, fled at the first sign of battle.

The steady hand of Sir Colin Campbell, who at 65 became the Commander-in-Chief of India at the invitation of Secretary of State for War, Lord Panmure, finally restored some direction. Campbell was born Colin Macliver, but took his name from his mother's family. He was a veteran of many conflicts and renowned for his personal gallantry. He had wanted retirement in 1849 but was persuaded to continue, and returned to England in 1853. The following year, at the outbreak of the Crimean War, Campbell accepted command of the Highland Brigade, which was prominent in the defeat of the Russians at the Battle of Alma. Promoted to Major-General, he served at Balaclava until peace was declared. Before leaving for England he addressed his troops, stating that he was old and would not be called to serve again.[3]

His plans, of course, were to again be disrupted by his Indian command, which he took up on 17 August 1857, reaching Calcutta, he waited instead of proceeding to the field. He was criticised for his delay and was called by his troops 'Old Khabardar,' meaning 'Old Take Care'. Campbell was seen as a capable officer but lacking in dash. He was not considered a born leader nor a gifted tactician, but respected he was, and his campaign would earn him great credit. He had the advantage of being accompanied on his part of the campaign by William Howard Russell, a journalist correspondent for *The Times*, who reported his successes to great public acclaim. This was not an advantage accorded Sir Hugh Rose and his force. It is seen as a reason for his lack of public profile, though regarded as one of the greatest of British Army generals by his close contemporaries and military historians.

To understand the circumstances under which Frederick Whirlpool fought and was singled out for his nation's greatest honour, it is important to appreciate too, those who would recognise him for his actions, as well as the great esteem in which they themselves were held for their gallantry, valour and leadership.

Hugh Henry Rose, the son of the Sir George Rose, essentially consul at the Prussian Court, was born in Berlin on 6 April 1801. His early military education was gained in Berlin and he entered the British Army in 1820. He served in Ireland and commanded the 92nd Highlanders in Malta, where he earned praise for his bravery and compassion when cholera broke out among his troops. He visited every one of his men in hospital, a practice he was to follow in other commands and campaigns.

In 1841, on special duty in Syria against the Egyptian army, he performed distinguished active service in the field, including leading an Arab cavalry assault which prevented a surprise attack on Omar Pasha, avoiding potentially heavy losses. He was awarded a sword of honour and the Nishan Iftihar from the Sultan and made a Companion of the Bath. He was permitted to accept the Cross of St. John of Jerusalem from Frederick William of Prussia.

Appointed British Consul-General in Syria, he took an active role, not within the scope of modern consuls. He rode between columns of Maronites and Druses, who were firing at each other and, at great risk to himself, stopped the fighting. Later, when other consular officials declined to assist, he rode alone to an area where civil war was intense. His personal intervention saved the lives of 700 Christians, whom he led to safety in Beirut, walking, to provide his horse to suffering women. Again, in Beirut, he was the only European, along with a medical officer and some Sisters of Charity, who remained behind to visit those afflicted and dying of cholera, as terrified people fled their homes. For his services in Syria, Colonel Rose was appointed Secretary of the British Embassy in Constantinople in 1851. In a telling move, when acting as Chargé d'Affaires, he took decisive action against attempts by the Russians, through their envoy, to subvert their treaty with Turkey, England and their allies. His actions did not receive favourable comment from England, but it has been claimed that had his efforts been accepted, the Crimean War would have been avoided.[4] This claim seems to have been an over simplification of arduous and detailed manoeuvres which were being thrashed out between Britain, France, Turkey and their allies.

When war with Russia did break out, Rose was appointed Queen's Commissioner at the headquarters of the French Army, with a local rank of Brigadier-General. He was commended for the manner in which he maintained the best relations with the French Commander-in-Chief and his staff and for tendering advice in accordance with the wishes of the government of Britain. Marshal

Canrobert recommended Rose for the Victoria Cross for conspicuous gallantry on three separate occasions during the siege of Sebastapole. Commentators have noted that Rose was denied the Victoria Cross, either because he was a general, or alternatively, because his was a general staff appointment with a foreign, though allied power.

The recently instituted Victoria Cross was open to all ranks, which was one of the reasons for its creation. His rank would not have been an impediment to the award, nor, it seems would have been his assignment to an allied force, where he performed meritorious acts in the face of the enemy. Indeed, in his early correspondence with Prince Albert on the subject of a new award to reward gallantry, the Duke of Newcastle stated, 'I confess it does not seem to me right or politic that such deeds of heroism as this war has produced should go unrewarded by any distinctive outward mark of honour because they are done by Privates or by Officers below the rank of Major, and it is impossible to believe that HM troops fighting side by side with those of France do not draw an invidious contrast between the rewards bestowed upon themselves and their allies.' ... 'There are some Orders which even Crowned Heads cannot wear, and it would be a military reward of high estimation if this cross could be so bestowed as to be within the reach of every Private Soldier and yet to be coveted by any General at the head of an Army.'[5]

So, from these earliest discussions on the subject in 1855, the intention was clear. All ranks would be capable of receiving the one award. Similarly, the original warrant, which instituted the Victoria Cross on 29 January 1856, made no mention of exceptions when serving with allied forces. The fifth rule of that warrant states, 'It is ordained that the Cross shall only be awarded to those Officers or Men who have served Us in the presence of the Enemy and shall then have performed some signal act of valour or devotion to their Country.'[6]

Rose's appointment to Marshall Canrobert's staff was clearly not an impediment to his receiving the Victoria Cross. It is more likely that he was the victim of a misunderstanding at the War Office, where it was still widely believed that the Victoria Cross was intended for lower ranks and the Order of the Bath remained the province of senior officers. This seems to be borne out by his being promoted to Major-General, created a Knight of the Bath and a Commander of the Légion d'honneur.[7] In the early years of the award and during its conception, Queen Victoria and Albert's intention, and those of some of her Ministers, were at odds with others who did not understand the change, or the reasons behind it. On 25 February 1856, Colonel Mundy of the War Office advised the Secretary of the Admiralty and the Commander in Chief of the Army, that the names of intended recipients of the Victoria Cross from the lower ranks should be advised. Lord Panmure, Secretary for War on whose behalf Mundy had written, was still of the erroneous belief that the Victoria Cross was to be reserved for the lower ranks and that the three orders of the Bath would be reserved for officers. 'The error was put right on 20th Mar, 1856 when Colonel Mundy wrote to Maj-Gen Sir Charles Yorke, the MS [Military Secretary] at the Horse Guards and the Secretary to the Admiralty. 'With reference to my letter of the 25th ultimo I am directed by Lord Panmure to request you will state ... that it is intended that the decoration of the VC may be bestowed on officers of all ranks, who have distinguished themselves by conspicuous bravery.' Despite this, however, the notion long lingered that this was not to be a commanding or field officer's decoration ...[8]

The Duke of Cambridge, as Commander in Chief of the British Army, however, set the precedent that senior ranking officers above major could not receive the Victoria Cross as the orders of the Bath were open to them. He is said to have generally resisted change in his army and led it into a parlous state. He did however, support Sir Hugh Rose and would later appoint him, Commander-in-Chief, Ireland.[9] Similarly, Sir Colin Campbell held this view when Lt. Colonel James Hagart was recommended for the VC for his actions in India, and was refused the award.[10] Again, in 1900 Colonel (local Major General) Hamilton was refused the VC because he was commanding a Brigade and therefore a General Officer. The precedent would not be breached until 1917.[11]

Rose, and many others, were denied the Victoria Cross because of their rank and the reluctance of their leaders to embrace the spirit of the award and the form of the Royal Warrant, which determined its terms. There can be no doubting Rose's bravery, strength of purpose, resolve and military prowess. Robson describes him as '...one of the most remarkable generals in British military history, but ... an enigma.'[12]

Similarly, Stanley is high in his praise for this enigmatic leader. 'While Campbell's "moveable columns" quartered Oudh, Rohilcund and Bundlecund, gradually engaging, pursuing and eliminating rebel forces, in Central India the last major campaign of the rebellion began. A Bombay army conducted the most remarkable campaign of the rebellion, introducing to the British Army in India the commander who was to influence more than any other individual the fate of the European force, Sir Hugh Rose.'[13]

Unlike Campbell, Rose was decisive. At the outbreak of mutiny, he volunteered for service in India and was appointed to command the Poona Division. No-one could have foreseen that this appointment would lead to his command of the Central India Field Force, as he had no field command experience. He had been liaison officer to the French and had observed warfare in other theatres, but had barely led troops in action. He was criticised for his lack of leadership skill and was considered frail and delicate — not suited to warfare. He was to prove otherwise, in spades.

Before the arrival of Rose, Brigadier C.S. Stuart was sent, in June 1857, as part of a greater force to relieve Mhow. He led the Malwa Field Force before re-forming as the 1st Brigade under Rose's, then named, Nerbudda Field Force. From early August until mid October, the fort there was strengthened and preparations were made to advance, when the wet season ended.

It was not until November 1857, that Brigadier Charles Steuart's 2nd Brigade began amassing at Sehore. That both brigades were led by Brigadiers Charles Steuart and Charles Stuart caused confusion at the time and no less so today, particularly when others, including Rose, added the name Stewart as an alternative in their correspondence. Our interest in this brigade rests mainly with the 3rd Bombay European Regiment and Frederick Whirlpool in its 5th Company. From General Rose's notebook of about 1 December 1857,[14] it is clear that the regiment consisted of 449 Europeans and was part of the Deccan Field Force, which was to become Rose's 2nd Brigade. A further detachment of 255 of the 3rd Bombay European Regiment were to join the force from Nuggur on 7 December, making a total of 704 men of a regiment that was raised in 1853 and had never seen active service. They were commanded by Colonel John Liddell. Rose, in a dispatch from Poona on 28 November 1857, to Lord Elphinstone, Governor of Bombay, thanks him for the opportunity of leading his force into Central India. He added an observation. 'I am just going to inspect the Troop of the 14th, at Kirkee which is to join Brigadier Steuart; they will be 90 sabres strong. The 3rd I am to see in a day or two; they are described as remarkably fine men; not so tall as broad and muscular. The country people say "England has now sent some of her peasants."'[15]

It is clear that Rose had been given a good appraisal of the 3rd Europeans, though tinged with a mild slight as to their origins. He would have cause to hold to the earlier part of that appraisal.

Brigadier Steuart's force left Asirgath on 15 November 1857, and made its way to Cundwah, some 24 miles distant. It then moved on to Hoshangabad on the Nerbudda River between Nagpur and Bhopal, before arriving at Sehore at the end of the month. In the meantime, Sir Hugh Rose, travelling by bullock gharry with Sir Robert Hamilton, political agent to the Governor General, arrived at Indore, where Tukojirao Holkar II, the Maharaja had disarmed his cavalry and infantry. He had begun courts martial and executing mutineers, the ringleaders being 'blown away from guns'. This gruesome spectacle, which was a Mughal punishment, had also been adopted by the British. It involved the offender being tied with his back to the mouth of a cannon, his arms secured and the charge, mostly without a projectile, being ignited by the port-fire. Death was instantaneous, with the head flying into the air and the burning trunk and entrails being scattered on the field. 'A word and a flash blew the head high in mid-air, without so much as displacement of the bandage from the eyes, the arms flew wide asunder, the legs beneath the gun and the chest, to fill the vacuum caused by the explosion, was driven back, bespattering gun and gunners.'[16] This mode of execution was usually witnessed by the troops of the offenders corps and of those in command, who were invariably spattered with the blood and gore of the victim, as were the gunners who had not taken care to protect themselves with sheeting.

Sir Robert Hamilton reported to Lord Elphinstone from Indore on 23 December, that the Amjeera Raja and three officials had been tried and sentenced to be hung. The Raja's sentence was commuted to transportation for life and the three others were hanged that morning.[17] By the evening of his report, eight more mutineers had been blown from guns. On the 27th a report was received from Asirgarh that five men had been hanged at Mhow and that Colonel Durand's, (Acting Agent to the Governor General), '… fun in hanging a lot of fellows at Indore was spoilt by the arrival of Sir Robert [Hamilton], who is supposed to be less viciously disposed.'[18]

Two days later, Rose reported to Lt. General Somerset that the Durbar of Indore (Ruler's Council) had not shown good faith or promptitude in punishing those responsible for the murder of 38 British subjects, plunder of the Residency, and the mutiny of Holkar's troops in July. 'With the exception of blowing one man away from a gun today a continuation of the same earnest representations was the cause of seventeen men being executed, not one officer was amongst them.'[19]

These short and savage reprisals, which followed equally rapid 'drum head' courts martial, meted out vengeance in the guise of justice. They were intended to shock and awe the enemy and no mutineer or rebel could be unaware of his fate, if captured alive.

Rose wrote to Steuart in January 1858, advising that they would meet on the 10th and outlined the composition of the siege train, which included two companies of the 3rd Bombay Europeans, and his intention to move with it to Sehore to prepare for the relief of Saugor (Sagar). The fort at Saugor contained one weak company of artillery, 40 officers of covenanted and uncovenanted services (Honourable East India Company civil servants), a large arsenal and 170 women and children. In the cantonment were 1,000 Bengal sepoys and 100 irregular cavalry, who were not trusted and not permitted to enter the fort. The fort was imperilled and Rose was receiving conflicting reports of the urgency of his intended relief. He would take 34 days to reach Saugor, after taking the fort of Rathgarh on the way.

Rose arrived at Sehore on 10 January, as planned, with his force, which included about 700 of the 3rd Bombay Europeans. The men of this regiment and Frederick Whirlpool had seen nothing of fighting before the outbreak of the mutiny in May 1857, though they had trained and drilled for combat since enlisting; they had been trained to kill. They saw conflict on their march to Sehore, and the flow of bloody executions, both summary and as the result of 'drum head' courts martial, which continued unabated.

The Bhopal Contingent consisting of about 600 infantry and 100 cavalry had mutinied, with only a few remaining loyal. They overran the nearby countryside, but for some inexplicable reason, they began to return in a steady flow. Sir Robert Hamilton had conveyed the government's intention of punishing the mutineers by proceeding to Sehore, with the loyal remnants of the Bhopal Contingent, whose evidence would be relied upon at courts martial. In early January, those who had mutinied were disarmed, stripped of their uniforms and over 400 were arrested. They had been ordered to parade and did so, no doubt considering that they had been allowed back into the fold. Of those who gradually returned to camp, were a number who had deserted their posts at Bursiah, north of Bhopal, through fear, rather than disaffection. They were accordingly each sentenced to 7 years hard labour, but Rose intervened and stressed that their actions still amounted to mutiny. Their sentences were increased to transportation for life. Rose considered them poltroons and not worthy of relief and it is clear that he would have preferred them to be executed along with the mutineers.

The courts martial needed to be conducted within three days and sat from morning till dark to deal with the volume of cases. Three mass trials were conducted in one day, but even then, some prisoners were not tried, as time for doing so had run out. From this, it would appear that the 'drum head' courts were conducted with some semblance of order, with bloody vengeance not wholly sought.

On 12 January, 149 men who had been tried by a drum-head court martial in the morning, were sentenced to be executed by firing squad. Their distress can only be imagined. That evening their fears were realised as they were taken to a parade as darkness approached. They were bound and blindfolded and forced to kneel in a single line before a shallow ditch. Some protested their innocence, others shouted insults at their captors and their former comrades who had given evidence against them, whilst others resigned themselves to their fate, knowing that this conflict rarely exposed compassion. A firing party of 149 men of the 3rd Bombay Europeans marched up close behind them and readied their Enfield's near the backs of the prisoner's heads. On the order to fire the crackle of shots rang out into the evening stillness, not in unison, but as the men felt able to do their duty. A pause would be as much of a liberty they could afford. To delay longer or fail to fire would bring terrible consequences. The smoke from the black powder engulfed the lines and 146 of the prisoners lurched forward, flailing and convulsing as their almost headless bodies gave up their sanguineous reserves in heavy, heaving spurts. Their blood pooled about them, filling the ditch by the gallon; pumping at first, then slowly oozing to envelope fragments of bone, hair, brain and gobbets of scorched tissue, until their rent bodies lay still, their futile, involuntary thrashing now quieted. The acrid smell of spent black powder and burnt flesh was kept low by the night air. The Enfield at close range was not a clean killer. No longer recognisable, these faceless, ruptured rumps of humanity were left in situ to stiffen then begin to bloat in their crimson congealing gore, which grew darker as it set and as night fell on the scene, sapping colour to black and grey.

Three of their number escaped, according to eyewitness, Lieutenant Bonus, who recounted the experience in a letter to his parents the following day.[20] Still blindfolded and bound, they ran off into the jungle, quickly melding into its verdancy and the fading light. Later that night, further shots were heard as 267 prisoners had attempted escape. Forty five were successful, 13 were shot and the remainder secured.

It is not known if Whirlpool was one of the firing party, but he would certainly have been forced to witness the massacre and may have been one of the men of his regiment who, with their officer, were ordered to stand guard over the bodies for the night.[21] It is hard to imagine why this guard was set, other than to ensure that the dirty task was finalised to military expectations of completeness. Completeness would entail burial, rather than any question of the nicety of protecting the dead from marauding hyenas, that would tear at their already defiled bodies. This would not be the case with prisoners hanged on the march as a warning to villagers. The longer they hung, the more effective the warning — and the hyena had its day, eating their legs to the knee.

Even by standards prevailing in India and England at the time, this incident caused horror in England and was the subject of great censure in the press. The tenor of their reportage can been seen in a report in the *Leeds Intelligencer* of Saturday 20 February 1858. 'At Sehore, Sir Hugh Rose had disarmed and punished the Bhopal contingents. After a little hesitation the whole of the contingent laid down their arms. Between 200 and 300 were then arrested and tried. Two days after 140 were executed. The firing party was not more numerous than the prisoners, consisting only of 150 men of the 3rd Bombay European Regiment, many of the shots failed to inflict instant death, and some missed altogether, rendering necessary further discharges, and even, it is stated, the sabres of the Dragoons.'[22]

The issue was to follow Rose into 1859. It caused the Court of Directors of the East India Company to write to Governor General, Lord Canning in March 1858, referring to newspaper reports of the executions. An explanation was called for and on 7 May 1858, Colonel Birch, Military Secretary to the Governor General wrote to Rose seeking the original proceedings of the courts martial of the Bhopal Contingent.[23] In 1859, the Governor General agreed with the actions taken by Rose, his earlier proclamation apparently having been overrun by circumstance.

Detail of the newspaper reports reached the men at the front. Lt. Bonus, writing to his parents in February 1858, reassures them, 'By the way do not believe half what you see in the papers about the doings of this force. I have been astonished at the lies I have seen.'[24]

Bonus described the executions in detail and made no mention of missed shots, or sabre attacks. He described one quick encounter and the prisoners lying dead on the ground. He also described the soldier's weapons as almost touching the backs of their heads, so the prospect of missing their target seemed remote. The Enfield rifle musket required manual loading of each shot and a good marksman was reckoned to be able to get three shots off in a minute. This would tend to make any second shots clumsy, time consuming and the cause of disarray. This did not happen. Like Bonus, Thomas Lowe describes the prisoners being brought out and ranged in single line, just as the sun was setting, and at the given signal, they were shot.[26] He reported that one man escaped. No mention was made of missed targets or sabring of the prisoners. As there was no correspondent with the Central India Field

Force, it can be safely assumed that as terrible as the incident was, it was embellished back in Britain.

If Whirlpool was in the firing party or the overnight guard, or even in file to witness the horror, it would have been a jolt to the man who aspired to be a schoolmaster and who had served quietly until the outbreak of mutiny. He had seen much of death en route to Sehore, in skirmishes or other executions, but as a certain witness to this mass killing he had seen the worst of human excess — or had he? A soldier of the 3rd Bombay Europeans identified only as HK, but certainly Private Hugh Kenalty, wrote to his parents in Birmingham on the 6th March 1858. 'When we got to a place called Sehore, we had to disarm a native regiment who had mutinied about three months previously, but afterwards returned to their duty. They were brought out on a large plain under the idea that they were going to be put through their exercise, and in the meantime we were ordered to turn out and load without a bugle call. We were marched up to them, and some artillery with loaded guns, and then they were ordered to leave their arms. They did not seem to like it much. After they were stripped 100 of them were made prisoners, and the rest were sent about a mile away. The next day they came back, and were all made prisoners. That same night we were suddenly ordered out, and when we got a little way from camp we found a line of prisoners some 149 strong, formed up beside a shallow trench. 149 of our chaps were then brought to the front, loaded, and then we blew their brains out. It was the largest execution I ever saw. We afterwards hung, blew away from big guns, and shot by musketry about 100 more. We then march on a large fort, called Rathghur; but we had a lot of prisoners with us, and at every village we passed we hung five or six, by way of warning.'

Again, no mention is made of second shots or sabre use as a *coup de grâce*. His account provides evidence that the regiment was called out to witness their comrades perform the executions. No mention is made in official records of the remaining 267 prisoners, 45 of whom escaped, 13 shot whilst attempting escape, or the balance of 209. Hugh Kenalty, if his account is to be believed, clearly indicates that the killing continued at Sehore with the hanging, blowing from guns, or shooting of about 100 prisoners and the remaining 109 or so, being retained for execution in batches on the road. India had become a charnel-house with savagery on both sides, and the sanctioned killings, both summary and under a thin veil of justice, continued in what must have looked like the harrowing scenes from Goya's,[27] 'The Disasters of War', from an earlier conflict, or Jacques Callot's,[28] 'The Miseries and Misfortunes of War', of 1633, which graphically illustrated butchery, cruelty, torture and the depths to which man is capable of descending. It appears that not all executions were officially reported. It was perhaps just as well that no journalist accompanied the force.

A final account is provided by Private James Flude in a letter to his parents of 25 February and published in the third person by *The Leicestershire Mercury*. As will be seen later, his assumed name was Private Few of the 3rd Bombay Europeans. '… he with his company left Sattara on the 23rd of November last, and joined the regiment at Sehore on the 15th of January, where they disarmed a regiment of Sepoys, afterwards shooting 149 of the rebels. They then marched to the relief of Saugor … '[29] No embellishment and nothing alarming about these terrible executions was mentioned.

From Sehore, the Nerbudda Field Force marched on Rathgarh on 19 January, arriving at 4pm the next day. Upon approaching the village, they were fired upon and the Dragoons and a company of the 24th Native Infantry skirmished with the enemy, forcing them into the village. Lieutenant Donne and his men camped for the night and established picquets on their outer perimeter, where they sustained fire from the enemy the night through. Fire was returned and at daybreak the rebels entered the fort. Shortly after, the 3rd Europeans led by Lieutenant-Colonel Liddell, with Major-General Rose, some cavalry and artillery, advanced up a hill some 350 yards from the fort. Two companies of the 3rd Europeans fanned out in skirmishing order and the force reached the summit undiscovered, and remained there for three days bombarding the walls of the fort until a breach appeared. Fire was returned from the walls but with little effect, slightly wounding three or four men.. A feigned attack on the town had been ordered by Rose under the direction of Brigadier Steuart, which was to draw attention from the real attack. On the third day, the firing from the wall ceased. The rebels in the fort had broken through another wall and lowered themselves by rope, passing the Bhopal native troops who had remained loyal, though perhaps not too enthusiastic in preventing them making good their escape. Rose estimated, from interrogated prisoner's information, that some 4,000 people were in the fort, but only a portion of them were fighting men. The 3rd Europeans entered by way of the incomplete breach and were met by the fire of some remaining rebels, who they killed.

When the fort was inspected it was found that the rebels had little ammunition and limited ordnance. Local Governor, Mahomed Fazl Khan, who had made a short escape, was betrayed by a servant to an officer of the Dragoons, and he and the Nawab Kamdar Khan were hanged over the gate of the fort at sunset. The next day, twenty six men were tried, seventeen of them were convicted and quickly hanged, showing again that some semblance of tenuous judicial oversight was in place. Lieutenant Shakespear's account gave a number of 25 shot on the night of the escape and 17 more hanged the following day.[30] Rose reported that despite all that had gone before and the discovery of an effigy of the head of a decapitated European woman, which the rebels appeared to have carried before them in battle, the 3rd Europeans upon entering the fort treated the women and numerous children of the rebels who were left there, '… with the humanity which was to be expected from their discipline and their faith. I had enjoined the troops, for the honour of their Country and the Army, not to harm a woman or child.'[31]

With Rathghur secure, Rose prepared to move on to Saugor, to relieve Europeans and their allies, who had been barricaded in the fort for months. Before leaving he telegraphed Lord Elphinstone, 'My second Brigade under the able command of Brigadier Stewart [Steuart] deserves all my thanks, surrounded by thick jungle and dangerous ground, attacked in the rear, and performing duties which according to rule demanded three if not four times their number … The 3rd Europeans young as they are have done credit to the Bombay Army. The women and children of the rebels were treated by the troops with the greatest humanity.'[32]

He was referring to their repulsion of an attack of about 1,500 rebels from Naraoili and Bhopal, who attempted to retake the fort, and a later, smaller attack. Eighteen rebels were executed. Those who escaped were later confronted and beaten at the battle for Barodia. As the force crossed a river and approached the village of Barodia, they were attacked by a large body of rebels, many of whom were cut up. The British suffered casualties, including eight of the 3rd Europeans who were severely wounded.

On 31 January, an attack was made on the fort of Barodia by Major Scudamore, who had called for a Howitzer to blow in the gate. Rose with a force, which included the 3rd Europeans, reinforced the attack and the gate was destroyed. The firing from the fort stopped and the rebels again made their escape through a small postern. Several British were killed in this attack.

The field force moved on, without further incident, to relieve Saugor, arriving on 3 February 1858, to the great joy and excitement of the inhabitants. The last station of the beleaguered British; 370 men, women, and many children had been relieved. Their survival would not have been possible without the loyalty of the portion of the 31st Native Infantry, which had not mutinied. Lowe noted, 'The Europeans looked very pale and care worn, and well they might, after having endured so anxious an imprisonment, cut off from all escape, and packed together within the walls of the fort for so long, surrounded by bodies of the enemy who constantly harassed them, and living in the midst of a vast population of disaffected natives.'[33]

The force remained at Saugor for a considerable time, to repair equipment and re-supply ammunition and provisions. By 9 February, sufficient supplies had arrived to allow a move on the fort at Garakhota. At about this time, the name of the Nerbudda Field Force was changed to the Central India Field Force to better represent the scope and breadth of its activities, rather than the area nearer the Nebudda River further to the south, which had been its original focus. The force found that the marauding rebels had decimated the countryside and had pillaged every conceivable remnant from the natives.

Observing operations before Garakhota, at Nurraullee (where the British had been repulsed) and at Sanoda, Lowe noted '... the villagers about Sanoda appeared to be in the deepest distress. They had been plundered of everything by mutinous sepoys and bundeelahs for months past, and were reduced to such an extreme condition of poverty as to wander through our camp seeking the undigested grains from among the dung of our cattle, and then and there to eat them!'[34]

The villagers were provided with large quantities of grain by the force and the cotwal who had assisted the enemy and inflicted great hardship on his charges, was arrested. He offered to provide valuable information to save his life. The following morning he remained silent and was hanged from a tree, apparently having had second thoughts, or having nothing to offer. The march to Garakhota continued and the force when within site of it, stopped at Shapore for breakfast, '... and to hang a few more rebels.'[35]

The rebels had left some two hours earlier, so the force moved on, cutting their way through thick jungle, avoiding the rebel reinforced road. When about four or five miles from Garakhota fort they surprised an infantry outpost, which was driven off by the 3rd Europeans and the 24th Native Infantry. The heat was terrific and engagements with the enemy were constant, taking a terrible toll on the troops who had to pause every few hundred yards as the heat overcame them. Despite this, the 3rd Europeans with the 24th Native Infantry and the 3rd Bombay Light Cavalry, preceded the columns as they neared the fort. The cavalry captured five men who Rose ordered to be taken to the rear and shot.

A camp was established and Rose rode out to reconnoitre the field, returning just before 8pm, with his exhausted staff. They had been in the saddle for 18 hours and had not eaten. At 8am the following day, Rose again rode out with his staff and an escort, including a company of the 3rd Europeans, to further examine the fort, from which they sustained fire. They returned to camp at 7pm and the fort was bombarded. By the next morning, again, the rebels had fled. The mutineers of the 51st and 52nd Bengal Regiments were pursued by the Hyderabad Cavalry for some twenty-five miles and were slain in great number, completing their rout. The 3rd Europeans guarded the fort as work to demolish it began.

NARUT, DHANONI AND MUDINPORE

To continue his move to Jhansi, Rose needed to cross a range of hills separating Bundelkhund and the Saugor districts, and through which were three passes. Narut was the the most extensive and had been heavily barricaded by its 8 to 10,000 defenders led by the Raja of Banpur and mutineers from the 31st and 42nd Bengal Native

Infantry, who had broken from their loyal counterparts in Saugor. Lowe provides an insight into this breach within the native regiments, through a recounted conversation with the commander of the 31st, Lieutenant Dickins, who had continued to lead his loyal troops. Dickins thought that the reason they had remained loyal was that the officers perhaps knew their men better than most. The loyal troops had been engaged against their former comrades and had been taunted for not deserting. It is notable that Dickins was a linguist and was well acquainted with the character of his men, which they appreciated. This would have been a salutary lesson for many of the Europeans then engaged in the fighting in India, had they bothered to learn it.[36]

The rebels considered Rose's likeliest approach to be centred on Narut, which they heavily fortified and barricaded with boulders and abatis. The second pass, and only a little more difficult than Narut, was Dhanoni. The other was Mudinpore, defended by the Raja of Shahgarh, about which little was known, but after reconnaissance by Major Orr, it was chosen by Rose for a breach as the ordnance map showed it suitable for guns. Rose ordered a feint attack against Narut and advanced on Mudinpore. He was forced into a rapid advance by the enthusiasm of one of his officers who advanced prematurely and precipitously approached an ambush. Rose later reported that the fire was as hot and rapid as he had ever seen. He retreated and the attack intensified with the 3rd Europeans charging against the front of the sepoys, then skirmishing the hills on each flank. The rebels were forced back into the village of Mudinpore, which was heavily fortified by masonry and earthworks from which guns had played on the 3rd Europeans as they skirmished on the hills.

The remainder of the siege train was brought through the pass and positioned safely, while the rebel guns were pounded by an 8 inch Howitzer and 9 pound artillery piece, forcing the enemy to retreat into the jungle and head for the fort of Serai. They were pursued by the 3rd Europeans and the Hyderabad Cavalry, who killed about 300 and took prisoners. The Narut pass was attacked from its rear and taken. After making the pass the brigade rested, as the heat was intense. The troops lay in the sun and slept soundly until ordered to move again. They then marched for almost twenty miles in searing heat and fell into their tents to sleep on the ground. The capture and destruction of Serai and the capture of the deserted fort of Marowra quickly followed, as did their annexation to the Crown. The road to Jhansi was clear.

Meanwhile the 1st Brigade under Brigadier Stuart was ordered to proceed by the Grand Trunk (Agra) Road via Goonah (Guna) and Sipri (Shivpuri) to meet Rose and the 2nd Brigade before Jhansi. Stuart was to receive the 86th Regiment, which following him up as soon as was possible. The Brigade included a company of 3rd Bombay Europeans (50 men) and Rose had also arranged for Captain Hare and the 31st and 42nd Bengal Native troops, nearly all of whom, it will be recalled, had remained loyal, to join the 1st Brigade at Goonah. This brigade saw severe action, firstly in taking the Kattee Ghattee, a tunnel that runs through the hills which surround the fort of Chanderi. The pass was breached and the force moved on the fort. The ancient town had once contained 14,000 stone houses, 84 markets, 386 caravanseras (caravan inns) and 12,000 mosques, but all lay in ruin brought about by Mahratta rule.[37] Rose had arranged support should it be required, and delayed his march accordingly. The assistance not being required and after an intense investment of the fort, its seizure was effected under very trying conditions. The 1st Brigade had prevailed and had opened the Grand Trunk Road to Agra, wasting no time in marching towards Jhansi to join Rose and the 2nd Brigade.

Hugh Kenalty, as HK, wrote to his parents. 'There is a very large force at Jhansi and we expect to be joined by the 2nd Brigade, under Brigadier Stuart, [Steuart] before we get there. I hope we shall, as our own force is very small, and they say that the rebels are all making for Jhansi.'[38]

CHAPTER SEVEN

JHANSI

'Who would true valour see,
Let him come hither...'

John Bunyan
'The Pilgrim's Progress' 1684

It took Rose and the 2nd Brigade a march of five hours to advance to within 10 miles of Jhansi, arriving at 7am on 20 March 1858. Rose immediately rode off with his staff to reconnoitre the field, city and fort. He had no plans of the fort and imprecise, erroneous maps of the surrounding area. He needed to see for himself how the land lay and where he should concentrate his attack. Jhansi was surrounded by thick walls 4½ miles in circumference, which were up to 16 feet thick and ranged from 12 to 30 feet high. They were interspersed with bastions of huge size, which were armed with artillery. To efficiently identify them, Rose tagged the twelve of them with readily recognisable names, such as *3. The White Tower Battery* or *4. The Black Tower Battery*, to avoid confusion. On the western side was a massive fort with more bastions and batteries. The enemy had removed any comfort or protection for the troops by levelling trees and other structures that might obstruct their line of fire, or provide shade and cover. Lowe reported that they were also short of firewood, water and grass.[1]

In their preparations at Saugor, the 3rd Europeans had been issued with uniforms especially suited to the climate in which they were serving. Their European cold weather uniform, which was totally unsuited to India, especially in the hot season, was replaced with a loose stone coloured cotton blouse, trousers, and puggaree of the same colour. This was an early use of khaki, an Urdu word meaning 'dust coloured'. ' ... [A] most judicious step, as the men could bear considerably more fatigue with comparative comfort while at a distance of half a mile they were almost invisible,' noted Lowe. 'Nothing could be more baneful to European troops in India than the dress worn by them in England and other temperate climates. It is amazing to think that the authorities did not alter this a century ago.'[2]

The 3rd Europeans thus became the envy of the other troops who called them 'brass heads' and similar names, for their ability to better bear extreme heat.

Jhansi fort was reported to be garrisoned by about 11,000 men, 1,500 of whom were mutineers. Rose's combined forces numbered about 5,000. He established seven 'flying camps' of cavalry and horse artillery around the city to prevent the garrison escaping and to warn of enemy advances. After further reconnaissance, main camps were established about 1½ miles apart to the south of the city and positioned for the establishment of breaching batteries. On the southwestern edge of the city wall was a prominent mound or mamelon, which ran up to a massive bastion. It was here that Rose decided to attempt his breach of the wall, which was one of the most powerful defences of the city. He planned to attack through this breach and by escalade at the Orcha Gate, east of the mound, to be well placed to attack the fort from within the city.

The bombardment commenced on 23 March, with the Right Attack Battery firing on the wall at the rear of the mound. The Left Attack Breaching Battery commenced its work on the 26th and despite heavy fire from the wall, exacted a breach on the 30th, and Rose was ready to launch his assault.

THE BATTLE OF THE BETWA

Later that day, Rose learned that Tantia Tope, the Nana Sahib's *aide-de-camp*, was approaching from the east bank of the Betwa River leading 22,000 men with 28 guns, to relieve Jhansi. Tantia Tope had styled himself a general and was one of the main leaders of the rebels. Rose knew that he had to maintain his investment of Jhansi and continue the bombardment, in preparation for a breach and to prevent the garrison escaping to provide aid to the approaching rebels. Still mindful of the planned escalade and storming to come, he ordered preparations for a feigned attack on the northern wall of the city, should it be required. Forty or more 3rd Bombay Europeans and Lieutenant Bonus, of the Bombay Engineers were to assist in this manoeuvre. Major Gall, in charge of one of the flying camps at the northern side of the wall, was to reconnoitre in preparation for its eventuality.

Rose took 1,500 men from his besieging force with 19 guns and marched 6 miles towards the Betwa River to meet Tantia Tope the next evening. He planned to lure Tantia across the river to make him fight with his back to it. He was successful in drawing his first line across the river by feigning a retreat on the evening of the 31st. In the meantime he received intelligence that part of Tantia's force was crossing the river, further to the north, in an effort to take his flank and prevent his retreat to the city. He split his force yet again, despatching Stuart with 900 troops to confront the northern attackers. At daybreak the following morning, Rose led four troops of cavalry and 400 native infantry with three heavy guns, four horse artillery guns and some field guns, about 600 men in all, to meet Tantia who had commenced his attack. Two troops of the light dragoons charged Tantia's right wing and a third troop with another of the Hyderabad Contingent Cavalry, the left. Tantia's force gave way and scattered. Confusion ensued and the enemy turned in disarray. Rose began a general advance straight at the centre of the rebels. The whole of the artillery and cavalry were sent after them. 'The fugitives — singularly or standing back to back — availed themselves of any shelter they could find. Maddened with bhang, they fought desperately; springing on the pursuers, matchlock and tulwar in hand, or lying down and cutting at them. The jungle, too, was set on fire by the fugitives ... '[3]

They were pursued across the Betwa for three miles losing 1,500 killed and ceding 18 guns, one an English 18 pounder drawn by two elephants of the Gwalior Contingent, whose mutineers were amongst Tantia's force. Other ordnance and two more elephants were captured. Stuart's force entered the action and aided in the completion of the defeat, taking five of the guns. Rose estimated that between 1,500 and 2,000 rebels were killed in the battle of Betwa. The European losses were 19 killed and 66 wounded. Exhausted, but elated by victory, the force moved back to camp that evening and rested the whole of the next day, as the cannonade continued on the city walls.

Not wishing to give the garrison ease after the defeat of their allies, Rose moved quickly to make the best of their disappointment. His worthy motto could have read '*bis dat qui cito dat*' — 'he gives twice who gives quickly'. He believed that attack should be followed by attack and when they fall back, go straight at them. He discarded many of the old precepts of warfare and in doing so, re-wrote the tactical manoeuvres to be adopted in India, and beyond. In fact, Rose, a complete novice to India, very quickly found his feet and understood the nature of his enemy. He wrote to Somerset in March 1858. 'The great thing with these Indians is not to stay at long distance firing, but after they have been cannonaded, to close with them, they cannot stand.'[4]

Half a century before, the Abbé Dubois commented on the fighting heritage and ability of the Hindu, particularly after the role of soldier had been wrested from the Rajput's sole and divine right. He noted in particular, 'Though the habits of the Hindus appear more likely to impair their courage than to make them good soldiers, the art of war nevertheless seems to be as well understood by them from very early times as any other, and those that followed the military profession have always been held in high esteem ... But however much the Hindus may have honoured the profession of arms, and however full their national histories may be of wars, conquests, sieges, battles, victories, and defeats, it is nevertheless remarkable that no nation has shown at every epoch in its history so little skill in military science.'[5]

THE ATTACK ON JHANSI

At 3am on 3 April 1858, the troops silently positioned themselves. At daybreak, the signal was given to advance the attack. Three shots from an 18 pounder of the Breaching Battery boomed out the signal and the attack was launched on Jhansi from three points. The feigned attack had been mounted by Major Gall on the north side, by cannonading as planned. He moved his troops and cavalry to deceive the enemy. The left attack of two storming parties, each of 100 men of the 86th Regiment and two of 50 men each from the 25th

Native Infantry Regiment, with 200 in support from both regiments, moved off. A reserve of a further 300 stood in readiness. Using the breach, the storming party entered the city with little loss and took the Rocket Bastion. The resistance though was fierce. Lowe, a member of the attacking force, would recount, 'The moon was very bright; too light, indeed for the coming work. We waited some time in terrible suspense for the signal, as morning was fast approaching. At length the word to advance was given in a voice a little above a whisper, the ladders were hoisted upon the shoulders of the sappers, preceded by the 3rd Europeans and Hyderabad Infantry as a covering party, and away we marched from our cover in three bodies — swords and bayonets glistening in the pale light. No sooner did we turn into the road leading towards the gate than the enemy's bugles sounded, and a fire of indescribable fierceness opened upon us from the whole line of the wall, and from the towers of the fort ... For a time it appeared like a sheet of fire out of which burst a storm of bullets, round-shot and rockets destined for our annihilation. We had upwards of two hundred yards to march through this fiendish fire, and we did it ...'[6]

Assailed by this fire, the right attack advanced under Lieutenant-Colonel Liddell. It comprised two storming parties of the 3rd Bombay Europeans, each of one hundred men, and two of the Hyderabad Infantry, each of fifty men. Two support parties of 50 men from each, stood prepared. Sappers advanced and placed three large ladders against the wall for the storming parties to ascend, but the fire increased and they wavered. Everything possible was hurled at them, rockets, stink pots, infernal machines, stone, blocks of wood and trees. As their officers began to mount the ladders, the men followed under the fire with the sounds of bugles and tom toms from within the walls showing that those inside were also awake to their efforts. The ladders gave way under the weight and a bugle sounded for the Europeans to retire. Again an attempt was made and Lieutenant Dick of the Bombay Engineers led the 3rd Europeans up another ladder only to be bayoneted and shot, falling dead from the ladder. Lieutenant Meiklejohn, also of the Bombay Engineers, reached the wall and jumping on it, was hacked to death and mutilated by the talwars of the enemy. Lieutenant Bonus was struck and fell from a ladder unconscious, later to make his way back to his lines. He would live to take an important part in the capture of the fort of Lohari where Private Frederick Whirlpool would be severely wounded only a month later. The escalade was carried in part, from some of the eight ladders now against the wall, but some of them were too short to reach the summit of the wall, whilst others were too weak and collapsed. The left column, under Captain Robinson, unable to escalade, found that they were able to enter by the breach and fought off resistance at the wall to allow the right column to escalade. They had earlier unsuccessfully attempted entry by blasting open a reinforced gateway. Fierce fighting followed and the rebels challenged every advance. Rose entered the breach with the 86th Regiment and under very heavy fire, which they could not return, made his way to the gates of the Rani's palace. As no plans of the city or palace were available, this landmark was settled as a rallying point for the troops. Fierce fighting continued through the streets and into the palace, room to room, where powder trails were ignited. Some rebels ignited their own powder pouches when cornered. The right and left attacking groups entered the streets of the town in larger numbers and savage hand-to-hand fighting continued at every door.

Beneath the wall before the escalade, the dead and dying of the 2nd Brigade Right attack lay exposed to incredibly heavy fire. Volunteers were sought to bring in the wounded. Private Whirlpool and Private Thomas Few of the 3rd Bombay Europeans rose to the challenge and each ran out to the wall under murderous fire to retrieve their fallen comrades. Whirlpool, not once, but twice. Between them, they brought in several dead or wounded comrades. Neither man received a wound in their forays to the wall, itself a remarkable stroke of fortune. Their recovery work done, they continued their duty and entered the city, amongst the bloody and terrible fighting. Whirlpool and Few would be mentioned in dispatches for their gallantry. Few was wrongly described as Fen in subsequent publications due to an apparent handwriting transcription error, but in any event he appears to have been yet another man who had joined under an assumed name.[7] He was James Flude who wrote an account of his exploits to his parents, in 1858, providing yet another eyewitness account of the storming of Jhansi and the intervening battle of Betwa.[8]

Flude's vivid account of the action at Jhansi and Betwa, accords very closely with the official line, although he gives an account of Rose making two forays to the river to entice Tantia. He obviously remained with the garrison at Jhansi and seems to have been given a field promotion for the recovery of Lieutenant Dick's body as a reward for his bravery. This in itself raises some interesting points. By his own account, he seems to have gone under the wall to recover dead and wounded only once, bringing back the body of Dick. It also gives weight to the fact that he was fighting under the name Few, as he was mentioned in despatches under that name and Few is shown thereafter as a corporal. He does not mention Whirlpool who had gone out twice and had not been promoted. He was already being considered for some other award.

Lieutenant Dick knew that he would die that day. He had been tried by court martial for protecting a native sergeant of the Sappers he believed innocent of a charge of looting and who was to be severely punished. Because of his righteous stand he was relieved of his command. Sir Hugh Rose sent for him to advise him of his penalty, saying, 'But I have heard of your high promise and good qualities, and I cannot subject you to a punishment which would be ruinous to your career, and deprive you of the honour of the assault. I therefore pardon you and I know you will do your duty tomorrow.'[9] 'On putting his foot on the step of the scaling-ladder Lieutenant Dick said to a brother officer, 'I never can be sufficiently obliged to Sir Hugh Rose: tell him how I have done my duty.' He ran up the ladder, received several shots, and fell mortally wounded to the ground.'[10]

The storming of Jhansi saw two soldiers awarded the Victoria Cross for saving wounded comrades, Private James Byrne and Captain Henry Jerome, both of the 86th Regiment of Foot, who rescued the badly wounded Lieutenant Sewell, Byrne receiving a sword cut in the process. Other members were mentioned in despatches for rescuing wounded comrades. Amongst them was Ensign Newport, who would feature with Whirlpool at Lohari. While Whirlpool and Thomas Few were mentioned in despatches, neither was nominated for the Victoria Cross at that time. Brigadier Steuart noted; 'Both columns behaved with great coolness and gallantry ... and also Privates Fen [Few] and Whirlpool, 3rd Bombay European Regiment, of whom Lieutenant-Colonel Liddell speaks in the highest terms.'[11]

Heavy fighting in the city and fire from the fort continued. Firing from houses was also taking its toll with each having to be forced and the occupants overcome. As Few reported in his letter, there was not a house where ten to twenty people were killed.

Rose, reporting to the Commander in Chief, through Major-General Mansfield, wrote on 30 April 1858. 'Having received no reports from the right attack, composed of the 3rd Europeans and Hyderabad Contingent, I made my way to them in the South-east quarter of the City. I found them engaged with the Enemy, and making their way to the Palace; the rebels were firing at them from the houses, which the troops were breaking open and clearing of their defenders.'[12]

The greater part of this was achieved on the first day of the attack, but pockets of heavy fighting maintained dangerous resistance. A body of more than 50 rebels, Vilayati sowars of the Rani's bodyguard, who Rose claimed were affected by opium, barricaded themselves in the palace stables and refused to surrender. Men of the 86th and 3rd Europeans broke into the stables and killed every man within, some of them suffering severe wounds themselves in the process.

Dr. Stack of the 86th had been shot dead whilst treating wounded men and Colonel Turnbull of the Bombay Artillery was mortally wounded by a sniper in one of the houses. By the following day, the rebels lay dead in great number. Private John McLachlan of the Royal Artillery described what he saw, 'When the 86th Regiment entered the fort the slaughter was terrible for two hours. I could hear nothing but the shouts of victory, and the savage yells of the dying heathen. My heart almost melted when I saw hundreds upon hundreds weltering in their blood, and calling upon their gods of stone and wood to save them.'[13]

McLachlan clearly described the taking of the city and palace, which had been captured, as the fort remained to be taken. During the next night the Rani and her retinue of 300 troops, her 10 year-old adopted son Damodar and her father, Moropant Tambe, escaped from the fort, unnoticed by the British forces. They were seen by one of the flying camps, which gave chase and killed 200, before losing contact as they spread out in differing directions. The pursuers did not know that the Rani was amongst the fugitives. It was not until the following morning that her escape was detected.

European casualties amounted to under 300 killed and wounded. Estimates of rebels killed, for there were no prisoners, stood at 5,000, which apparently included those killed on the field at the hands of the flying camps, but not those killed at Betwa. About 400 rebels ran into the hills only to be rounded up by the 24th Native Infantry, who killed all but about twenty of them. These climbed higher, inflicted casualties on their pursuers, then blew themselves up.

On 18 April, the Rani's father Moropant Tambe and the Jhansi *bakhshi* were taken prisoner by a loyal landowner, after being found wandering the countryside hopelessly lost, some 12 miles from Jhansi. Emaciated and wounded in the leg, he and his companion were taken to the spot at Jokun-Bagh, near where the British soldiers and their families had been murdered, and promptly hanged. Private John McLachlan again described the scene, 'It was a woman who commanded the blacks in the fort, but she is called the "Ranee" … Her father … is a very old man … I had the pleasure of seeing the old man hanged along with the paymaster of his army … He seemed very reconciled, and asked General Rose if he had got his dinner. He answered, no. The Rajah then told him to go home and take it, and then come back and hang him.'[14]

Vengeance was the victor's. Almost eighty men women and children had been seized by the mutineers and assorted rabble at Jhansi. Like those killed at Cawnpore, they had surrendered under promise of safe passage. The men, women and children were separated into three lines where the men were hacked to death, followed by the women and then the children. They were left to bloat in the sun before being buried in a mass grave near the mamelon mound outside the city. Rose had given an indication in a message to Brigadier Stuart on the 18th of March, of his intentions when taking Jhansi. His blood was up, as it was among his troops. 'Except Cawnpore, there was no place where there was a more numerous and awful assassination of the English than at Jhansi, the horrid Ranee being at the head of the atrocities; the people assisted in hewing down the English officers, ladies and children, then dragged their naked bodies through the town and danced round them. I will therefore not let if possible, a man escape, who was concerned in these wholesale [?butcheries].'[15]

The finer detail and the involvement of the Rani may not have been as described, but the basic facts would not have made any difference. Vengeance was sought, and in this case there was little opportunity to wreak it with forethought, during intense fighting. It would have given the troops cause to fight without pause under the most trying conditions, in a manner over and above normal effort, or the will to survive.

Fierce fighting raged in the city and palace for 13 hours on the first day, and for a further three days, the killing continued. Sir Robert Hamilton declined to take possession of Jhansi for the Crown as it was still considered unsafe to move about the city, due to snipers still actively shooting from the houses. An extremely hot *simoon* blew dust over the plain and the city, so fiery, that the troops could have been excused for thinking that it had come directly from the mouth of Hades. They sweltered in their uniforms. The 3rd Europeans would feel only slightly better off in their khaki's than their comrades in other regiments. Their discomfort can only be imagined; the long forced marches, the investment of the city and fort, the siege and cannonade, all in tremendous heat, which continued while a third of them were drawn away to fight at the Betwa River against overwhelming odds — about 1500 against an estimated 22,000 enemy. Returning to camp, the Betwa force was allowed to rest while the cannonade continued, but cleansing and hygiene were scant. They had not been able to bathe or change their clothing for 17 days. By the end of the fighting, a further four or more days lay ahead of them and the heat would increase as the season progressed towards the monsoons. Temperatures of 117°F in the tents had been recorded and at the end of the campaign, still some months off, more troops would be dead from heatstroke, cholera and malaria, than would fall to enemy aggression.

It is tempting to call the fighting inside the walls of Jhansi as 'mopping up', but it plays too lightly on the mind when considering the depth of the action taking place. Unlike their earlier victories, some of which were achieved with little resistance or quick flight, the rebels at Jhansi fought to the last. Rose wrote to Lord Elphinstone on 10th April, 'All the people in Jahnsee, one and all, took arms against us. They all thought, last year, that the English Raj & People were extinguished in India.'[16]

Nine days later he was able to advise that he had lost 340 killed and wounded in the siege and capture of Jhansi and in the battle of Betwa. As a consequence, he was not able to leave more than 400 native troops for the protection of the Jhansi fort when he moved towards Kalpi, and then only to protect the fort itself and not the city where he resorted to leaving his sick and wounded as the buildings of the fort had been destroyed. He also advised that the estimated enemy losses from the battles of Betwa and Jhansi totalled 7,000.

Earlier in the campaign Rose was a pains to report that his men had spared the lives of women and children, acceding to his wish that they should do so, for the honour of their country and the army. In a telegram to Elphinstone on 3rd February, he assured him that the 3rd Europeans had done credit to the Bombay Army and that the women and children of the rebels were treated with the greatest humanity.[17] In describing the treatment of women and children at Saugor, Rose was setting a pattern, both in expectation of the proper behaviour of his men and reaffirming that his orders had been obeyed.

Sylvester noted that at Jhansi, 'It took several days to clear the place completely. During the whole siege the greatest forbearance was shown to all who would fully surrender, and yet the estimated number of killed was four thousand: in fact there was an amount of forbearance and Christian kindness displayed by the Europeans to unfortunate women and children, and to aged men, that reflected more credit on their already lustrous arms ... It is no fiction when it is said the soldier shared his meals with some of the people found destitute in the city; and many of the women I believe, joined the English camp.'[18]

Lowe described the streets stained with blood. The street fighting went on all this time in a terrible way. Those who could not escape threw their women and babes down wells, and then jumped down themselves; they were dragged out, the women and children taken care of, and the men then despatched ... but I also know that the rough and bearded soldier behaved most kindly to the women and children. It was an awful sight to see these poor creatures follow out of their houses some rebel husband, brother, or son, who was at once shot, and then to see them huddled together, pale and trembling, beneath the walls, helpless and alone in the world. But the soldier was as compassionate to these poor wretches as he was unrelenting to all male inhabitants found in arms. Many I saw dividing the contents of their haversacs among these half-starved women and children, and every woman was treated with kindness and respect.'[19]

Burne corroborates Lowe in observing that, 'The victors treated the enemy's women and children with humanity. "Neither the desperate resistance of the rebels nor the recollections of the revolting and wholesale murders perpetuated the preceding year at this place," said Sir Hugh Rose, "could make them forget that, in an English soldier's eyes, the women and children are always spared. So far from hurting, the troops were seen sharing their rations with them."[20]

Compared with Sylvester's diary entry of 25 October, of the previous year, questions arise as to whether the official line and heart-warming accounts of contemporary observers didn't sanitise the seedier side of the happenings during other parts of the campaign. Even Sylvester gives his public account in glowing terms, but his private, opposite observations were confined to his diary, albeit six months or so earlier.'
… ye Brigr who issued no order of any kind the village was not properly occupied even though he was advised to do so. The consequence was the men off duty & even some of the native soldiers but chiefly the 86th and Artillery were frightfully drunk having seized the native liquor shops. They then commenced looting and killing everything black, old men, young women and children!! This of course was to be deplored but I had anticipated this. They shouted Cawnpore, Delhi and down they went. [Indecipherable] says he saw a room full of dead women with children sucking at their breasts. Other women brought out dead, children supplicating for mercy. Officers rushed down, the Provost Marshall & some Dragoons & they soon put a stop to it and destroyed all the liquor.'[21]

No punishment was noted, nor arrests for murder or other atrocities. The episode seems to have been seen as a drunken aberration, which was swept under the carpet and withheld from public scrutiny. Those who knew of this incident, which must have included Brigadier Charles Stuart, conveniently overlooked it. Any claim to it being an isolated incident is debunked by Sylvester's observation that he had anticipated the bloodbath. How could one anticipate such behaviour without knowing that it had either happened previously, or was a natural consequence of frequent drunkenness and the uninhibited quest for vengeance? Sylvester noted in his diary, not three weeks after this terrible event, '(17 November 1857) A Drum Head Court Martial sat immediately on the 78 prisoners taken by Major Orr's people. They were sentenced to be shot. We paraded that evening at 5pm, 74 prisoners had their hands tied behind them, their eyes bandaged, were shot by one detachment of the 86th. Most fell dead instantly, some having their brains shot out, others shot through the heart, the blood came pumping out & some shot in ye abdomen showed signs of agony afterwards & so received an extra bullet. I walked past them lying in a bloody line. We dined in the open air...'

This passage shows immense disdain for human life and dignity and probably provides the reason why the 86th Regiment offenders were not brought to account. There was much more bloody work to be done, before they dined 'in the open air'.

The 86th regiment went on to fight at Jhansi, where atrocities against women and children, if they occurred, were negated by the glowing praise of the behaviour of the troops. In the hand-to-hand fighting, which raged for days, from house to house, we have already seen that the men were forced from the houses and shot whilst their allegedly suppliant women looked on. The difference here though, was the absence of drunkenness and the watchful eye of a stern leader.

Rose wrote to Canning in April, after taking Jhansi, that the Indians feared their wives and children falling into the hands of their enemy. 'They know that English troops would respect them. But still the Connection in their mind they would rather kill their women than that they should fall into submission.'[22]

Why did the Indians hold these fears? Was it because it was their practice; had they experience of it from the British in earlier clashes, or was it because of the atrocities committed against the British at Meerut, Delhi, Cawnpore, Jhansi and elsewhere? It is more likely to have been the ancient rite of *juhar,* which was practiced by the warrior class of Rajputs, in which the women and children of their besieged menfolk, either suicided by immolation or were killed by their men, rather than face capture, before the men engaged in a final and hopeless battle. Sylvester provides an account of this occurring at Chanderi in 1528.[23] It must also be recognised that many of the men who died in front of their families, did not kill them upon the approach of the troops. It may be that the rite of *juhar* was confined to a section of the garrison who identified with it. Or was it because their defeat was so rapid, that time did not permit completion of this rite? An account provided by Indian eyewitness, Vishnu Godse as related by Tahmankar,[24] during the fighting in the city of Jhansi, exposes a version of the ferocity and indiscriminate killing as the troops moved from house to house. He talks of starvation and the pleas of neighbours to assist with the disposal of their dead husbands who were beginning to putrefy. People were flushed from their hiding places by fire or were shot when throwing themselves into wells. Alternatively, they burned to death or drowned. The troops looted, killed families in their homes and ransacked temples, stealing sacred ornaments. This observer does not mention the killing of women and children directly, until the end of his discourse when he mentions the ladies being put to the sword in Kothipur. He seems to mention this as an exception.[25]

This account relates some of the terror and horror experienced by the inhabitants of Jhansi, but must be seen against the backdrop of house to house fighting, shells dropped through the roofs of houses, snipers shooting from houses, dogged resistance to the last, and active participation in the fighting by women.[26]

On the 4th, Sir Robert Hamilton entered the city and went to the palace. He noted, ' … and round through the outhouses. I came to a Coach House, the doors were fastened. I had it opened. The place was full of women, 100 odd with children. The heat suffocating and the cries for water piercing. I got a water-carrier at once and he poured it out in a cup to a very respectable woman with child at breast and 2 little ones at foot. She asked his name. She would not wet her lips with the water but gave it to her children, and I had difficulty in finding a hindoo with lotah to give her a drink.'

Comparing Hamilton's observations with those of Sylvester, Lowe and Burne, it is difficult to reconcile the women sharing their rations and food, or even joining them in camp. It may have come down to a question of caste; the lady refusing water for herself from the *feringhee*, pariah-caste English, through a low caste water carrier, may have been a high caste Brahmin, whereas the others may have been of a lower caste, but even then, eating with the conquering enemy who had just killed family and other kinsmen is curious, if not unlikely; let alone joining them in camp. Later, Hamilton wrote, without mention of nourishment. 'Not a woman was ill treated anywhere. I saw them sitting in crowds in the different *bugeechas*, gardens, and *hatehs* — and not one complained of ill usage ... When the town fell — they herded together in open spaces. Not a man with them, the most extraordinary sight I ever beheld — not a sound did they utter — many went home to find themselves widows and fatherless.'[27]

It is probable that the administration, Rose, and his officers were sensitive to the need to be seen to protect women and children, after the horrific excesses committed by the British at the recapture of Delhi. There, murder and rape was widespread and committed under the approving eye of officers.[28]

'The attitude of many of the British to the people who fell under their sway was well put by one soldier, who wrote from Delhi to the *Bombay Telegraph* decrying what he called General Wilson's "hokum" that women and children must be spared. This "was a mistake" he wrote, as they were "not human beings but fiends, or, at best, wild beasts deserving only the death of dogs." All the people found within the walls when our troops entered were bayoneted on the spot; and the number was considerable, as you may suppose when I tell you that some forty or fifty persons were often found hiding in one house. They were not mutineers, but residents of the city, who trusted to our well-known mild rule for pardon. I am glad to say that they were to be disappointed.'[29]

This is just one account of the many horrors, which occurred in the retaking of Delhi, and which was common knowledge at the time.

Some direct and unfettered evidence emerges of the standard expected of the storming troops at Jhansi, from the words of the soldier's themselves. Sergeant A. G. Alexander (Corporal Adam Alexander of the 3rd Bombay Europeans) wrote to his friends in Scotland. 'By this time some of our men had gained the top of the wall, and it was not long until the whole were over it and in the city, and then came our time for mowing them down. What with the sight of our dead and dying comrades, and the officers address to us — 'Remember the slaughter committed here by the Ranee on our poor countrymen and the ladies! Spare no man with arms, but spare females and children'. We were ripe for the work of destruction.'[30]

Similarly, Private Peter McPherson of the 3rd Bombay Europeans, writing to his parents in Glasgow, noted. 'On the 3rd, at break of day, we were ordered to scale the walls of the city and the officers gave us a final speech before we started. One of them said that the time had come when we were to avenge our countrymen and women, 72 in number, who were murdered here, and that we were to show no mercy to the men, but to spare the women and children.'[31]

Women and children died in the conflagration, shelling and confusion at Jhansi, and it is possible that amongst those killed were people who had been loyal to the British and had even assisted them in a time of great danger, as had happened in other cities, such as Cawnpore, but it is clear that an official stance was taken to spare them.

The public at home also sought vengeance, but even as the wounds of the great slaughter of their countrymen were still festering, that vengeance did not include retribution that extended to women and children. Despite calls for blood and the healing effects of a muscular introduction of Christianity, a cautionary verse was published as early as September 1857, in *Punch* magazine, which was addressed to the general public as much as it was to soldiers:

A WORD TO THE AVENGER.
SOLDIER! When thou, beneath thy bayonet,
Shalt get a devilish Sepoy, save the wretch,
Safe if thou canst but make him, for Jack Ketch
His howls, which none who heard them should forget,
Were lost amid war's uproar; rather let
The miscreant swing in exemplary throes
Upon the gallows; but if thou suppose
That show uncertain, then exact our debt,
And there, in full: but not thou defiled
In imitation of the accursed beast,
Who babes and women slew with lingering pain.

Upon the wretched slave thy vengeance feast;
There stop : nor let his guilt thy manhood stain,
But spare the Indian mother and her child.[32]

The soldier was urged to spare the sepoy for the hangman. Where it was not possible to do so, only then should the debt be exacted by slaughter. Though English women and children had been hewn down, the soldier was beseeched not to be defiled by imitating the acts of their enemy, and to spare Indian women and children.

These events have been examined to posit the possible causes for the way Whirlpool held himself liable to eternal punishment, which stemmed certainly, from his time in India. The carnage inflicted on an enormous section of a community would leave its enduring effects on those sensitive enough to be so afflicted, even without the wanton abuse of women and children. Ample evidence is available to show that the official line was to spare the women and children before the onslaught. Accounts, after the event, of them being spared, abound, but many must have been killed during the fighting and the sight of this would be have had a terrible impact on some of those responsible. The widespread killing of men in front of their families, though officially sanctioned, must have had an impact on those required to actually perform the acts. In much the same way as Private John McLachlan's heart 'almost melted' when he saw hundreds upon hundreds of his enemy 'weltering in their blood', as they were massacred.

What drove the men was undoubtedly the desire to avenge the deaths of the Europeans in Jhansi the year before, but the behaviour of some, upon securing the palace indicated they were also driven by a lust for booty and in doing so, they were, for a time, beyond the control of their officers. Looting was forbidden, but happened, and in Jhansi it had got out of hand and order had to be enforced to quell the greedy enthusiasm of some. It is not to be wondered that this would occur when it was official policy to seize plunder, appoint 'prize agents' whose role it was to audit the seizures, sell what could be sold for the proceeds to be divided up; quantum according to rank. As Lowe reported. 'The prize agents were busily engaged daily in taking stock of the money, jewels and other valuables found in the palace and town, and sales were going on daily in camp for disposal of prize goods and the property that once belonged to officers who had died in action.'[33]

It was a great motivator to fight, for both sides. It is also possible that if looting could not be controlled in the heat of the campaign, then the abuse of civilians cannot be discounted. It is here that we can be fairly certain that Humphrey James was above such vile behaviour. It simply does not fit with a shy and retiring person, incapable of accepting charity or favour, who sought neither fortune or fame. His established willingness to risk his life for others, does not accord with one concerned with his future. What happened in the heat of the moment or what he saw, may be another matter. He undoubtedly was with his regiment as they made their way to the Rani's palace, clearing houses of their occupants, amongst whom were rebels, who had been firing on them. This would have been no pleasant task, not only because of the dangers involved, but for the killing of the men in front of their families. If nothing else played on Whirlpool's mind after the battle, this surely must have.

Whatever happened in Jhansi and at the previous conquests, and perhaps at those to come, it had a profound impact on Humphrey James, serving as Private Whirlpool. In all probability it was the cause of his belief that he had confided to his sister Deborah, that he was 'damned and going to roast'. In other words, he was certain that he was going to Hell. He still held this view near the end of his life, so severe was his self condemnation. But that was yet to come; he was to have a foretaste of a personal Hell, which would end his military career. There is no doubt that he was heavily involved in the fighting, as he had been since leaving Indore. He had been part of the failed escalading party and had redoubled his efforts as a 'forlorn hope' volunteer, who twice braved almost certain death to rescue wounded comrades. This done, he entered the city with his force and continued to fight for four days under the most trying conditions. He would have needed the spur of vengeance to maintain him. As Lieutenant Henry Clifford, who won his VC at Inkerman in 1854, explained after killing a Russian and severing the arm of another, '... the excitement was certainly tremendous while it lasted, and it is well perhaps it is so, for I am sure in cold blood I could never strike a man as I did.'[34]

Whirlpool would have been at the forefront and used his bayonet unsparingly as he had already shown and would later show at Lohari. He may have been part of the attack on the Villayets in the palace stables. In any event, he had no escape from the killing, as his sense of duty dictated. It would not be until much later that he would reflect upon his actions, here and elsewhere. With time on his hands after his campaign had finished, and later in life, like so many other former soldiers, before and since, his recollections would visit him, unbidden and unwanted. He would never forget what he had done; the things that he could not have done in cold blood.

Though Jhansi had been secured, the Central India Field Force was compelled to remain garrisoned there for lack of provisions and threats from enemy outposts, which could not be met until properly equipped. Work went on as city squares were lit with pyres of the burning dead in their thousands. Sylvester had noted that, ' ... outside in the streets, the smell of dead bodies and the bloated carcasses of bullocks, horses and other animals was sickening: one day's exposure in the heat we were then enduring was sufficient to induce decomposition.'[35]

To add to their unpleasant work, 'In the squares of the city the sepoys and soldiers collected hundreds of corpses in large heaps and covered them with wood, floorboards and anything that came handy and set them on fire. Now every square blazed with burning bodies and the city looked like one vast burning ground. By another order the people were given permission to take care of their dead, and those who could afford to give a ritual cremation took away the bodies of their relatives and friends, but the others were just thrown on the fire. It became difficult to breathe as the air stank with the odour of the burning human flesh and the stench of rotting animals in the streets. The carcasses of thousands of bullocks, camels, elephants, horses, dogs, cats, donkeys, buffaloes and cows were strewn all over the city. These were collected and removed to the outskirts of the city where a huge pit was dug into which they were all pushed and the pit covered with earth.'[36]

When the fuel ran out, the rendered fat from the putrefying corpses kept them burning for days until the remaining ash and bone could be disposed of outside the city walls. The clean up was necessary, as the fort would be garrisoned, initially by a small force, once the Central India Field Force was able to proceed. Rose had spared the palace from bombardment as he planned to use it for his troops, as a headquarters and particularly, a hospital. His garrison force was only able to use the fort and the sick and wounded remained in the city, presumably until the palace was fit for habitation after the fighting and looting frenzy had damaged it. The garrison was commanded by Colonel Liddell of the 3rd Bombay Europeans with the headquarters wing of his regiment, four companies of the 24th Native Infantry Regiment, left wing of the 3rd Light Cavalry, 100 men of the Hyderabad Cavalry, half a company of the Bombay Sappers and 3 guns of the Bhopal Contingent, in all, about 800 men. Rose spent three weeks at Jhansi, fearful that marauding rebels would attack his rear if he left, as he was not yet prepared for an engagement or to endanger his garrison, which was too small to mount a strong defence of its position.

The officers and men of the 3rd Bombay European Regiment were so moved by the loss of comrades who died in the taking of Jhansi and other battles, that they each gave one day's pay to enable the erection of a monument to their memory. That monument still resides in the Cantonment Cemetery at Jhansi. It reads:

'Erected by the officers, non com officers and Privates of the
3rd BOMBAY EUROPEAN REGIMENT
To the memory of Their Gallant Comrades
Who Fell During the Campaign in Central India
Under Maj Gen Sir H Rose K.C.B. 1857-59'

CHAPTER EIGHT

———

LOHARI

'Out of suffering have emerged the strongest souls;
The most massive characters are seamed with scars …'

Edwin Hubble Chapin 1814 - 1880
'Living Words'

Strengthened slightly and wanting to pursue his objective, Rose moved towards Kalpi with his 1st Brigade on 26 April, followed by the 2nd Brigade a day later. His force had been depleted to about 4,500 men but was reinforced by 500 of the Headquarters Wing of the 71st Highlanders. Likewise, the Kalpi rebels, who had been defeated at Betwa, were reinforced by the Nawab of Banda's troops. Rose forced his way towards Kalpi.

He telegraphed Somerset from Poonch on 6th May, ' … I sent Major Gall from here against the garrison of Loharee, a ghurree with one gun belonging to the Rajah of Sumpter because they had betrayed an outpost of the Hyderabad Cavalry to the rebel cavalry in Koonch — Major Gall blew in the gate, stormed the Ghurree and killed the rebels in it, 71 in number. They were disguised sepoys of the 12th B.I. and fought to the last.'[1]

Lohari was a small village with a mud and brick fort about 6 miles north west of Koonch (Kunch), which was garrisoned by about 90 mutinous sepoys of the 12th Bengal Infantry. The garrison had betrayed a picket of native cavalry, who were forced to cut their way out of an ambush, losing two killed and several wounded. Rose ordered Major Gall to march on the fort with the left wing of the 3rd Europeans, left wing of the Bombay Native Infantry and 20 sappers. They were supported by 220 dragoons and irregular cavalry and four guns. His task was to punish the garrison for their treachery. His orders were given verbally. On 2 May, the force marched to Lohari. Gall, in a letter to his brother several days later, explained the events. ' ... I was sent for and verbally instructed to proceed with [his force] to Loharree, bring in the Commandant, Munohur Singh and all his garrison, about ninety strong, prisoners of war, or if they refused to surrender, to blow the fort about their ears and destroy them. With the above force I marched accordingly, and on arriving near Loharree, halted in battle order on the plain in full sight of the garrison on the walls. Then rode, accompanied by one officer and a native official, through the village up to the gates of the fort, and summoned the Killedar — whoever he was. I was insulted by having an inferior person sent out but after a while discovering that Munohur Singh, the Ranee's brother, was himself in the fort, I summoned him to come out. After many delays caused by fear, and perhaps by other causes ... he came out on foot, with an armed retinue of seven or eight, with his sword in both hands which he presented to me, at the same time his retinue laid down their arms at my feet. When he came out I upbraided him with the delay, and he exclaimed that I was dishonouring him. To which I replied "Is it a dishonour to a Shakoor [thakur] holding a petty fort like this to be called upon to surrender to an army like mine?" He then begged to be allowed to retain his sword, which I returned to him. He was in a great state of alarm. I now called upon him to make the garrison lay down their arms. This he tried to do, sending in several messengers with the order, but it was clear that he had no power over them. They positively refused to obey him, so I sent him and his retinue as prisoners to Poonch. And after vainly endeavouring to induce the garrison to surrender at discretion I proceeded to attack the place, in the full expectation that whilst engaged in reducing the fort I should be attacked from the side of Khullea, said to be occupied by 800 of the enemy. General Barr will let you see a copy of the report I sent in of what followed, but I could not but leave much unsaid. To wit that when the General heard the guns he became excited and feared I might fall, and wrote a letter in which he peremptorily forbade me to risk an unsuccessful assault, which I received just as Bonus, the engineer, was closing the powder bag, and we were in doubt whether or not it would be necessary to blow in more than one gate; and how I concealed the purport of this note from all except Thompson to whom I gave the command of all outside, while I went in. Nor could I dwell on the uncivil treatment I personally received during the assault. Once I was knocked head over heels by a rush of my own men the wrong way under the influence of an ignited bag of powder that made its appearance among them. Twice I was knocked down by stones thrown by the enemy ... I may live many years and see many strange things but I shall never see such a fight as that again. I could never bring more than twenty men at the outside against the seventy or eighty that assailed us.

'The gateways being both uncovered at the top and the garrison could throw what they pleased on our heads. At the trees I had a melee with about twenty of them and then the inside of my left hand was just touched by a talwar and the sleeve of my right arm cut by another; and I had, using my sword with both hands, the satisfaction of reducing an opponent to equal terms of combat by nearly severing his left arm at the wrist. Nor could I allude in my official report to the ludicrous effect of so many dirty faces, all begrimed with the dust and smoke of the explosion.

'When I got into the place the breast of my coat was drenched with blood streaming from my forehead and head, giving me the appearance of having been shot. I am still sore from the bruises I had got and can still scarcely yet lift my right arm without great pain. A stone struck me upon the shoulder point and sent me reeling against the wall. At one time I though we must lose the day, and cried out "If you are Englishmen come on now and never come back, men." They did come on and never returned to that gateway until every opponent had been slain.'[2]

Sylvester provided a slightly differing account in which his number of ninety killed accords with Gall's estimation of the garrison in the fort and Gall had only one howitzer, not two as he reported. He was not an eyewitness to the events.[3]

More importantly, Gall's own description of his injuries prove inconsistent with the oft suggested claim that some of the breaching force had inflicted his wounds by throwing bricks at him, as they resented him leading instead of their own Armstrong. Armstrong had been rendered senseless by a blow from a brickbat and was in no position to lead. Gall suffered a talwar cut to his hand and sleeve. He received a serious blow from a brick to his shoulder, which threw him off balance and another to his forehead, which bled profusely onto the breast of his coat, a wound which must have been sustained from in front of him. Gall describes following his men and being knocked over by their rush in retreat, all of which means that they, or most of them were in front of him and not in a position to assail him, even had they had the time or opportunity to do so in the heat of the battle. He also clearly states that he was twice knocked down by stones thrown by the enemy. This little myth, I think had its roots in an attempt to embellish the 'devil may care' attitude of the Irish members of the 3rd Europeans, by some revisionist's.

Lieutenant Bonus's eyewitness account must be given credence, as he played such an intrinsic role in the breach and fight. Writing to his parents on 4 May 1858, he outlined the events. 'Since my last was posted, I have had I think a more narrow escape than I had at Jhansi. Let me tell you about it. A picket of Native Cavalry was posted in a village, Loharee by name, about six miles from this place. One morning they found themselves beset by the enemy's cavalry, they had to cut their way through and lost two killed and several wounded. A strong force consisting of a wing of the 3rd Europeans, a wing of the 25th N.I., a H.A. battery, a troop of the 14th Dragoons, 100 irregular cavalry and my company of Sappers were ordered out. We started at 2am on the 2nd. There is a fort at Loharee. When we arrived we found this occupied by the enemy, we summoned them to surrender, they refused, so it became necessary to turn them out. But how was this to be done? Our guns opened fire and our infantry rushed the outer gate, but the next was closed. We seemed to be in a bit of a fix. I rode right around the fort to see if I could find a place where escalade would be possible but I could not see any, the wall seemed to be too high for our ladders and in good condition everywhere; I was certain that escalade would not do. I reported my opinion to Colonel [sic] Gall who commanded the column; he did me the honour to ask my advice, I said that there seemed to me only one thing to do and that was to blow open the gate, not that I liked giving this opinion for I knew that the very unpleasant job would be mine. Colonel Gall agreed. I had not come prepared for this adventure, so I had no materials. I went into the village which of course was entirely deserted and hit upon a smithy where I found a leather bellows. The bellows of the native is a leather bag, the complete skin in fact of a goat. This I saw would answer my purpose. Then I got 50 lbs of powder from the Artillery and soon my bag was ready. I took three men with me, two to carry the bag, the third a European, to fire the charge should I be knocked over. We rushed to the gate while the Infantry poured a furious fire on the defences. I propped the bag against the gate, lighted it, and bolted back to cover. The thing was done so quickly that I do not believe the enemy knew what was up, at any rate not a man of the party was touched. After about half a minute which seemed like half an hour, the charge exploded, smashing the gate to matchwood. The Europeans rushed in, there was some desperate fighting but soon the place was ours. We had two officers severely wounded, one man killed and about 20 wounded. All the rebels, about 60, were killed. We returned to camp in the evening after a very hot and hard day, during which we had no food.

'The heat was terrific, several Europeans were overcome and were brought in in carts. Colonel Gall thanked me warmly and he mentioned me in flattering terms in his report to the General.'[4]

Major-General Sir Owen Tudor Burne also related his knowledge of the event. 'Before marching to Kalpi, Sir Hugh Rose detached Major Gall with a small force to attack and take the strong fort of Lohari, held by Valaitis, six or seven miles on his left flank. This was done with great gallantry. The fort was too strong to batter with field artillery, and the only entrance was a difficult one, built on the old Maratha plan of a double gate with a small postern in an angle. Here the 3rd Europeans particularly distinguished themselves. A desperate struggle took place when they got into the first gate. Two officers were severely wounded and several men killed. A soldier named Whirlpool*. received no less than nineteen wounds. "Take care lads", he said, as they put him into the dooli, "and don't shake my head, or else it will come off." '[5]

* 'He had been mentioned in despatches for saving the lives of two comrades who had fallen wounded from the broken ladders at the siege of Jhansi. He himself lived to receive the Victoria Cross and sixpence a day beyond his usual pension...'

It is in this account, retold to Burne by Rose, which included the anecdote about Whirlpool's parents visiting him in Ireland, that some truth resides. The occupants were not *Valaitis (Walayatis)*, but mutinous sepoys of the 12th Bengal Infantry, although this was not discovered until after their rout. Otherwise, the bland facts seem to accord with those of Gall and Bonus, apart from there being only one man killed and several dangerously, or seriously wounded. If so, it is a recollection of what Rose was told shortly after the operation. It is the only account which mentions Whirlpool's actions and this may be because it is retold many years after the event when his Victoria Cross was announced and later, presented. Some thirty years in fact. The other accounts were more contemporaneous and either the writers did not know of the impending award, or a decision had not been made to join the actions of Jhansi and Lohari in Rose's recommendation for Whirlpool to be awarded this signal honour. This would quite plausibly be due to the action, under severe circumstances, in which Rose and his force were then engaged. It may also have been the case that as the Victoria Cross could not at that time be awarded posthumously, his survival needed to be ensured before the recommendation could be made.

Major Gall reported on the action against the fort of Lohari, through the chain of command to Rose and thence to the Commander-in-Chief, Campbell. As was the norm, that correspondence was released and published as a supplement to the *London Gazette*. In this report Gall brings to the notice of his superiors the actions of his men and in particular, Private Frederick Whirlpool.[6]

By June 1858, Lieutenant Donne had recovered sufficiently to write to his father who, in turn, wrote the following day to his old friend from his days at Trinity College, Cambridge, Richard Chenevix Trench. Trench was the Dean of Westminster and Professor of Divinity at Kings College, London, and would shortly become Archbishop of Dublin and Primate of Ireland. 'My Dear Trench, We had a letter from Frederick yesterday. He describes the attack of the Fort very vividly, and though he admits of having received two shrewd cuts on the left arm and just above the elbow of that arm, makes light of his wounds, and appeals to the good spirits in which he writes as a token that he is not much hurt. However this morning Mrs. Newport, the mother of the brave fellow that was cut down beside Fred, has enclosed to me letters from Sir Hugh Rose, Col. Liddell and Major Gall, from which it is plain that Frederick is severely but thank God not dangerously wounded and that his and Newport's conduct is looked upon as remarkably gallant. Major Gall says that he never saw anything pluckier than the way they dashed in, and fought against tremendous odds, and that the regiment has lost for a time "two of its bravest officers". The wounded pair were doing well at Ghanzi [Jhansi] when the mail was made up, and Fred speaks of the luxury of being under the shadow of canvas and in a recumbent posture after the toil of the summer campaign. Unless he recovers too quickly he will probably be sent down to Bombay and so be exempt for a time from the dangers of battle and the sun. He had just before he was wounded been put on the staff: this however is only suspended, and his wound will not be unfavourable to his promotion eventually, so we rejoice with trembling and are desirous to be most thankful for his escape from worse and for the credit he has done his name. With many thanks for kind inquiries, Affect. yours W B Donne.'[7]

A week later Lieutenant Donne's concerned father wrote to Fanny Kemble, the noted author and internationally popular actress, who was the sister of another of his old Cambridge colleagues, John Mitchell Kemble. '... I enclose a letter from Fred. You will grieve to hear that he has been severely wounded, but rejoice that he has gained himself great credit as a good and gallant soldier. Little of this appears on the slip of newspaper: but after receiving the letter from Fred we got others from Sir Hugh Rose, Col. Liddell and Major Gall all mentioning in high terms of praise of "Donne and Newport". They seem, indeed, to have led a sort of forlorn hope. After getting in front of the gate which they blew up, and after blowing it up, the prospect before them was a narrow passage turning off at a sharp curve. Major Gall describes the rush made by these two lads as one of the most gallant things ever witnessed. As soon as they were past the gate-way they were surrounded by the enemy, and Major G. says he saw Donne and Newport cutting away at about six black fellows apiece. He laments their temporary loss for active service as "the loss of two of the best and bravest officers in the force". A Lieutenant Armstrong, who was also engaged and temporarily blinded by a stone, writes, "on partly regaining my sight and consciousness I saw Donne and Newport come thundering up the passage surrounded by swords and bayonets and cutting clean through them all." Sir Hugh Rose's letter was to say that he had received the report of their gallantry and conduct and should certainly report it to the Commander in Chief ...'[8]

Breaching the gates at Lohari had involved ingenuity on the part of Lieutenant Bonus. He prepared a powder bag from a goat-skin bellows and destroyed the barricaded third gate under fire, which was diminished by rapid fire from the 3rd Europeans. Lieutenant Armstrong had managed to open two other gates preceding it, apparently without great force, where he waited with his 25, 3rd Europeans while Bonus completed his work. 25 men of the 25th Bombay Native Infantry waited behind them in support. Once the gate was destroyed and smoke filling the passageway, Lieutenants Armstrong and Donne with Ensign Newport led their men past the burning timbers and into the unknown, for they had considered the possibility of further gates barring their way. Pushing their way through the smoke they found a fourth gateway, a postern, turning at right angles to their right.

They met the enemy in a curved uncovered passageway with low walls on either side, and were hacked and shot at, forcing them back. The passageway was narrow and would not permit more than three or four men to advance abreast. As they advanced again, they were showered with missiles, brickbats and anything else the enemy could muster. Lieutenant Armstrong was felled by a brickbat and was for a time insensible. His men moved past him, following Donne and Newport until a lighted cloth, or bag, which appeared to contain gunpowder, was dropped among them. Fearing an explosion, the Europeans retreated, colliding with Major Gall, at their rear. When it was realised that no explosion would occur, the men rallied and again moved forward. While still in this passageway, the rebels made a stand and vicious fighting felled both Donne and Newport, who suffered dangerous sword wounds. Whirlpool, who was at the front of the charge and immediately behind his felled leaders, fought the rebels with his bayonet, not the most flexible of defences in the tight space. He stood between the enemy and Lt. Donne and would not retreat. As the rebels sought to thwart the advance upon them, Whirlpool still refused to yield. He was repeatedly cut by their *talwars* and did not fall until he had received seventeen sword wounds to his head, body, arms and neck. It is almost unimaginable how this man stood his ground, receiving cut after cut to his head and upper body. Yet he did not only that, but continued to parry and thrust with his bayonet at every opportunity, using his rifle to deflect the *talwar* blows, which were raining down on him from the front and above him at each side. The neck wound was the severest cut, but his skull was also fractured by a blow. These and his other cuts were later described as desperate wounds. He had held the enemy at bay long enough for his comrades to rally and emulate his determination. As his Victoria Cross citation would later include, '*The gallant example shown by this man is considered to have greatly contributed to the success of the day.*'[9]

The great contribution Whirlpool made to the efforts of the day was to stand his ground, not only to protect his officers, but also to prevent a further retreat, which could have proved a serious setback to the operation. In doing so, he showed the way to those who followed along the narrow passageway, and there would be no retreat. That passageway would only allow the advance of at most, four men abreast and as Gall had stated, allowed no more than twenty men to attack the 80 or so enemy at any one time. Donne and Newport were said to be fighting six men each, and when they fell, Whirlpool too would have faced those men and many more, with limited support, as the soldiers who followed made slow progress into the final gateway. That 57 rebels were killed in the gateway gives an indication of how outnumbered Whirlpool was as he stood his ground. Armstrong fell, Donne fell, as did Newport. Then Whirlpool fell too, but only when his stand was complete and assistance had been gained. He was conscious until placed on a dhooli and well aware that victory was close at hand.

Gall's force overcame the enemy, slaying those in the gateway before moving into the fort where the remainder were overcome, including those attempting to escape from the bastions and walls. A remaining few were also killed at the gate. Whirlpool's actions were seen by Gall, and he would later bring them to the attention of Major-General Rose, who joined them to his actions at Jhansi.

The account provided by Frederick Donne, which play down his own injuries, revealed the action in great detail, but sadly, Whirlpool was not included in his or his father's letters. Letters from Colonel Liddell, Major Gall and Sir Hugh Rose spoke of the gallantry of Lieutenant Donne and Ensign Newport. Lieutenant Armstrong gives a vivid account of Donne and Newport rushing into the narrow passageway to confront the enemy. No mention is made of Private Whirlpool or his being in the foremost part of the advance, the third of its kind, before entry was achieved. Whirlpool's attacking at least twelve of the assailants, who had felled Donne and Newport, was not mentioned, nor was his eventual wounding and dangerous condition. This, despite him being carried back to Jhansi with the wounded, including Donne and Newport. The reasons for this must be viewed in the context of time and place. Rose, Gall and Liddell were writing to the families of Donne and Newport, who were officers. Armstrong also wrote of his fellow officers. Whirlpool was a private and would not have entered the conversation because of his lack of rank and therefore, his lack of importance to the families of the other wounded men. He would never have entered the conversations of this class, any more than would the loyal sepoys or their achievements. It was just the way it was.

Of more interest are the observations of Major Gall, who witnessed the attack and participated in it. He reported Private Whirlpool's actions to Colonel Liddell and Sir Hugh Rose, and they clearly surpassed the gallantry of these officers. His actions were valorous in being at the forefront with his officers, in defending Lieutenant Donne from further attack and at the third attempt, 'contributing greatly to the success of the day.' These soldiers, regardless of rank and station, recognised Whirlpool's valour as a combatant and that, coupled with his actions a month previously, led to their recommendation of him for the Victoria Cross. He was dogged and thought nothing of his personal danger. He had to make a stand to protect his officer, knowing that although the entranceway was tight and restrictive, assistance would come. Severely wounded, only his death would have prevented him receiving the award.

Whirlpool was placed onto a dhooli and carried from the scene where he is reported to have uttered the words about his head falling off. It was later reported that his neck wound had almost severed his head from his body. His remarks and serious and bloody wounds may have given rise to a belief that this was the case. They certainly laid the foundation for the folk memory adhering to the incident. On closer analysis this had to be an overstatement, or at least acknowledgement of the potential for such an eventuality. It is hard to reconcile his neck injury being so severe as to have almost decapitated him. He suffered no spinal injury, so any cut to the back of his neck was not so deep as to have caused major damage. He was able to speak, indicating that his trachea had not been severed. Similarly, his jugular veins and the deeper carotid arteries must not have been damaged, as almost certain death would have quickly followed. It is more likely that he suffered a deep laceration to his neck, which added to the horrific spectacle of his serious wounds. Leaving that aside, as it in no way detracts from his valour, he was very seriously wounded. He was taken to the rear where his bleeding wounds were stemmed, and where he lay until the action was complete and he could join the other wounded. They, including Donne and Newport, and those suffering from sun stroke, would be taken back to Jhansi by cart. Whirlpool was fortunate that the mutineers in the fort had been routed and his immediate medical needs could be met by his regimental assistant surgeon, O'Brien and Assistant Surgeon Skipton of the 78th Highlanders, who was attached to the 14th Light Dragoons. In other protracted battles the wounded had been known to have endured their injuries in the field for days on end.[10]

The severity of Whirlpool's wounds may be measured against those sustained by Lieutenant Donne who arrived back at his father's home at Blackheath on 14 September 1858, on 18 months leave. Writing to Fanny Kemble later that day, Donne senior described his son's wounds. 'My Dear Friend. I am always sure of your sympathy in any happiness of mine, and, therefore, though I have written so lately, send you a line to say that our dear Fred arrived this afternoon from Bombay with 18 months leave of absence. He is in good health, though his wounds look ugly, and his left arm is a mere appendage to the shoulder. He is grown very handsome, and wears a beard that might become the father of the faithful. He made so light of his wounds that I had no idea, till he threw his shirt off, that he had, like St. Francis, been wounded in five places, and ghastly cuts they look still, although cicatrised. On his shoulder you might put your fist into the scar ...'[11]

Donne's wounds were severe, but he was able to undertake the homeward journey to England within a month or so of them being inflicted. Frederick Whirlpool had months of treatment still ahead of him.

At Jhansi fort, where a hospital had been established, Whirlpool was provided the best possible treatment available at the time. Chances of his wounds mortifying in the intense heat and filth were extremely high. He was given the services of a native servant, who kept the flies from his wounds and attended to his needs. His care must have been excellent, as evidenced by his very survival. His wounds were kept clean and his dressings changed regularly. His major wound was a serious fracture to his skull, which, once the bone fragments were removed in an operation similar to trepanning, a silver plate was affixed to close the gap. That this operation did not cause major infection is again testament to his good medical care.[12]

On 29 June 1858, the *Bury and Norwich Post* carried an article, which again gives voice to Lieutenant Donne. 'We rejoice to find that Lieutenant F.C. Donne, 3d Bombay Europeans, though severely wounded in the attack on the fort near Poonch, on the 3rd of May, writes to his father from the camp at Jhansi, on the 9th, that he is "doing wonderfully well" and hopes " in a few weeks to be all right again." He was gallantly leading the storming party into the fort, after the gate had been blown open, up a passage so narrow that only three or four could go abreast, with a raised platform on each side, on which the rebels had concealed themselves behind a parapet, and was cutting at a fellow who had cut down one of our men, when he received a wound at the back of the left shoulder and another on the left elbow, which obliged him to fall to the rear. Severe execution was done upon the rebels: "Every man in the place was killed — not one lived to tell the tale." Our loss was one man killed, 2 officers and 18 men wounded.'[13]

By early October 1858, however, Whirlpool was still in Jhansi. His recuperation was lengthy and his progress was slow; five months at this time. When he did regain some strength, he was moved to Poona to await a decision on his future in the Bombay Army.

As it transpired, the Government in England had decided to withdraw the Honourable East India Company's charter — a reflection on its director's bad management in India and an admission that its time had come to an end. With the demise of the Company, its army would be dissolved and in many cases subsumed by the British Army. This caused consternation amongst the troops and resentment amongst them and their Queen's counterparts, who saw them as inferior specimens, though battle hardened and not wanting in bravery, still not up to their disciplined force. Sir Hugh Rose would soon become Commander-in-Chief in India and be responsible for the transformation of the armies.

Whirlpool's position would not have been comfortable. To be transferred to a British unit might entail his return to Britain, or more particularly Ireland, which was not what he desired. In any event, he was spared the decision about his future by his medical officers determining that he was unfit for further service. This meant that he could not pursue the role of schoolmaster at Poona, a goal he had been working towards before the outbreak of the mutiny. On 2 February 1859, he was discharged from the Company's service, medically unfit. His pension was determined at 1/3d (one shilling and threepence) a day and presumably included his £10 a year once his Victoria Cross nomination was confirmed and gazetted, but would date from the actions which earned it.

Frederick Whirlpool, though he seems to have lived a lifetime, was just 27 years of age when discharged. He made arrangements to travel to Australia, to add an antipodal flavour and distance to his peripatetic lifestyle. It is not known why he chose Australia, but Ireland was out of the question; he was still on his quest. He made arrangements for his pension to be paid to him in Victoria.

It was exactly ten months since he had received his wounds. His regiment had fought on without him and their condition had deteriorated markedly, as they marched and fought under the most appalling conditions, spent, disheartened and almost at the end of their endurance. But endure they did, destroying all before them through Kalpi to Gwalior. By August 1858, Rose was back in Poona having defeated the main forces of the rebels, though bands still roamed the plains fighting a guerrilla campaign. Tantia Tope had been betrayed, captured and hanged in April 1859. Corporal Few wrote to his parents, ' … one of our columns caught the villain Tantee Topee he was hung his head is embalmed and is to be sent home so the yarn goes.'[14] Whilst this account may have been apocryphal, it does show that nothing was too gruesome to ensure that vengeance was not only seen to be swift, but was very widely desired in its worst form.

It is more than likely that Whirlpool, 'seamed with scars', was visited in hospital in Poona by Rose, as it was his custom to do so. He may have told Whirlpool of his nomination for the Victoria Cross, but it is not likely, as its award was still not certain, after all, Lieutenant Armstrong of his regiment had been nominated for the Victoria Cross on three occasions and was never to receive it. Rose would not have raised his hopes.

Rose had another battle on his hands; recognition of his force and its successes. Campbell had played down the tremendous successes of the Central India Field Force and Rose thought that it was due to jealousy. He also had to fight for a Central India campaign clasp, which had been denied by Campbell. It is thought that Rose made a personal appeal to Canning on this account, which led to the issue of the 'Central India' clasp to the Mutiny medal.

Burne throws more light on this period by revealing, ' … the keen disappointment that was felt in the Service when the troops of the Central India Field Force were not only forbidden to accept the silver star which the Maharaja Sindhia desired to give them, but received no *batta*, and no decoration, for a series of brilliant successes untarnished by a defeat or retreat, except the general clasp that was given promiscuously to all the troops in Central India, some of whom had done little, or nothing.'[15]

It is likely that, had Whirlpool's actions been conducted under the command of Campbell, instead of Rose, he may never have been recommended for the Victoria Cross. It was well known that Campbell favoured Scots regiments and promoted their efforts at the expense of others. Whirlpool was unmistakably Irish. Campbell was a Scot and highly partisan. He would become 1st Baron Clyde of Clydesdale.

Rose was also a Scot, but far more urbane than Campbell — and fairer. His Victoria Cross nominations bore no taint of partisanship. He would be created 1st Baron Strathnairn of Strathnairn and Jhansi. Though not a wealthy man, he never sought or received a pension, and according to Burne, lost an estimated £30,000 in prize money, despite his claim to it being adjudged fair by the military, and government at home and in India.

The randomness of life and events, that embellish or diminish it, is highlighted by the actions and attitudes of Rose as much as did Whirlpool's own decisions. His decision to join the Indian army, his subsequent engagement in the mutiny, Rose's appointment as Commander of the Central India Field Force, the rebel's stand at Jhansi and the call for volunteers to rescue the wounded and recover the dead, placed Whirlpool randomly in the way of history. His move to Lohari, because the rebels there had betrayed part of Rose's force, the saving of Donne's life and perhaps Newport's, impacted, of course, on their lives, on his and on those of the defeated rebels. What was not randomly undertaken were his decisions to volunteer to go to the wall, and to move to be at the front of the attack at Lohari, standing his ground, despite receiving dangerous wounds. These were clearly spur of the moment decisions he made, over and above his being required to be in a place at a particular time. The decisions set him apart from being a random participant, especially as they were not made to exploit the situations for his own ends. His actions, which resulted from his own decisions, drew valour from deep within him, making him a most worthy Victoria Cross recipient.

On 19 April 1859, Prime Minister Stanley, 14th Earl of Derby, rose in the House of Lords and gave the following tribute:- 'In five months the Central India Field Force traversed 1085 miles, crossed numerous large rivers, took upwards of 150 pieces of artillery, one entrenched camp, two fortified cities and two fortresses all strongly defended, fought sixteen actions, captured twenty forts; and never sustained a check against the most warlike and determined enemy, led by most capable commanders then to be found in any part of India.'[16]

The campaign was vicious and vengeful on both sides, but militarily, Rose led the Central India Field Force magnificently. This 'griff' of delicate stature, was not expected to achieve much, but he had excelled, and more. As Burne put it, '… Sir Hugh Rose showed that military talent may, after all, be sometimes preserved under the black cloak of the diplomatist, and that peaceful avocations do not necessarily rust the facilities of a true soldier.'[17]

Many critics had forgotten that Rose had been taught his military skills by the Prussians, and diplomacy by his father. Tenacity and courage were part of his upbringing — they were not negotiable. Under this man, Frederick Whirlpool was allowed to bloom and be recognised for his actions; the praise higher still because of the man it came from.

Two years after the end of the campaign, the Duke of Cambridge spoke in the House of Lords of his friend. 'Certainly if any officer ever performed acts of the greatest valour, daring, and determination, those acts were performed by Sir Hugh Rose. I personally had an opportunity in the Crimea of seeing what manner of man my gallant friend was, and of what stuff he was made; and I was satisfied at the time that if ever the right occasion presented itself, he would be found to distinguish himself in the extraordinary manner which he has lately done. Permit me to say that he was at the head of a very small European force, and that a very large proportion of the troops under his command were natives, regular Sepoys; and I have reason to believe that these troops on all occasions conducted themselves with a valour and bearing equal to that displayed by the Europeans.'[18]

CHAPTER NINE

VICTORIA

'In his new existence, a man's good and evil acts
Follow him like his shadow, and the consequences thereof
Make his life either pleasant or painful.'

Mahābhārata, iii. 183. 78.

Whirlpool organised his affairs, obtained his discharge papers and the balance of monies owed him, and bade farewell to his comrades, many of whom had, like him, survived serious and dangerous wounds. Their physical wounds were healing, though many would suffer psychological damage known only at the time as 'nervous shock', 'mental shock' or more loftily, 'neurasthenia'. In the next major conflict, the war to end war, it would become known as 'shell shock' and later, 'war neurosis' and 'combat stress reaction'. Today it is commonly known as post traumatic stress disorder and it continues to take its toll. The long road from less than adequate diagnosis through the First World War, and the second and subsequent conflicts, passed by earlier sufferers amongst Whirlpool's contemporaries. They were left to their own devices; the dulling effects of alcohol, helplessness and seclusion. Others, who may have shown outward signs of distress in the field by leaving their posts, throwing away arms, disobedience, or desertion, opened themselves to the death penalty. Treatment in Whirlpool's time was almost non-existent. Rest was proffered to the fortunate; usually officers. Otherwise, overt reactions were often attributed to cowardice and lack of character. Whirlpool had a severe head injury, other critical injuries and he had seen a great deal of action and bloodshed. It can only be imagined what effect these things might have carved into his being. It is highly probable that he was so affected by his experiences in India, that he fell within the ambit of those suffering from 'nervous shock'. His mood changes, which were brought on by things unknown to us, but which tormented him, probably led to his sporadic drinking excesses. This has led some latter day observers to declare him an alcoholic. This is an easy appellation, which has overlooked his own assessment and the way in which he conducted his affairs. His admissions, several years after arriving in Australia, included the observation that he was not addicted to alcohol, nor did he use it habitually. He had the means to indulge himself more frequently, but he didn't. He managed his life, his comfort and his finances and never permanently surrendered self-control.

Whirlpool sailed to Melbourne from Bombay, but of the few arrivals there in 1859 or 1860, he is not recorded on any of the contemporary ship's lists. There is little doubt that this was because he chose the cheapest mode of travel — steerage — where passenger's names were rarely considered. Embarkations from India were not recorded once a soldier had left the service. By 1863 he was to claim that he had arrived in Melbourne on the *Cambodia* in 1860. There was little reason for obfuscation on this point, although on the same form, which was completed by another who had asked him questions, he claimed his birth year as 1833, not 1831, and his native place as County Cavan. There is no record of the *Cambodia* arriving in Melbourne in 1859 or 1860; its last recorded voyage to Australia being in 1855. It was, however used as a troop transport ship taking soldiers to Calcutta in late 1857.[1] It also sailed the Pacific, foundering in New Zealand in late 1866,[2] indicating that it did spend time in local waters. He at least would have known of the ship and was obscuring his movements. On the same entry he used the name Frederick Whirlpool, although under the circumstances, as will be seen, this was unavoidable. He was again covering his tracks.

Victoria, as a colony of England, was a place of resort for many from Britain and the Indian Army, after its disbandment. Arrivals had slowed when the goldfields ceased to yield as they had in earlier days, but stories of this southern *el Dorado* were common currency in India, as much as they were in California and elsewhere. Perhaps Whirlpool followed those stories or indeed, countrymen who had preceded him, although fortune never seemed his goal. It may simply have been that he needed to make a decision after his army career had suddenly vaporised. Whatever the reason, he had made solid plans to travel to Victoria. A notice in the Supplement to the *Victoria Government Gazette* of Thursday, 1 December 1859, announced that a letter had arrived for him by ship in the week ending 23 November, and awaited collection at the General Post Office, Melbourne. It is probable that this was his pension for the September quarter. It had commenced from the date of his last pay certificate, which was about the time of his discharge.[3]

Whirlpool arrived in Melbourne some time after his discharge and before 15 October 1859, according to his written application to join the Victoria Police made on 15 October 1860.[4] In his application he professed to have been in the colony for more than a year. This is at odds with his later account of arriving in 1860, but as the *Bombay Standard* of 21 December 1859 reported:

'Private Frederick Whirlpool, whose achievements we shortly narrated on Monday, in noticing that the Queen had graciously awarded him the Victoria Cross, may congratulate himself on having received such "honorable mention" as he may well prize next to the favor of the Queen herself. We are assured that Sir Hugh Rose has declared (in conversation, we believe, with the Commander in Chief) that if he were asked who was the bravest soldier in his whole force, he should point to Frederick Whirlpool — he has never seen such wondrous daring as his. Whirlpool is now in Australia, having accepted a pension. It was 9d per day, but by the special representation of Sir Hugh Rose has been raised to 1s3d. The rules of the service are no doubt necessarily very stringent. We must hope the gallant fellow's wounds will not incapacitate him from adding to his fifteenpences.'[5]

This clearly indicates that at the time of the Indian publication, — December 1859 — he was already in Australia and in receipt of his service pension, which was to be paid to him in Melbourne from 1 March, 1859.

This report might have caused acute embarrassment to Whirlpool, had he read it. There is no doubt that his actions were probably more significant than those of the others that Rose had nominated for the Victoria Cross. There were not many, but it is hard to imagine him publicly favouring one over another, no matter how impressed he may have been with him. He was after all, a diplomat. It just wasn't politic to make these comments publicly and it is more likely the source was from Campbell's office, where the comments may have, indeed, been made. It was, however, another bright light shone on someone who did not fancy illumination.

Between his arrival and the application for police employment, Whirlpool claimed to have been employed in various labouring positions and was fully restored to health and strength. He advised that he had served in the '... late Honorable East India Company's Army in the late War under Lieutenant General [sic] Sir Hugh Rose. That he was present at every brilliant action fought under that distinguished Commander from the commencement to the capture of Lahoree fort, in which Applicant's military career was ended through severe wounds received in close conflict with the enemy, That Applicant has been awarded the Victoria Cross for his fighting conduct at the storming of Jhansie and Lahoree.'

Clearly, Whirlpool knew by 15 October 1860, that he had been awarded the Victoria Cross and was already in receipt of the £10 annuity it carried. Chief Commissioner of Police, Captain Standish, confirmed this in an addendum to the application the following day, when he advised that he had been in contact with the Deputy Commissary General of the Army, who had confirmed that the applicant had lost his discharge papers and that he had made an affidavit to that effect. He also advised that he was in receipt of 1/3d a day pension, which was 6d a day over and above his 9d a day service pension. The extra sixpence *per diem* was that brokered by Sir Hugh Rose. The application was marked 'This man's name has been entered on the list of candidates for the Police Force.' The application also revealed that Whirlpool had offered himself, '... for the Mounted or Foot Police, humbly considering myself eligible physically and mentally for that employment.' He also professed to be a fair clerk and correct accountant, had some knowledge of elementary mathematics, was thoroughly disciplined as an Infantry soldier, '... and will be most happy to place himself and his humble talents wholly at your honor's disposal, for the service of the colony'. It is notable that he claimed that he had been awarded the Victoria Cross for 'his fighting conduct', rather than 'for valour'.

He made no mention of seafaring, which will be explained later. Nor did he mention that he had been teaching, because in that capacity he was employed under the name, Humphrey James.

About three weeks before he made his application to join the police, Whirlpool enlisted in the Hawthorn and Kew Volunteer Rifle Regiment. This regiment was formed in September 1860. As he lived and taught in the Kew and Hawthorn area, he may have naturally gravitated towards membership and the companionship it offered and perhaps, to fill the void after his sudden departure from his army 'family' in Bombay. He may have joined at the instigation of James Conly, headmaster of the Bell Street Model School, who had been a volunteer for a considerable time himself. Alternatively, he could have joined Conley at the school as a teacher after meeting him at the regimental parades and drill. Either way, at about this time he was a teacher at the Bell Street School and had reverted to the name Humphrey James. He also joined the volunteer regiment under his real name.

Conly[6] was the same age as James and also an Irishman. He came to Australia in the 1850's and took a position at the Hawthorne Denominational School, leaving twelve months later to work at the Bell Street School in Fitzroy. He was asked to manage the school in the absence of Mr. Bell who had travelled to England for a holiday. He eventually bought Bell out and managed the school himself. By 1859 it had become a National School and under new ownership and perhaps a new direction, Humphrey James was engaged as a teacher. Also teaching in the area was Alfred Brunton, a Londoner who had been head teacher at St. Mark's Church of England School and a teacher at the National School in Hawthorn. It would not have been unusual for the men to know each other socially, or as they ebbed and flowed between schools.

Brunton had come to Australia at age 19 in search of gold, but instead, had become a teacher. He was also an evangelical preacher whose lively sermons attracted the inquisitive young James, who was still open to new and pragmatic beliefs. Brunton waxed and waned between denominations and eventually moved to New Zealand where he relieved as a Congregational Minister in Dunedin, before becoming a preacher for the Plymouth Brethren. He was able to draw huge crowds by his oratory, but unfortunately one who gravitated to him was Henry Rouse, a former convict in Tasmania and Norfolk Island, who, as Henry Beresford Garrett, bushranger, held up the Bank of Victoria in 1854 and robbed it of £6,000. He fled to England and when captured, was returned to Australia to serve a further ten years gaol. By 1861 he had obtained his ticket of leave and left for New Zealand where he was again imprisoned. He aligned himself with the Plymouth Brethren, perhaps to enhance his chances of early release. When it came, he was pushed backwards and forwards from New Zealand to Australia before settling into Brunton's congregation. With one eye on his Bible and the other on the chemist's shop in the same building as the chapel, he made plans. Returning at night, he burgled the apothecary, thereby throwing doubt upon his religious fervour.

At the Sir Robert Nickle Hotel in Burwood Road, Hawthorn, on 20 September 1861, the Hawthorn and Kew Volunteer Rifles sought to extend membership. At its inception the period of enlistment was for only twelve months, but at this meeting, Colonel Pitt had advised them that the new period of enlistment would be for two years in order to get more wear from their government subsidised uniforms. He stated that he considered the period of two years enrolment would be no more binding on them than had the previous twelve months.

The Hawthorn and Kew regiment was not large and at its best, had 68 men 'on paper', well down from the allowable 100. New members were enthusiastically sworn in by Colonel Pitt, as the presiding magistrate. He extolled the virtues of membership, apart from patriotic duty, and announced £1,700 in prize money for competitions to be held at their next encampment.[7] Just 46 members were sworn in, but Humphrey James was not among them. He had been part of the original intake of volunteers who had been swept up in the fervour of the moment on 27 September 1860,[8] when a meeting had been held at the same hotel, presided over by local identities. Days later, another meeting was convened at the Prospect Hotel in Kew, to form the Hawthorn and Kew Volunteer Rifle Company. About 60 members were enrolled, including Humphrey James. The volunteers carried out drill and sentry duty at Brooks' paddock opposite the Sir Robert Nickle Hotel.[9] It was whilst serving in this Company and teaching, that one of Frederick's former pupils, J.J. Bradley, was so impressed with him, that he was able to attest more than thirty years later, 'He was a man of fine physique, but singularly modest and retiring.' He was also to throw light on the manner in which James was to be presented with his Victoria Cross. '… had it not been for the interest taken in his case by Captain Rodd of Dandenong, then Sergeant and drill instructor to the Hawthorn Rifles, who, on ascertaining the facts, took the matter up *con amore* and communicated with the military authorities in England, the emblem of gallantry would most likely never have been presented.'[10]

Either James had mentioned his VC to Rodd (he didn't seem reluctant to do this at the time) or Rodd had fallen across his name in despatches from the *London Gazette*, or reports in local newspapers, leading him to pursue the matter. The *Argus* correspondent, James Bradley, of the Melbourne Custom-house, had reason to recall that had Rodd not intervened, the presentation may never have happened. It is clear from this account that James had either not bothered to pursue the matter, or did not know how to approach it. The latter scenario is unlikely as he was well able to arrange the transfer of his pension from state to state and was articulate, so we are left with the unavoidable impression that he simply had resisted any attempt to obtain his meed. It would not have been because of dissatisfaction with the army. He had, after all, volunteered in the colony. It was probably more to do with his 'singularly modest and retiring' persona.

Augustus W. Rodd was an auctioneer who had resided in Dandenong for 30 years. Community minded and with a high business reputation, he was appointed a Justice of the Peace by the Executive Council later in his life. He was described as fair and urbane by his friends, and it was thought that that, and his impartiality, would serve him well on the Bench. His fairness and sense of duty certainly ensured that James would be recognised.

Another *Argus* correspondent, M.H. Mortimer of Lyndhurst-park, Cranbourne, recalled serving with a volunteer force and attending a special parade at Melbourne's Albert Park to witness Private Whirlpool's VC presentation. 'Some 35 years ago, when I was a member of the old volunteer force, I attended a special parade at the Albert-park parade ground to witness the presentation to Private Whirlpool, of the Hawthorne Rifles, of the Victoria Cross for distinguished bravery and determination during the Indian Mutiny. In one fight Whirlpool received some 27 sword-cuts and bayonet thrusts, and yet survived. He passed (in the rifle company here) under an assumed name (Smith I think). It may be worthy of record in your history of the Mutiny that the VC given to a brave actor in that great tragedy was bestowed upon Victorian soil.'[11]

Both correspondent's had responded to a series of articles in the *Argus* titled 'Deeds that Won the Empire' by Vedette, the *nom de plume* of the Reverend William H. Fitchett, who had embarked on his tales in an attempt to instil a sense of history and military purpose in the raw colony. He was a co-founder and president of the Methodist Ladies' College, a preacher, educationalist, and religious and secular editor.[12] His series in the *Argus* flushed out responses from correspondent's in all the colonies and we have to thank him for publishing those of 'M.H. Mortimer' and 'J.J. Bradley', as they allow us a small glimpse of the purposefully enigmatic Humphrey James. The former claimed that Whirlpool had used an assumed name, Smith, he thought, after the passage of almost 40 years. As Whirlpool was an assumed name, we are left to ponder why he would again change it. The fact is that he hadn't. His 'assumed' name was 'James', in reality, his birth name, to which he had reverted in his role of teacher. He simply began to use his old name. His problem was that he still received his pensions in the name Whirlpool, and had applied to join the Victoria Police in that name. He decided to do no more, until his circumstances changed after his Victoria Cross presentation, which of course had to be made in the name, 'Private Frederick Whirlpool'.

In a communiqué from the War Office in London of 9 February 1861, it became clear that Rodd's solicitations had been fruitful. It contained the Victoria Cross and read, 'As this man's absence from England prevents his receiving this high distinction from Her Majesty's hands, I have received Her Majesty's commands to desire that you will take the earliest fitting opportunity, after the receipt of this instruction, of presenting to him the enclosed cross in such a public and formal manner as you may consider best adapted to evince Her Majesty's sense of the noble daring displayed by him before the enemy, and to testify her wish that a distinction in which the officer and soldier may equally share may be highly prized and eagerly sought after by all, of whatever rank and degree, in Her Majesty's naval and military services.

'I have it especially in command to desire that the discharge of this duty, you will take care that nothing is omitted which may tend to redound to the honour of the man for whom this cross is intended, and to enhance the value of the decoration; and I have further to request that you will transmit to me, without delay, a report of the proceedings which you may adopt on the occasion, together with a copy of the general order which may be issued, for the purpose of being recorded in the registry of the decoration.

I have &c

(Signed) S. HERBERT'

The occasion chosen was a review of the entire volunteer force planned for the Queen's Birthday, but this was postponed due to the death of Her Royal Highness, the Duchess of Kent, the Queen's mother. The new date, 20 June was the 24th anniversary of Queen Victoria's accession. Over two thousand men paraded with their officers, joined by some regular troops and naval forces. Among them, of course, was Private Frederick Whirlpool, no doubt overawed by the unfolding drama and wishing to be anywhere else. Even the support of his escort, Sergeant Atkyns, would offer little comfort.[13] The crowds came and at 11am the volunteers took up their positions in line. By midday the spectators had swelled to between 13 and 14,000. Commentators described the field as the Emerald Hill racecourse, others, simply the ground between the Butts' Station on the St. Kilda Railway and the Sandridge Battery. About 700 or 800 boys from local schools were run through their drill under the watchful eye of Colonel Pitt, who commanded the whole of the volunteer force.

Major-General Pratt and his retinue arrived shortly before midday and took up their positions with Colonel Pitt and his staff. His Excellency, Sir Henry Barkly, Governor of Victoria and Lady Barkly, who was Pratt's daughter, arrived soon after to a royal salute. The Governor inspected the troops on horseback, after which another salute was fired. The troops then marched past the dignitaries and formed into three sides of a square, a manoeuvre not unfamiliar to

Private Whirlpool, who had seen it many times in India preparatory to executions. One wonders what was going through his mind as Major-General Pratt called for him to come forward.

A *Bell's Life in Victoria* correspondent wrote, 'Mr. Whirlpool is a well built man of middle age, and his wiry frame appears capable of great endurance. The effect of the wound on his neck is still apparent. On his name being called, he stepped out of the ranks, and with shouldered rifle stood in the attitude of attention.'[14]

The *Age* correspondent took this moment a little further. 'Private Whirlpool having been summoned from the ranks, appeared in his gray uniform, shouldering his rifle.'[15] This is the only clue to the appearance of his uniform, for which the government sought frugality, apart from the *Argus* correspondent noting, 'The 40th Regiment, and the new scarlet uniforms of the Royal Engineers, in the centre of the line, agreeably relieved the more sombre hues of the volunteer ranks, whilst the cavalry on the extreme right and the artillery next to them looked admirable.'[16]

Lieutenant-Colonel Carey then read the General Order, which Queen Victoria had commanded.

'GENERAL ORDER. Head-quarters, Melbourne, June 20, 1861. Extract from the *London Gazette*, of Friday, October 21, 1859:- Private Frederick Whirlpool, Third Bombay European Regiment. Recommended for the Victoria Cross — for gallantry volunteering, on the 3rd April, 1858, in the attack on Jhansi, to return and carry away several killed and wounded, which he did twice under a very heavy fire from the wall; also for devoted bravery at the assault of Lahore, on the 2nd May, 1858, in rushing to the rescue of Lieutenant Donne, of the regiment, who was dangerously wounded. In this service Private Whirlpool received seventeen desperate wounds, one of which nearly severed his head from his body. The gallant example shown by this man is considered to have greatly contributed to the success of the day.' In publishing the foregoing extract from the *London Gazette*, the Major-General Commanding the Forces will but carry out Her most gracious Majesty's wishes by giving publicity, at the same time, to the instructions he has received as follows.'

He added. 'No words from the Major-General can add honour to the terms above-quoted, but it gives him the highest satisfaction to be the medium of conveying to Private Whirlpool the high distinction which has been awarded to him, and which he has richly merited; and under the impossibility of receiving the decoration from Her Majesty's own hands, it will be placed on his breast by the wife of Her Majesty's representative in this country, and the daughter of a very old soldier. The whole force will then give three cheers for the brave recipient of the "Victoria Cross" ROBT. CAREY Lieutenant-Colonel, Deputy Adjutant-General.'

Lady Barkly then spoke, addressing her comments directly to Frederick. 'Private Whirlpool — Had you returned to England after your gallant services in India, the value of this cross, which you have so nobly won, would doubtless have been immeasurably enhanced by your receiving it at the hands of your Queen. As, however, you have chosen this country for your home, and joined the ranks of its defenders, the honour of presenting it devolves today on me; and I cannot but feel doubly proud that this the first occasion on which the highest distinction British valour can attain is bestowed in Australia, I should have to affix it to a volunteer uniform, and in presence of comrades so capable of appreciating your heroic exploits.'

Lady Barkly stepped forward and affixed the cross on his left breast. Whirlpool raised his hat and said a few words. Again *A Bell's Life in Victoria* reported, 'Private Whirlpool was so much moved by the receipt of his well deserved reward that he could hardly express his heartfelt acknowledgements.' The lily seems to have been gilded and some license used by this correspondent who added, 'He was understood to say that he was gratified with the distinction awarded to him for doing his duty, and that he would always be ready to do his duty to his sovereign and his country to the laying down of his life.'[17]

Whirlpool baulked at the attention he was receiving before such a large audience. Three cheers were called for and when he fell back into the ranks, his comrades continued to cheer. Had he known that the majority of the crowd had no idea of the proceedings, he may have drawn some comfort from it. Most had come for the parades, bands and pomp. There had been no warning that the presentation would be made.

Lady Barkly had noted that this was the first occasion on which a Victoria Cross had been presented in Australia. Or was it? Two Victoria

Cross presentations were made in Sydney in 1858, to Sergeant John Park and Private Alexander Wright, who had arrived in Sydney with the 77th Regiment of Foot in late 1857, to relieve the 11th Regiment. Most of the 77th were recalled in early 1858, to be hurried to India to reinforce Queen's and Company armies in the suppression of the mutiny. Theirs was not a public presentation, and although the *London Gazette* Supplement had been reproduced in the *Sydney Morning Herald* earlier in 1857, most of the public would not have been aware that two of the many recipients of the decoration won in the Crimea were in their midst, let alone know of their hasty presentation. The Whirlpool presentation was certainly the first to a man wearing an Australian uniform, and presented publicly.[18,19]

After the Whirlpool presentation, the dignitaries departed and the volunteers were marched to the Exhibition Building, which had been decorated for a levee for the gentlemen of the colony, hosted by Governor Barkly, to belatedly celebrate Queen Victoria's birthday. James was among those assembled, as were most of the volunteers, but he was well down the pecking order, with senior military figures, diplomats, church leaders, judges and other worthies further along the perch. Interestingly, the Commissioner of Police was present, as was Justice Sir Redmond Barry, who had presided over the trial of the Eureka Stockade rebels and would sentence the murderer, Edward 'Ned' Kelly to death in 1880. Commissioner Standish didn't have to look Whirlpool in the eye, and it is just as well, for as will be shown shortly he knew full well that the man who had just been awarded the Victoria Cross, which was still pinned to his breast, may never take up a position with the Victoria Police. The levee ended at 3.45pm and the invited crowd and those observing from outside, dispersed. James' company was dismissed. He quietly pocketed his small gunmetal cross and made his way back to his lodgings. It was the only time he wore the decoration.

Humphrey James continued to teach, but the connection was drawn with his Whirlpool persona and decoration. In his small circle, anonymity could no longer be assured. His award was news across the colonies, in India and in Britain. Strangely, none of the Australian newspapers mentioned that he was a teacher, though this fact was not missed by the *Aldershot Military Gazette*, which relied on a correspondent from the *London Times*. 'On the same occasion Lady Barkly, on behalf of Her Majesty, presented the Victoria Cross to Private Frederick Whirlpool, late of the 3rd Bombay European Regiment, now a schoolmaster and volunteer in Victoria, for services in India.'[20]

His application, as Frederick Whirlpool, to join the Victoria Police was still active, though he had been waiting to be called up for eight months without word. His interest was waning by this time and his teaching had been satisfying enough for him to continue it. In any event, the good burghers of Hawthorn had other ideas. He was still newsworthy and there was nowhere for him to hide from this unwanted attention. On 26 June, not a week after his investiture, Mr. Embling, Member of the Legislative Assembly for Collingwood in the absence of Mr. Stephen, rose in that chamber to speak and asked, '... whether the Government had any objections to bestow some office, for which he might be qualified, upon Private Whirlpool of the Kew and Hawthorn Volunteer Rifles (recently honoured by Her Majesty with the "Victoria Cross" for his extraordinary bravery during the late Indian campaign), as a means of providing for a gallant soldier who had been severely wounded in the service of his country, and thereby been disabled for active bodily occupations?'

Chief Secretary, Richard Heales replied. 'The name of Private Whirlpool was entered on the list of candidates for the police force a short time since; and in consequence of attention having been drawn to his bravery during the Indian campaign, he has been permitted to take precedence, and would be appointed to the first vacancy.'[21]

James wasted no time and on the morning after the parliamentary question, he hand delivered his response in a letter to the editor. It was couched in terms which convey the impression that it had been written on his behalf, but he was more than capable of composing the polite but pointed letter, which was simply signed 'W'. He considered himself in rude health and wrote, 'I am authorised by Private Whirlpool to say that he has had no communication whatever with Mr. Stephen respecting the notice of motion given last evening in the House of Assembly; that he has no intention to importune Government for employment; and that so far from being "unfit for active bodily occupation", he is "able to handle an axe with anybody." He thanks Mr. Stephen for his kind intentions, but feels that this explanation is due to himself. I am, Sir, your obedient servant, W. June 26.'

And that was the end of the matter. Two weeks later, James wrote to General Pratt, asking that his name in the Victoria Cross Register be changed to 'Frederick Humphrey James' and that his pensions be paid in that name. On 11 July 1861, General Pratt wrote to the Secretary of State for War in London to pass on the request, attaching the application. A reply written by Sir Edward Lugard, the Under-Secretary of War, in October 1861, indicated that before the matters could be considered, Private Whirlpool would have to provide evidence to support his application, '...either by the production of a copy of his baptism certificate, or such other evidence as he may be enabled to bring forward.'[22]

It is evident that James' application expressed his desire to revert to his given names, or Lugard would not have sought a baptism certificate. All of the James children had single given names according to lists they prepared for the information of the Director of Intestate Estates in New South Wales, but as Samuel, living in Philadelphia, used the name Samuel Robert, the more formal full names may not have been used in the lists. It is therefore possible that Whirlpool was born Frederick Humphrey James, but used the name Humphrey. His siblings all referred to him as Humphrey. It is more likely though, that he wanted to include the name Frederick by which he had been known for so long. In doing so he would have made it difficult to produce a baptism certificate. He must have seen other difficulties in providing the certificate. He did not falter because of any fear of contacting his family, he had already done that, but Carlow is some distance from Dundalk and he may not have wanted to put them to the trouble. Alternatively, he may never have been baptised, unusual as it was for the time, but then again, his parents were nonconforming liberals.

Crook,[23] indicates that Frederick Humphrey Jones, [sic] who had won the VC as Frederick Whirlpool, had had his request to change the name on his cross and medal denied. This does not accord with the record. James sought to change his name in the Victoria Cross Register and to have his pensions paid in his birth name. He did not request that his name be altered on the Victoria Cross, or on his

Indian Mutiny Medal, which he had received in October 1861.[24] In any event, he let the matter rest and left the Hawthorn and Kew Rifles, resigned his teaching position and disappeared into Tasmania sometime after 6 October 1861, obviating the need for the War Office to deny his request.

He was acutely modest and could not tolerate being a curiosity, or to be fawned over. His pride would not allow it, as it would not allow him to take a benefit from a well-intentioned government. But still the press did not let up. *The Star* newspaper of Ballarat helpfully proposed that a job be found for him. 'We will give the Ballarat Volunteers a hint in reference to this matter. They require a drill instructor, and where could they get a more gallant one than this brave fellow, Whirlpool. We presume he is perfectly qualified for such a post, and if he is not, he must at least be well acquainted with military matters as only to require a very few weeks instruction in some of the later developments of drill to be able to take the position of drill instructor; such a delay we have no doubt the Ballarat volunteers would most willingly submit to, if by it they would secure the services of one, who, like Whirlpool, would be an honour to the Corps ... '[25]

It seemed that gallantry might be helpful to a drill instructor who may not be able to conduct the latest drill. It is not known whether James saw this gratuitous and patronising advice; one can only hope not.

The *South Bourke Standard* of 24 January 1862, covered the prize night at the Hawthorn Model School where Master James Bradley, (presumably the latter day correspondent, J.J. Bradley), was awarded a silver medal for proficiency and where an announcement was made that, ' ... the unexpected retirement of Mr. James had, however created a vacancy, which had not since been taken up.'[26]

So, after four months, the schoolmaster's vacancy had not been filled and after eight, nor had the Victoria Police been in contact. It seems the wheels of state turned slowly in 19th century Victoria. There was a reason, however, for the delay on the police list and a rather sinister one at that. Chief Secretary O'Shanassy had a penchant for interfering with the management of the police force. Unlike his predecessor, Chief Commissioner McMahon, who resigned because of it, Chief Commissioner Standish, in a breathtaking display of apostasy did not, and bent to the will of his political overlord. 'Collusion between Standish and O'Shanassy as Catholics involved the compilation of a special list of candidates for the police force. By using it, O'Shanassy and Standish circumvented the normal recruiting procedures and were able to give favoured candidates almost instant entry into the force. Standish did not particularly like the special list, but lacked sufficient principle to resign or take a stand over it. So he maintained two lists of applicants, a general list containing the names of more than seven hundred men who waited, on average, fifteen months for a place on the force, and a special list of men who received almost immediate appointment, most of them being Catholics who had served with the Irish Constabulary. Some men on the general list never gained a place with the police ... '[27]

What appears as more galling in James' case, is that Standish was a military man who had spent nine years in the Royal Artillery. He was a hedonist, roué, heavy gambler and played favourites with his subordinates, giving preferential treatment to cronies over worthy officers. He was obviously corrupt and protected his favoured acolytes, including Superintendent Frederick Winch, the head of the Police Depot, who endorsed Whirlpool's application with the telling and dismissive 'This man's name has been entered on the list of candidates for the Police Force.'[28] Standish knew that Frederick Whirlpool had been awarded the Victoria Cross, after serving with valour in the field of battle. He knew that he had been severely wounded, yet had recovered sufficiently to again seek active service within the police force. He noted on 16 October, in a memo added to the application, 'With reference to a candidate (whose name I forget) but whom I directed Mr. Winch to enter on the list at the Depot only if he produced his discharge from the Indian Army, I have seen the Deputy Commissary General who confirms this man's statement that he had lost his discharge, but that he had made an affidavit to that effect. This man is in receipt of 1/3d per day pension and rec'd the Victoria Cross for great gallantry. Mr. Mylrea informed me that though he knew nothing of this man personally, he had seen his testimonials of character which are most satisfactory.'[29]

Despite his 'great gallantry', 'most satisfactory character' and education, he was placed on the general list because he was not a former Irish police officer and was not a Catholic. James had completed his written application to Standish with the words, 'Trusting that your Honor, as a military gentleman, will graciously consider this application, your Applicant, as in duty bound, will ever pray.'[30] It is clear that Standish was without honour, was not a military gentleman of any note and was far from gracious. One can only speculate upon what Major-General Sir Hugh Rose would have made of Captain Standish.

Not until his case was raised in the parliament and an assurance was given that he would be given preferential treatment at the head of the list, that James' circumstances could have changed. It is a measure of the man, that he would not take advantage of his situation to pass over other candidates who had been on the list for much longer periods; periods he would have been familiar with, even if he didn't know of the 'other' list of favoured candidates. He refused the offer and left his aspirations behind as he crossed Bass Strait for Tasmania.

He also left behind a police force severely crippled by its dishonest recruitment processes, where the best candidates were overlooked for a particular 'type', many of them illiterate. Even James' handsome copperplate handwriting and articulate application had not swayed this toady. Standish did not favour formal training, rather preferring on the job experience through trial and error.[31] James rejected the offer publicly with grace and left with honour. In an intriguing squirm, Standish had himself applied to join the Victoria Police in 1853, under an assumed name, but was refused entry by McMahon on the grounds, '… of his having held a position in society which would render him unfit for such a comparatively humble office.'[32] Five years later he was drawn from the smoky depths of the Melbourne Club gaming rooms, to become Victoria's third Chief Commissioner. He was considered a gentleman despite coming to Australia to avoid gambling debts, but as far as the measure of a gentleman was concerned, the bar was apparently not set very high.

James' time in Tasmania must have passed agreeably, as he remained there in relative anonymity for about eight months. He probably used his original name to avoid further unwanted attention, although the duality of his identity had to continue in order to receive his pensions, and it was here that he worked as a surveyor's labourer. He had already said that he could use an axe with anyone, and this type of work would have taken him away from settled areas to his familiar tent accommodation, sleeping rough and eating off the land. He may also have taken advantage of specific surveying studies at his Dundalk school. No record of him has yet surfaced in Tasmania apart from his pensions being forwarded there, from 1 January, 1862[33] and his departure. Interest in him had died down and he now sought a new beginning. He secured a passage on the *Alarm* bound for Sydney on 4 September 1862, and although relegated to steerage, the manifest did record his name. He was listed as Thomas Whirlpool, though this may have been a clerical error. It is hard to imagine him seeking anonymity by changing his first name, rather than his unique surname.

CHAPTER TEN

———

NEW SOUTH WALES

'I have done one braver thing
Than all the Worthies did;
And yet a braver thence doth spring
Which is, to keep that hid.'

John Donne[1] 1572-1631
'The Undertaking'

The *Alarm*, a brig of 196 tons, was cleared for sailing on 4 September 1862, and left as soon as conditions permitted, arriving in Sydney on the 11th of that month. A new horizon, another city, and another purpose had set James a new target. He made his way to police headquarters in Phillip Street and applied to join the New South Wales Police Force. The Police Regulation Act of 1862 had enabled a single, uniform body to be established, drawing together the threads of former forces in much the same way as had occurred in Ireland 25 years earlier. Much of the Irish model was favoured by the legislators, as it had been by Sir Hugh Rose, who had called for it to be established in India.[2] 1861 was the year of reform for the police and word must have been abroad that recruits were welcome. In just a few years 60% of police in New South Wales were Irish born;[3] a trend that had emerged across the western world. It may be that, as Haldane suggests, some contend the Irish took to policing naturally, but others hold that Ireland got its policing model right, from the county forces to the unified force of 1836. The model was agreeable to the landlords of Ireland, as much as it would be for the squattocracy of Australia. It would be the model used for the establishment of the unified New South Wales Police of 1862. It is also the case that Australian born men declined to join the police force in any numbers, as it was seen as a disadvantageous and socially unacceptable move.[4]

The Royal Irish Constabulary, the font of policing, was subject to wild fluctuations in its authorised strength, depending on the prevailing political circumstances. In the latter part of the 19th century it comprised more than 10,000 men. During the late 1850's and early 1860's, more than 6,000 men resigned, eventually leading to attrition outpacing recruitment by the mid 1860's. Poor wages and working conditions partly explain the attrition rate, and many quit Ireland for much better pay in America and Australia.[5]

Regulations in the Royal Irish Constabulary prohibited men from marrying until they had served for seven years, and even then, they had to show means capable of maintaining a married state. Only a quarter of Irish police were allowed to be married and there was a long waiting list for those wishing to enter into matrimonial bliss. Dismissal would follow the offences of criminal intercourse, extramarital sex and marriage without permission. Although permission was required to marry in Australian police forces, it was rarely refused and none of the other Irish restrictions applied.[6] Little wonder that distant shores beckoned.

Frederick Whirlpool was appointed to the New South Wales Police Force, as a supernumerary officer, on 22 September 1862, less than two weeks after arriving from Hobart Town, suggesting that he may have made a written application from Tasmania. On the other hand, if the force was recruiting from the street, as it were, 12 days from application to appointment was incredibly swift, and may have reflected avid recruitment to the newly formed force. Upon appointment, his particulars were entered into the *Register of Police Appointments* simply as 'Frederick (1024) Whirlpool, supernumerary; date of appointment — 22nd September, 1862; age — 29; eyes — grey; hair — brown; complexion — sallow; height 5' 7½ ; single; Country — Ireland; Religion — Church of England; read and write; Previous Occupation — Soldier 3rd Bombay Europeans; Remarks — Transferred to the Murray District.'[7] His Victoria Cross was not revealed.

In another register his general appearance was described as 'commonplace', which was somewhere between 'dull and heavy' and 'ordinary', 'smart', or 'intelligent' appearing against the names of others on the list. After reverting to his real name while teaching in Victoria, it is to be wondered why he chose to enter this new phase of his life in the guise of Frederick Whirlpool. Perhaps it *was* his *nom de guerre.*

He was on his way, seemingly having achieved one of his goals; to be a policeman. Teaching had taken a back seat, perhaps because it too, like clerking, seemed too placid and unchallenging after the trials and excitement of battle in India. Restoring normalcy after war was a theme amongst ex-soldiers, many of whom, unable to cope with the routine of civil life, rejoined for more of that to which they had become accustomed. His brother Benjamin enlisted three times, campaigning in the Mutiny and US civil and Indian wars, only to end his days in the Patton Lunatic Asylum. Policing offered the excitement and challenges of a combative and adversarial role, balanced against life amongst a basically well ordered people. This was not a new experience for Whirlpool. He had seen policing first hand at the arm of his father, who had been at the forefront of the new police in Ireland. That he was immediately posted to the Murray district was a measure of the acute shortage of police in that region, who were being criticised and derided for their inability to rein in and arrest various bushrangers, including the infamous Ben Hall, Frank Gardiner and Dan Morgan.

The Murray headquarters were at Albury, on the border of New South Wales and Victoria. Once attested, Whirlpool attended the Police Depot at the Carter's Barracks on the site of the present day Central Railway complex, in Sydney. The Barracks had been built circa 1819 to house convicts who were used to draw cartloads of bricks from the kilns at Brickfield Hill, into city building projects, as there were as yet insufficient draught animals to do the work. By 1862 the barracks housed the police depot, a police station and the police paddock. The depot held a commissariat for the whole of the state wide force, which was responsible for an area covering 809,444 square kilometres or 312,528 square miles. It held harness, saddlery, stores, stationery, uniforms and every other conceivable accoutrement for the supply of officers in the field. It was overstocked, to meet the needs of a mercurial population, which was likely to move in the tens of thousands, in search of gold. The store even held sufficient material for the construction of police stations, including nails and tools, as the constables were often required to build their own stations and accommodation. It was here Whirlpool was fitted with his uniform and equipped with his horse, tack, saddlery, arms and other equipment that would see him prepared for his trip to Albury. His uniform would not have differed much from that of the Union Army in Civil War America, worn by his brother Benjamin during that campaign. The changes in uniform and equipment made in 1862 must be noted. A troopers outfit now comprised a blue cloth jumper, grey cloth riding pants, blue cloth overalls, a waterproof cape and cloak of military pattern, and Napoleon boots. For bush service the mounted man's dress was less precise. Red tape, fortunately, did not prescribe any hard and fast regulations in this respect. One new feature that was universal, however, was the adoption of leather leggings.'[8]

The New South Wales *Police Gazette* announced Frederick H. Whirlpool, as a new supernumerary appointment in the Murray District, on 24 September 1862. He was confirmed as a Constable in the *Police Gazette* of 7 January 1863. His next appearance in the *Gazette* was on 17 June 1863, in which he was shown as Constable Frederick Whirlpool No 1024 — Dismissed on 10 June. The year 1863, as it happened, was the nadir of police dismissals for misconduct in the 10 years between 1862 and 1871, when 68 fell foul of regulations and the law,[9] although it was also the year of the highest intake for the period.

Whirlpool appeared at the Wagga Wagga Court on 9 June 1863 charged, 'In default of sureties to keep the peace.' His sentence was one calendar month imprisonment, and he was dismissed from the police force the following day. The Wagga Gaol Entrance Book entry for his admission, indicates that he served the month and was released on 9 July.[10] It was in this book that he had provided answers to questions about his arrival in the Colony. He stated that he had arrived in 1860, aboard the *Cambodia*, that he was born in 1833 and was a native of County Cavan. His religion was shown as Church of England and his occupation as 'soldier'. He had hit a brick wall and his aspirations to serve as a police officer were finished. His false answers to his questioner may have been an attempt to muddy the waters to ensure that his family did not learn of his predicament. This is the first indication that Whirlpool was troubled by alcohol abuse as there must have been an incident on a previous occasion, for which he had been placed on a recognizance to keep the peace. The exact circumstances are, so far, lost to time. It is clear though, that whatever the original offence, it was not of sufficient seriousness to attract instant dismissal, or incarceration. Detention was not an unusual practice in the latter part of the 19th century. Drunkenness was a major problem, in society, in the military and no less so in the police forces of the colonies. It was normal for constables to be placed before the courts on charges of drunkenness, punished, even gaoled, and allowed back to duty. This was also the case for other minor infringements. The police force accepted the process and the public thought nothing of it. Robert Haldane found that, 'Police drunkenness was a perennial problem, partly because habitual drunkards within the force were not dismissed but briefly gaoled. Drunken police were charged publicly in open court and their prior convictions were read to the court before sentence.'[11]

While Haldane was discussing Victoria police, he stressed that this methodology was adopted across the colonies. Examination of the police strength in Wagga Wagga in 1861, assuming that Whirlpool had been stationed there as part of the Murray District staff, indicates that it comprised one sub-inspector, one sergeant, one senior constable and seven constables. To do other than reinstate sheepish and chastened constables for their baleful habits, would have left the local force woefully weakened. About half of all cases coming before the court in Wagga Wagga at this time were for drunkenness.[12] In this, it would not have differed from most towns in the colonies and partly explains the tolerance of the people. In some areas, special cells were established for police drunks, not unlike the 'congee cells' in the Indian Army, though the latter were designed to keep drunken soldiers away from senior officers and NCO's to avoid them being sentenced to death for striking their superiors.

Whirlpool had shown no propensity to overindulge in alcohol while teaching in Victoria and was comfortable to use his former employers and colleagues as referees, when he did go on to train as a teacher in the National system. No indication exists of his having fallen foul of the volunteer company in his time with the Hawthorn and Kew Volunteer Rifles. What had changed was that in the Murray District, as a constable, he had the time and opportunity to drink to excess. On patrol and alone, there was no-one to supervise him. He would not have been permitted to overindulge in alcohol in his parent's home, if at all. His short army service before the outbreak of the mutiny, would not have seen him suddenly alcoholic, though long periods of inactivity in Poona could have lent itself to him joining his fellows in the mess, or the bazaars where native arak, rum, brandy, wine and beer were plentiful. It is probably here too, that he took up smoking.

Whirlpool's offence would have involved alcohol abuse and disorderly conduct of some kind. He was given a second chance and he gave his assurances that he would behave and 'keep the peace'. He formally entered those undertakings and when they were not kept, the court would have taken a very dim view of this failure. It would have been considered a greater failing than his original offence, or indeed, the second offence, which caused his fall.

Whirlpool's taste for alcohol probably developed in his quieter time in the army, and perhaps during the latter part of his long convalescence in India. It made the time pass, the company of colleagues more enjoyable and perhaps blurred unwanted recollections.

The ease with which one could over indulge in country New South Wales is shown in an incident only one month before Whirlpool's downfall. The *Wagga Wagga Express* reported in May of 1863. 'Shooting the Pigeon and killing the crow — on the 11th instant, Sir Frederick Pottinger preferred a charge against two of his troopers for a misdemeanour in laying a wrong information to the police. It appears that they were under orders to proceed to Eugowra and becoming rather thirsty called at Mr. Rogers' public house to refresh themselves, a process which they effected powerfully. On resuming their journey one of them perceived an emu and having a natural turn for sporting, drew his revolver and fired. The bullet took no effect on the bird however, but grazed the neck of the sportsman's charger, inflicting a rather severe wound. His companion immediately made back and reported to Sir Frederick that they had been stuck up by five bushrangers, two of whom were O'Meally and Gilbert, and that some 15 or 20 shots had been fired, one of them striking the horse. The other constable corroborated the report of this gallant encounter with the consequence that the entire police force in the neighbourhood were turned out to scour the country — of course without effect. We wonder whether any other of the extraordinary shooting matches, which we have heard of between police officers and bushrangers, are equally founded on fact.'[13]

That the press could make light of this incident, tells of the enduring patience of the public to alcohol-fuelled stupidity within police ranks. It was merely a reflection of the abuse of alcohol within the community they served and of which they were a part. They were not so kind, however, to the more sober police efforts against the better mounted and better armed bush-ranging gangs. Public tolerance was all the more puzzling as only 11 months earlier, Australia's largest gold robbery had taken place near Eugowra, when Frank Gardiner and his gang — including Ben Hall, John O'Meally, Bow, Manns and Fordyce — robbed a Cobb & Co. coach of 2,719 ounces of it (77 kilograms) and £3,700 in cash.

The emu hunting troopers, William Neilson and John Chambers, who had left the Nowra barracks for Eugowra before their undoing, appeared at the Nowra Court on 18 May 1863, and pleaded guilty, claiming drunkenness in mitigation of penalty.[14] They were fined £5 each, which was not an insubstantial amount, but were dismissed from the police force the following day.[15]

Cold comfort though it was, Wagga Wagga Gaol had been constructed in 1862, so was not in the vile condition which saw its demolition in 1919. It was made of brick, but the cells were timber lined and would eventually fall to white ant infestation. His time there would have been somewhat more hygienic than at some other locations. Its recent completion would not have allowed time for the permanent infusion of rancid, stale, tobacco and alcohol laced human stench, which is so familiar to those who have known such places, and which no amount of cleaning can obliterate. His time was taken up in the light labour of teasing out curled horse hair, for which the gaoler was paid three farthings per pound weight, by local saddler W.A. Mitchell. His saddle and harness making business was opposite the Court House, and he used the teased hair to pad his saddles.

On one occasion, in 1863, Mitchell, happy with the work, increased the payment to 2d a pound and the gaoler, Robert Monteith, retained the extra money received to purchase tea for his prisoners, before remitting the balance to the treasury.[16]

How Whirlpool fared upon his release, can only be imagined. He had had a month to consider his position and ever the fatalist, he moved on, but not without regret it is certain. He never considered levering his reinstatement into the police force by disclosing his possession of the Victoria Cross. He would not consider it and never did, on this occasion or at a later time when he was confronted with a similar dilemma. On one hand, Constable Frederick Whirlpool VC, was absolutely unwilling to further himself through his holding of the Victoria Cross. It was not in his nature and it would have been dishonourable for him to do so. He valued the cross, as shown by his attempts to have his name changed in the Victoria Cross Register and by eventually placing it with the pension office in Sydney for safekeeping. He did not expect or seek advancement through his high honour and was certain that he would not again be placed in public focus through holding it. He kept it hidden. This was consistent with the way he had earned the cross. On each of the two occasions, he did his duty and did it with valour. He was modest, unassuming and unambitious, unlike many of his cohort who outwardly coveted and sought the award for the advancement it would bring. 'Of the 182 VC's awarded during the rebellion, 66 went to members of the Company's service, mostly of the Bengal Army. No less than 42 of these men were officers, most lieutenants ... of the eighteen soldiers awarded the VC only two secured promotion, from bombardier to quartermaster sergeant and from private to sergeant.'[17] Eighteen of the officers who received the VC achieved the rank of general. Although the award was intended for all ranks, those without class, entitlement or connections, would never gain preferential promotion. Whirlpool's main early ambition was to teach, not to fight and not to seek promotion, other than what a teaching position would bring, but when called to arms, he volunteered for the 'forlorn hope' as a chivalrous and selfless act, not for advancement. Nothing in 1863 was going to change that attitude.

On the other hand, a man the same age as Whirlpool and who was born in India, came to the colony of New South Wales, like Standish, to avoid the ignominy of a lost fortune and gambling debts. He joined the police under the assumed name of Frederick William Parker and worked on the gold escorts. In 1856 he had succeeded his father, an East India Company veteran, to his baronetcy as Sir Frederick William Pottinger, 2nd Baronet Pottinger. Once discovered, his elevation and status enabled his almost immediate promotion. He became the Clerk of Petty Sessions at Dubbo, then the Assistant Superintendent of the Southern Mounted Patrol, before being installed as an Inspector under the new act in 1862.[18] He was a dilettante, though an effective leader, who was much maligned in his day, and since. He was prone to overindulgence of alcohol, as much as many of his men, and was himself charged before the courts. He was also eventually dismissed, in 1865 for behavioural infractions, which may have given former troopers Neilson and Chambers some comfort. Upon travelling to Sydney to face a parliamentary inquiry, he accidentally shot himself, whilst boarding a moving coach at Blaxland, in the Blue Mountains. He died some days later. Pottinger had absolutely no qualms about furthering his position in the police by use of his newly revealed title. Frederick Whirlpool would never do so by declaring his coveted cross. Again, it must be remembered, that he was still a young man, having turned 32 whilst in custody. A lesser man might have considered his future more selfishly.

Whirlpool left Wagga Wagga as soon as he was released from the local gaol, and disappeared from view. In a little over a year he was in Sydney again, where he had one friend of worth, Robert Bayley, proprietor of the Sydney Riding School and former Drill Sergeant of the New South Wales Police Force.

CHAPTER ELEVEN

———

TEACHING, LOWER MACDONALD RIVER & WISEMAN'S FERRY

'All I have achieved was
carried off on the golden boat -
only I was left behind.'

Rabindranath Tagore (1861-1941)
'Song VII of Gitanjali'

Frederick Whirlpool was no more. Vestiges of his former persona had been expunged; no longer just to avoid unwanted attention for his deeds in India, but because of his fall from grace in Wagga Wagga. His father, one of Ireland's earliest constables, had served through to retirement age and a well-deserved pension. He would be disgusted by his son's fall and this would add salt to his son's wounds. Although still corresponding with his father, he would ensure that he never heard of it. He had decided that the whole Frederick Whirlpool episode would be erased so far as he could manage it.

In Sydney, he re-acquainted himself with Robert Bayley, former constable number 7, who also hailed from Dundalk. Bayley too, had fallen from grace. The pattern was not unfamiliar in the force of the time. After some early setback, Bayley had taken charge of the Sydney Riding School in Pitt Street, Sydney, not far from the old Carter's Barracks and police complex. He took his countryman in and housed him in return for work in the school. Bayley was younger than James and had joined the New South Wales Mounted Police as a Trooper on 30 September 1860,[1] two years before the new police was formed. He was 24 years of age, married and a member of the Church of England. His education was classed as 'good' and his previous occupation was noted as 'Irish Constabulary'. He was stationed at Sydney and therefore the Carter's Barracks Police Station. He had been promoted to senior constable in 1862, only to be reduced to constable on 19 September 1862, perhaps as part of a reorganisation of the new force six months earlier. His employment register entry indicates that he resigned and left five days later on 24 September 1862, two days after James had been appointed. Second thoughts, on his part or on the part of his officers, must have prevailed as he was promoted on 1 December 1863, from senior constable to sergeant 2nd class. His reprieve was short lived, however, as he resigned on 12 September the following year. James would not have crossed the path of Bayley whilst in the police force, but could have have known him in Ireland, where he must have been acquainted with his father. It is likely that James senior orchestrated their introduction to each other in Australia. By 11 February 1865, five months after his resignation, Bayley advertised in the *Sydney Morning Herald*, 'SYDNEY RIDING SCHOOL, Pitt — street. — Mr. R. BAYLEY begs to inform the ladies and gentlemen that wishes to learn the noble art of horsemanship that they can be taught. Terms moderate.'[2] The riding school was under new management and customers were eagerly sought, but James' tenure had run its course. On 4 January 1865, he had applied to the Board of National Education in Sydney, to be a teacher in the National School system. The secular National system was based on the multi-denominational Irish National School model, which would become the Council of Education, and later, Department of Education.

His *pro forma* application indicated that an attached certificate had been signed by two responsible persons 'who have known me long enough to enable them to testify concerning my sobriety, and general moral conduct.' Portentous comments, indeed. The form also indicated that he would receive an allowance whilst training, of £7 per month. This figure provides some sense of the worth of his £10 per annum Victoria Cross pension. His application indicated that his name was Humphrey James, was not married, 30 years of age, born in County Carlow, his religion was Society of Friends, had trained as a teacher in Melbourne and his referees were Alfred Brunton and James Conly, schoolmasters. The certificate was signed by R. F. Bayley and T. Donohoe, baker of George Street, Sydney, who had only known him for about three weeks. On the same day, James was referred to the Training Master, Mr. Wright, who reported on his suitability two days later, 'Mr. James has undergone a preliminary examination with the following result:-

Grammar 7, Geography 9, Arithmetic 8; Average 8 out of ten. I have no hesitation in stating that Mr. James will be able to pass the required examination at the end of a month's training. I consider he is an eligible candidate.

James also completed a statement that day:

'Statement of Mr. Humphrey James a candidate for a situation under the Board of National Education.

I Education

1. Educated chiefly at the Dundalk Institution, Ireland, for a period of four years.
2. I was taught Grammar, Geography, Arithmetic, History, Euclid, Mensuration & Algebra.
3. I consider my attainments when leaving school were fair.
4. I have kept up and improved my previous knowledge, except in Euclid.
5. I have studied in the evenings after work.
6. My present attainments are fair.

II Previous History

7. Since leaving school I have been occupied as clerk, sea-faring man, Surveyor's labourer & School-teacher.
8. I have been engaged in teaching in Melbourne for two years.
9. They are both in Sydney, Robt. Bayley the proprietor of the Sydney Riding School and Mr. Donohoe a Master-Baker.
10. Mr. Bayley has known me for the last two years and Mr. Donohoe about three weeks.
11. I am not related to either of them.

III Present Circumstances

12. Unoccupied at present.
13. I consider I am naturally adapted for being a teacher.
14. I have a knowledge both of the responsibilities and difficulties of the teacher's office.
15. I applied to the Board because I prefer the National System of Education.
16. I am acquainted with the principle on which the National System is founded.
17. I have studied the Statement and therefore have a knowledge of how Candidates are received into training, paid &c.
18. I have the means of supporting myself during the period of training.
19. I can support myself a second month if I fail at the first examination.
20. I am not now in the position of an insolvent nor have I ever been.
21. I am willing to take a situation in the Country.

Sydney 6th January, 1865 Humphrey James'[3]

On 1 February, James received a pamphlet containing the Board's instructions to candidates and a book required while training. His application statement is telling in a number of its details. It firstly confirms that he had attended the Dundalk Institute for four years and outlines the subjects he undertook. His modesty, or lack of ability to self promote, shows in his comments classifying his attainments as 'fair'. He correctly claims to have taught in Melbourne. That he provided referees from that time, proves that he taught under his birth name. He correctly asserts that he had been a clerk, but the claim to being a 'sea-faring man', is obviously designed to extinguish his period in the Indian Army, the events in Melbourne before leaving for Tasmania and his short-lived police career. His claim to be a schoolteacher is not listed chronologically, unlike the other positions, and this was done to avoid the anticipated question; why he would leave teaching to go to sea? He indicated that he had the means of supporting himself and would have fallen back on savings, had he been impolitely pressed to answer how. His pensions could not be disclosed. James was a saver and somewhat frugal. Tellingly, he asserted that he considered himself to be 'naturally adapted for being a teacher'. The important things missing from his application and statement are his army service, Victoria Cross and his police service. The latter is understandable, for it would have rendered him unsuitable for a teaching position, as sobriety was a major concern. The army service and decorations were part of his past that he did not want to resurrect, and could be the cause of more unwanted attention. Disclosure could also lead to revelation of his recent past, which was lived under the assumed name, Frederick Whirlpool.

On 3 February 1865, the Head Master at the National Training School at Fort Street, Sydney, reported on 'Mr. James' to the Secretary of the Board.

1. *Conduct and Demeanour*
    Very correct and satisfactory.

2. *Discipline*
    Fair. He manages a class moderately well, is quick of eye, prompt but somewhat theatrical and noisy.

3. *Method and Value as a teacher*
    Graphic and correct in description, and combines the simultanious [sic] and the individual with fair success. From what I saw of him I am of opinion that habit of thought and speech will render him unsuitable for the instruction of young children.

4. *My estimate of him is as follows:*

Discipline	*Method*
(1000)	*(1500)*
700	*1000*

J W Allpass
Head Master'[4]

James was sent to the Balmain National School for practical training and assessment. The Headmaster hurriedly wrote to the Secretary on 3 March 1865, 'Your note of yesterday requiring a report on Mr. James' qualification has but just come to hand. I have not therefore time to enter into details.

'As regards his attainments I should imagine that they are above those generally found among candidates. He has shown a very fair amount of tact in the management of the classes entrusted to him, and I believe his teaching to be effective. He is certainly an earnest teacher.

All things considered I should assign him 750 marks. I am Dear Sir, Yours respectfully,

Th. Bradley'[5]

His examination paper estimates gave him 2,500 marks from a possible 3,500 for 'subjects' and 5,590 of a possible 7,000 for practical skills entitling him to teach at Class III B. He had passed the Board's requirements and was on his way to a permanent position. His theatricality and noisiness was assessed by Bradley as him being an earnest teacher.

On 1 February, the parents of a number of children in the Lower Macdonald River region, near the township of Wiseman's Ferry on the Hawkesbury River, had petitioned for a National School to be established. The representations were fruitful, particularly as the land and building were provided by the parents. It was a building of slab, 23 feet long and 14 feet wide, lathed and plastered internally, shingled and properly warmed and ventilated. An additional room of 14 feet by 8 feet was to be built and made available to the teacher as a sleeping apartment. Thirty children were expected to attend from both sides of the Macdonald River, manoeuvres not without their difficulties. The new school was about 2½ miles from the Wiseman's Ferry School. The first teacher at the school was appointed on 10 April 1865, and books and materials were shipped from Sydney to the river wharf. The new teacher remained about three weeks and made a midnight flit, owing money in Wiseman's Ferry and, '... other acts in no way recommendable.' He was last seen heading in the direction of Maitland.[6]

On 22 May, Humphrey James was appointed as the new teacher. Some discussion had taken place concerning a replacement for the teacher at the Wiseman's Ferry school, who had recently been dismissed, and it was proposed that James should teach half a day in each. This was in no way practicable, as the parents for one thing, would baulk at sending their children to either school for only half a day. Then there was the question of needing a boat on standby to cross the 500 metre wide river. In good conditions this would have been difficult enough, but there were no wharves on the Macdonald side and entry to the boat would entail walking through mud. The proposal was reluctantly dropped and the Wiseman's Ferry School remained closed.[7] A week later the Lower Macdonald school secretary, Henry Wilson, reported that the local patrons were quite pleased with the selection, and that the new school building was almost ready. Pending the completion of the new schoolhouse, Wilson provided a building he owned as temporary accommodation. James completed his form of engagement, in which he agreed, 'to observe all the Regulations now in force, or that hereafter may be adopted, by the Board of National Education, for the management of Non-Vested National Schools.' He completed his name as simply Humphrey James, and indicated that he was not married, was 30 years of age and was born in Carlow, Ireland. He was in fact approaching 34 and the missing years seem to accord with the expunged part of his former life. He reiterated that his religion was Society of Friends and that he had completed his teacher training in Sydney. His signatures were witnessed by James Sullivan, Christopher Douglass and the man who would become his *bête noire,* antagonist and deliverer of a Judas kiss, Henry Wilson.

His theatrical and noisy teaching methods may not have overly endeared James to his tutors, rendering him unsuitable to teach smaller children. Loud and scarred they might have said. He was loud because he was enthusiastic and may have, not unnaturally, been emulating his own teachers in Dundalk. He came from a large family, which are often noisy and perhaps he hadn't quite recovered from the mess-rooms and barracks of India. His scars were visible and he must have had a stock answer for the inquisitive. Notwithstanding this, he did teach smaller children as his class, which, by necessity, ran the gamut of ages; and he did it successfully, to the great satisfaction of their parents. He progressed for several months, completing his monthly reports and more importantly teaching his pupils soundly. But then he fell into a trap set by the devious and ambitious secretary, Henry Wilson, who James was later to describe as a despicable knave.

According to James, whose version was later supported by some of the parents who were not beholden to Wilson, the secretary had tried his best to cause his new teacher to side with him against settlers and to act on his behalf, as he had done with others, to write letters for him to show his worth for the magistrate's position he coveted. Wilson had developed himself into a local worthy; secretary of the school board, trustee of the road board and similar positions. He had beheld very early that James' weakness could be alcohol and James was later to claim that it was Wilson himself who first invited him to drink with him. He also claimed that Wilson, when attending what he described as 'grand' meetings, imbibed to excess himself, to the extent that he would have to take to his bed to recover. James was not taken in or fooled by Wilson's lies against other community members, but he was suckered into his occasional binges, the first in February 1866, when Wilson, after drinking with him, quickly reported him for being drunk and for not opening the school for two days. This had allowed time for Wilson to engage the school inspector, Johnson, and with him, make an unannounced visit to the school. The inspector reported that he had found James 'recovering' from some state. Johnson allegedly told James that he had insufficient grounds to report him and he would not do so. This may have been his intention when face to face with him, but when safely away, or upon being inveigled by Wilson, he did report the matter. This no doubt attracted some form of censure, but beyond that James felt betrayed.

He called the Board's bluff by submitting his resignation on 21 February, to take effect from 1 May, if the Board withheld his salary or brought in another teacher. He allowed himself some leeway by asking that should the latter occur, he would seek another posting. 'Sir I have the honor to state that in consequence of the last official document addressed to Mr. Wilson, I have in accordance with Regulations, given this Local Board three months notice — date 1st Inst. — of my intention of leaving their employment on 1st May next, should the Board's intention of withdrawing the salary be carried out, or should the L. Board have provided themselves with another teacher.

'I have the honor to request that the Board will immediately upon hearing this situation — provide me another or release me from my obligation according to agreement.

'I have the honor to be, Sir, Your most obed't. serv't. Humphrey James Teacher of above school.

12/2/66'[8]

This is an angry letter in which James' normal copperplate is hurried and becomes looser as the letter progresses, and larger until the final chapter is heavily written in uncharacteristic script, but polite verbiage. None of his extant letters take this approach as they are generally neat, tempered, polite and well constructed. This man had been told one thing and his tormentors had done another and he was very, very angry. At least part of that anger was self directed, for again falling victim to his own foibles and exposing himself as easy prey to his rancorous enemy. He had been used to an identifiable enemy, armed and worthy; not this ethereal, malevolent, backstabbing usurper who wove his plots abstrusely and unseen. In the end the matter was to rest, as the parents of children at the school persuaded James that he was valued and that their children needed him. He withdrew his resignation and demands, and continued to teach until almost a year later, when all hell broke loose again.

Before looking at that next episode it should be noted that James would have been, and would have known that he could be, under the scrutiny of Wilson and perhaps some of his acolytes. He toed the line and provided no cause for complaint, which is one of the interesting things about his condition. He was a person who, as he was later to state, went teetotal for weeks or even months, but occasionally weakened. It was when opportunity and circumstance and perhaps even stress and mood collided, that he let his defences down and drank to excess.

The confluence of these circumstances fell together with the heavy rainfall that was to keep the children from the school between 6 and 8 February 1867. James crossed the river to the post office side, as he would later describe it, perhaps to play down the fact that the Wiseman's Ferry Inn was also located there. Wilson reported to Secretary Wilkins that James had been drinking at the Wiseman's Ferry Inn on these days and had left the school unattended, as he was unable to teach. The charges were substantially correct, but James, whilst not denying his behaviour, lamely stated that he had not opened the school on Friday, though it was no longer raining, as being the last day of the week, parents would not bring their children. This was probably correct, as roads were scant and rough and would have been difficult to traverse in the muddy conditions and the swollen river, dangerous. But it did not excuse him taking advantage of his vacant school to home in on the temple of his undoing. James was being watched, but not by Wilson, who he later stated he had not seen during this time. One of his acolytes had no doubt reported to him that James was drinking and drunk; information that he was later to convey to the School Board in Sydney. This is supported by Wilson's erroneous reporting of the dates on which the school was closed, which included a Saturday; hearsay information at best. James had been 'dry' for a year and circumstances had again enticed him to entrap himself and allow his career to be wrought asunder. It was now only a matter of time before the sword would fall and his life would need to take yet another turn. Wilson wasted no time in writing to the School Board, after he had allowed James enough rope to hang himself. He penned his dogged letter on 11 February. 'I regret having to draw your attention to the conduct of Mr. James, Teacher of our school at Lower Macdonald who has been drinking and drunk from the 5th to the 9th Inst. at the Wiseman's Ferry Inn, and unable to teach. I therefore beg to submit the above for your consideration and further beg to recommend his removal from this school. I have the Honor to be, Sir, your obedient servant, Henry Wilson.'[9]

No quarter seems to have been given, no confrontation with James and no thought of dealing with the matter locally. Wilson had waited for his moment and it had arrived. He was within striking distance. To ensure that his letter had its desired effect, as he might have wondered that no action seemed to have been taken, he confronted school inspector Roberts who was on his way to St. Albans via Wiseman's Ferry. Roberts wrote to the Board, ' ... this gentleman requested that I would urge upon the Council the pressing necessity of the speedy removal of Mr. Humphrey James, the present master of the school, 27-2-67. The details of the complaint against Mr. James are, I believe, before the Council; and should Mr. James be removed, I am requested to say the people would prefer to have as the master a married man; and further they are willing to do what they can towards building a Residence for his accommodation.'[10]

Wilson was not going to let his opportunity slip. He now turned the knife and without waiting for a response from Sydney, intimated that the matter was a *fait accompli* and needed to be speedily resolved. As it happened, the School Board had written to James on 19 February, suspending him and presumably, outlining the allegations against him, by asking him to show cause why he should not be dismissed. Cornered, James replied on the 25th.

'Sir. In reply to your letter of the 19th inst. I have the honor to request that you will do me the favor — which I believe is usual in similar cases — to cause the hostile letter to be sent to me, that I may be in a fairer position to defend myself.

'Having for a considerable time been exposed to the unscrupulous malice of the writer of that letter, on account of having detected him more than once in his attempts to injure others, by lying to me against them, that he might make me a partisan of his, I feel the greater necessity for this request.

'On the former occasion when he reported me, and abruptly visited me in company with the Inspector, neither party had ocular demonstration that anything was wrong — save the closing of the school for two days, which was duly registered, for they found me quite well and holding school; and being quite well, the Inspector was not justified in reporting that I was recovering from any state — especially as he assured me when leaving that he did not consider that he had sufficient grounds to report me, and further that he had "no intention of doing so". With that assurance from the gentleman, I have found it impossible to reconcile his subsequent action; and could only account for it by attributing it to my enemy's urgent request that the Inspector should do so, — he, Mr. Wilson, being anxious to have me removed, because I had become fully cognizant of his foul play towards his more simple neighbors, and had convinced him that he could not make a political tool of me: the man who would request others to write political letters to Members of Council in his name, that he might be though qualified to write such letters and might thereby be appointed to the magistracy, is — I hardly need to say — a despicable knave, and sufficiently mean for anything. If being plausible in speech, rather illiterate — though by no means ignorant — cunning and unscrupulous, tolerably deceitful — as was made manifest at the settlement for the building of this school, to which he had agreed to contribute an equal share with two others, but which he positively refused to do when called upon in presence of a large meeting of the inhabitants, at which I was present, and which he has not since done, — both spiteful and avaricious — excluding his poor but honest neighbors from employment on the roads, for which he is a Trustee, and placing strangers thereon at one third of the stated wages, thereby appropriating two-thirds of the same, — and — for I must not forget the miserable fact, or crime, or misdemeanor, with which he is ever ready to charge his opponents — getting very unreasonably intoxicated at meetings of Trustees or Committee-men, so much so, as to be quite incapable of making an effort to get home from some of the grand meetings of that very intellectual body of public servants, and afterwards having to lie up for a week under medical treatment, but fortunately for the physical constitutions of those public-spirited and, of course most interested committee-men, their grand meetings are not very frequent:- If, I repeat, this preceding be the essential qualifications for the Bench, it is very much to be regretted that his stupidly absurd ambition has not be gratified by an appointment thereto.-

'Sir, In reference to the portion of his statement repeated in your letter, I beg to inform you that there were three days — Wednesday, 6th, Thursday, 7th, and Friday, 8th, on which school was not held, the first two days being wet and no children coming on that account, of which I was fully aware, and none coming on Friday — that being the last day of the school week. And, as that person neither saw me, nor I him during those three days — nor for several days previous and subsequent, I infer that he founded his adventurous statement on the fact of my crossing the river to the Post Office side during the time. I have further to add that the school has been constantly open since then, to this day, on which I have proclaimed it shut, in accordance with the notice of suspension.

'Sir, in concluding, I beg to remind you that my two years' engagement will terminate at the end of May next, that is three months hence; and if the Council should deem it advisable to dispense with my services — for which I shall be very sorry — they still have it in their power to secure the lasting gratitude of a poor, bush, school-teacher by permitting me to complete my term of service, and thus to rescue, at least, a portion of my honor, so that my only enemy may not completely triumph over me. Trusting to the magnanimity of the Honorable Council, and humbly requesting that you will be so kind as to read this to the Honble Members of same.'[11]

As the situation stood, James had been reported by the local school secretary, who used hearsay evidence to allege that he had been absent from school and drinking to drunkenness at the local inn. Without reference to his version of the events, he was suspended and called to account to save his position. It is evident that James did not want to deny that he had been at the inn and had been drinking heavily as alleged, for five days. Had this not been the case and the informant was incorrect in his observations, it would be a reasonable expectation for James to rail against the allegations as fabrications, or at least misinformed errors. But he did not acknowledge that part of the allegation at all. He sought to explain why he had closed the school for three week days only, not the five claimed, during which time he had crossed to the post office side of the river. His omission screams for want of attention.

On the other hand, he attacked his attacker it what may have been truthful observations, but they were also largely irrelevant to his situation. A short sharp observation of his mendacity and spite would have been enough. Instead, James' pent up emotion about past wrongs and his own bad judgement came across as not only irrelevant filibustering, but as a diffuse rant. It overwhelmed the story he could have told and the *mea culpa* that was yet open to him to propose.

The letter was to no avail and was to sound the death knell for James' career with the simple word 'Dismiss' written on its covering page, in censorious blue pencil. He had been denied natural justice, and this despite entreaties from the parents of his student's who had written a letter of support on the same day he had written his reply. James had been suspended and had therefore to close the school and turn away the children. The parents quickly learned of his dilemma and rallied to his cause, remarkable in itself as twelve fathers from outlying properties managed to sign the document on the same day. The community, most barely literate themselves, wanted better for their children and saw their advancement possible under James. They wasted no time in getting their letter off to the Board. It read, 'To the Honorable Members of the Council of Education. The following Address of the undersigned Local Patrons and parents of children connected with the Lower Macdonald Public School is most respectfully presented, and humbly sheweth.

'That, being just made acquainted, by the closing of our school, with the steps taken by Mr. Wilson against our Teacher, and being for a long time aware of the spiteful attempts made by him to render the Teacher unpopular amongst us — in which he has completely failed — and also being pretty well aware of the cause of his spiteful proceedings against the Teacher, whom he has found to be too independent to suit his purposes, we hereby unanimously protest against the whole of Mr. Wilson's proceedings towards the Teacher — not to say anything of other parts of his public behaviour towards a great many of ourselves — and beg to assure the Council that the usual regularity and energy with which the school has been carried on, along with the fact that the merest babies have been made able to read, write, and count better than some of ourselves can do, have given universal satisfaction, and made many regret that they live too far to send theirs. And we further wish to state — for regard for our school — that some are so much provoked with Mr. Wilson's general style, and late spiteful behaviour, that they now vow not to send their children while he has any authority in the matter. Should our present Teacher, then, be dismissed — and we humbly remark that we cannot see reasonable cause, as there was no loss or inconvenience on the three days reported about, during which the rainfall was pretty abundant and children stopped at home — and should Mr. Wilson continue to be Local Patron, we see plainly that our successful little school is doomed. Trusting, and earnestly praying that your Honorable Council will overrule and prevent such a grievous result.'[12]

The letter was signed by Christopher Douglass and James Sullivan, both members of the School Board and ten other fathers. It was received at the Council of Education on the same day as James' reply, and was ignored. Tellingly, these men had no reservation about publicly calling Wilson 'spiteful' and antagonistic towards their teacher. It says something of their fortitude, but alas, it was of no avail to their teacher. Not to be thwarted, Wilson, on hearing of the address prepared and sent by the parents, including two of his board, wrote another letter the day after theirs, which reached the

Sydney office of the Council of Education on 27 February, ensuring that the three letters could be considered together. He would not be outdone or beaten. He wrote in a style and manner, which supports James' contention that his literacy was wanting.

'Wiseman's Ferry

Feby 26th 1867

'Sir I beg to state that since my report against Mr. James, teacher of the Lower Macdonald School which I forewarned about the 12th Inst. his conduct is anything but satisfactory, he is trying to injure the school in every way he can — parents keep there children away owing to his conduct he has closed the school on his own responsibility and will remain closed until we have your dissision.

'I beg to request that in the event of Mr. James being removed that you will not keep us long without another — if long closed it would have an injurious affect to the school.'[13]

Another turn of the knife, which was so obviously malignant, it is a wonder that the School Board did not question his especial and fervent interest. James had not closed the school of his own volition, he had been suspended and the parents were forced to keep their children from the closed amenity.

James was dismissed shortly afterwards and a new teacher was appointed. He must have remained in the area for a couple of months and this was not unexpected as he had formed close bonds with some of the families there, especially those whose children he taught. There was no future in Wiseman's Ferry for him and certainly none at Lower Macdonald River, but by 6 April he had lingered there and had written another letter to the Secretary of the Council of Education.

'Sir. I have the honor to acquaint you that I have this day delivered to the Local Committee of Lower McDonald Public School all the property of the Council and of the Committee — as shewn by the enclosed receipted Inventory, which was lately in my charge. With respect to the few books absent, viz — 1 First, 2 Second, 1 Third, and 2 Scripture Lesson Books — they were lent by me occasionally to Parents, at their request, that they might appreciate their non-sectarian character, and have not as yet been returned, but are to be made good as stated in Inventory … I have now to request, Sir, that you will have the goodness to cause the amount due to me accompanied by

papers deposited by me at the Office, and the late Board's Certificate of Classification — to be forwarded to my next address as promptly as may be convenient. Pardon me for doing myself the justice to add that I leave this place with reputation for honesty — at least — unblemished, having paid every person with whom I had any dealings, to the utmost of his claim, and caused each to sign a statement to that effect — that the tongues of slander may be silenced. I may be excused for regretting that some of the people here have not been so punctilious towards me, as more than £5, being due to me as School Fees, I shall never recover, having little taste for legal proceedings. With respect to my future career — pardon this digression — I have under consideration the advisability of joining the noble army of Total Abstainers, though I am by no means an habitual inebriate (weeks and even months elapsing of pure teetotalism in my habits) yet, sometimes, I am induced to taste — and sometimes more than taste, but very rarely — by meeting some enthusiastic friend, and of this a professional man's foes eagerly take hold. I regret to have to say that the first person who induced me to take an imprudent step here was the first and only man to attack my character on that score. However, I am pretty well convinced that there should be no such salient angle in the habits of a teacher or of a preacher, or, indeed of any respectable man. I do not meditate the step, referred to, through regard for any man's good opinion — save my own, — but through a desire to raise myself a full step, at least, above the thoughtless, grovelling trash of humanity, and through a still higher motive. As it is likely that this is my last communication, I beg leave, Sir, with profound respect for your high & irreproachable character to bid you farewell. I have the honor to be, Sir,
Your obedient servant
H. James (late teacher)'[14]

This letter is the most lucid example of how James really felt. His inner feelings are laid bare, with no hint of self pity, no second plea, no complaint against the Board and a raw admission that he sometimes abused alcohol. He had had two months to reflect on his situation and he wanted to have one last say in his polite and articulate way. He made it clear that he had been led astray by Wilson under the guise of friendship, leaving the impression today, that this minor Machiavelli had worked out James' strengths and feared them, but had also discovered his vulnerabilities, and exploited them. James mentioned that his debts had been settled, leading to speculation that some in the town were slandering him and he was still fighting a rear guard action by gaining receipts for the payments he had made. That he lent non-sectarian scripture books to parents is also interesting and reinforces his pragmatic approach to religion and his interest in its various forms. He mentioned having little taste for legal proceedings and perhaps this is a hangover from his days at the Poor Law Union prosecutions, or could it have been that his last court appearance was not a happy one? He claimed that Wilson was the first, and only person to have ever attacked his character on the grounds of his drinking. This is the most interesting observation, which adds weight to James' low key sporadic drinking. He, of course, omitted the infractions in Wagga Wagga. He owned that there should be no such 'salient angle' in the habits of a teacher and others, meaning divergence from the straight and narrow, though he did not ponder the opinions of others, only his own. He considered joining the 'noble army of total abstainers', which was probably a reference to the Total Abstinence temperance movement.[15]

The still higher motive he referred to is puzzling and may refer to the redemption he sought. He wanted to step up above where he had fallen, not for the opinion of anyone else but himself. He had already shown that he did not need the opinion of others and shied away from adulation, but still had to measure up to his own standards. Only he knew what he had done and approbation or censure was within his own remit, to a point. Being a believer, he still feared his end. Believer or not, he could never forgive his enemy. The ' … thoughtless, grovelling trash of humanity … ' were epithets likely reserved for Wilson.

James stayed in the area long enough to become involved in the great flood of June 1867, which washed away the Lower Macdonald settlement and ruined most of the signatories to his letter of support. The newly built inn at Wiseman's Ferry had also been washed away. The flood was devastating. It had destroyed a wide area of the Nepean/Hawkesbury Valley and drowned 12 members of one family near Windsor. At this time James had little choice but to leave when the floodwaters subsided. The only high ground in the valley were those parts identified by Andrew Thompson to Governor Lachlan Macquarie early in the 19th century, which were to become known as Macquarie's five towns. Pitt Town was the closest of these settlements to Wiseman's Ferry. This led James to this spot, where he settled and engaged in menial work, for there was plenty to do rebuilding and reclaiming the land from the river.

James learned over the ensuing years that Henry Wilson would indeed be appointed as a magistrate and then, chief magistrate. He became Commissioner of Affidavits and head of the Wiseman's Ferry School Board. He served as President of the local progress association and became Guardian of Minors. Wilson, also an Irish-born Protestant, built his property, Riversvale into a showpiece. He and his wife produced four boys and four girls, some of whom became teachers and one, a school inspector. One became President of the Colo Shire, in the Hawkesbury, and another an Alderman of the Sutherland Shire Council, south of Sydney. The family had prospered under their wily patriarch who died on 11 December 1904, in his 78th year. Over 150 people attended his funeral, but of those listed as attending, none who supported James' cause are mentioned. They knew that he had been 'collateral damage' along the path to Wilson's success.

CHAPTER TWELVE

PITT TOWN, GRONO PARK
SCHOOL AND BEYOND

'Courage was mine, and I had mystery;
Wisdom was mine, and I had mastery;
To miss the march of this retreating world
Into vain citadels that are not walled.'

Wilfred Owen 1893-1918
'Strange Meeting'

Pitt Town offered high ground and shelter from the flood and its aftermath, giving James reason to settle there. Either through happenstance or a serendipitous meeting with local families, it also offered him a chance to become a teacher. The need for extra schooling over and above that offered by the local Church of England, known then, as now, St. James', had been recognised. The children in the area were too numerous for the church school alone, not that the church authorities would concede this point. The church had long since railed against the secular National School system, although its arguments were wearing thin. Within a radius of two miles from the school there were estimated to be 44 boys and 60 girls between the ages of 4 and 14 years. A new school was not a priority at this difficult time, but had been mooted before the flood. The church offered schooling in the old Georgian parish hall and it was here that James conducted evening classes. He collected his fees, as he had done on behalf of the Lower Macdonald School, and this sustained him. To be teaching again, free of Wilson and the National system, was a pleasure and it was what he was meant to do. Denys Croll was fortunate in the 1960's, to interview Tom Ryan of Pitt Town and his sister Elizabeth, both of whom remembered their father talking of 'old Humphrey James' when he was a young man teaching him at evening classes in the parish hall.

Their father, who died in 1945 at the age of 93, remembered that he was about 12 years of age when taught by James.[1] The arithmetic doesn't quite support this, as Mr. Ryan would have been 12 years old in 1864. He was 14 or 15 years old in 1867, the earliest date that James could have come to Pitt Town and it may have been at this age that he gained extra tuition at night. The Official Post Office Directory of NSW of F F Bailliere, published in 1867, listed Humphrey JAMES, teacher of the National School Wiseman's Ferry, reinforcing that he was teaching in that area at that time, though not at the Wisesman's Ferry School. Despite this, Mr Ryan's recollection was clear, that he had been taught by Humphrey James at the hall. This may have continued for several years, as James is listed in Greville's Official Post Office Directory of New South Wales, in both the 1872 edition and that of 1878-79, incorrectly as was often the case, with his name being reversed. He is shown in both instances as HUMPHREY, James — teacher of Pitt Town. His occupation is the same over the six or seven year period covered by the directories, which leads to the conclusion that he was teaching during that time. There is evidence from the Ryan's that he was in fact teaching earlier, so there is no reason to think that he was not teaching for quite a lengthy period in some capacity. But there is just the hint that the latter listing may not have been updated when the directory was re-printed. It may also have been that Humphrey James identified himself as a teacher, whether employed or not. This was his right and if the practical nomenclature was not really important, the symbolism certainly was.

On 7 February 1871, the parents of the district formally applied to the Council of Education for the privately conducted school at Grono Park, near Pitt Town, to become a state school. Its teacher was Humphrey James. It was a rough slab hut 24 feet by 16 feet. It had two rooms, presumably the second adding to the dimensions at 12 feet by 6 feet. This room may have been for the accommodation of the teacher. The school managed to enrol 19 boys and 20 girls and their parents had done all they could, morally and materially, to educate their children. But they needed state assistance. On 13 February, the Secretary of the Council of Education directed Mr. Forbes, Inspector of Schools, to make an inquiry and report on the position of the Grono Park School. James had been the teacher at the private school since it was built at least two years earlier, but possibly longer.

Sometime after his arrival in Pitt Town in 1867, James' teaching at evening classes brought him to the attention of the community, and the small school was built on a farm of 90 acres, known as Grono Park, which was worked by Joseph Brown. It may have been built to allow James to become foundation teacher. His history at Lower Macdonald would have been known to the parents as some of them were related to people from that area. The Lower Macdonald parents had been forgiving and were not particularly concerned by the allegations that had been levelled against him. The Pitt Town community did not concern themselves with the matter either. Most of them would have taken it in their stride; their own antecedents, though immured, were not forgotten.

James was engaged as teacher and continued until the parents, quite naturally, decided to seek entry into the public system to gain the benefits that would ensue. On 28 March 1871, Mr. Forbes attended the school, where all of the pupils were present. Twelve heads of family attended, accounting for 31 of the pupils. James was also in attendance. It must have crossed his mind that if the school was embraced by the Council, his job would be in jeopardy, although he entertained some degree of hope that he would be acceptable, after the passage of time, given his record of achievement and the support of the parents. The upcoming meeting must have played on him, as would the uncertainty of his position. Had he not toiled to re-establish his reputation, both as a teacher and as a temperate man, and largely succeeded? Had he not enjoyed his role of teacher, something to which he knew he was intrinsically drawn and suited? Had he not worked with the parents to make the application, which was initially successful, only to have to put his shoulder to the wheel again, when some of the committee of the Church of England Denominational School had raised an objection to its establishment? Burdened with doubt, James attended the meeting between the parents and Mr. Forbes, where it became apparent that he would not be considered for the head teacher's position. His fears had become manifest and his pent up apprehensions, disappointment and sheer sorrow, burst forth in a torrent of invective and indecent language. Forbes was to write in his report from his Richmond office of 1 April. 'The present teacher, who was scarcely free from some exciting influence and who conducted himself in a rather offensive manner, has I am informed been since placed under arrest for having carried his excitement too far in Pitt Town.'[2]

While Forbes stated that he was 'scarcely free from some exciting influence', it is doubtful that he meant alcohol. He was well within his rights to say outright that James was affected by drink, yet he didn't state that possibility in any form. The exciting influence may well have been his emotional state and that, said Forbes, he had carried too far. When James was arrested by Windsor Police, he was charged with 'Using Indecent Language' only. No mention was made of drunkenness. He was not arrested until the 29th of March, the day after the meeting, so someone had to have laid a complaint against him. He was arrested on a Friday and spent the weekend in custody until he appeared at the Windsor Court on Monday 1 April. Even after spending time in the cells, he was fined five shillings, which he paid immediately.[3] Despite this setback and the loss of any hope that he might instruct at the school again, James continued to teach there until 5 April, when he closed for the Easter break. Secretary Wilkins had assumed control of the school by this time and James tendered his resignation the following day. This tends to indicate that none of the parents reported him to the police for his outburst and this is supported by him continuing to teach and, after his resignation, to assist them to have the Council of Education reverse a decision not to proceed with the school, due to the objection of the local Church of England. This leaves only Forbes as the complainant; he after all, was still affected by the incident when writing his report on the day that James was sentenced, four days after the event. One wonders what the offensive words were! How straight had been his aim?

Proper as always, on 14 April, two weeks after parting with his five shillings and a week after resigning, he felt the need to write to Secretary Wilkins,

'Sir I beg to inform you that this

'School was closed for the Easter Vacation on the 6th Inst., and that I resigned the position of Teacher at the same time.

'Mr. Joseph Brown desires me to add that , he anxiously awaits the decision of the 'Council' as to whether this is to be a Public School, so that the repairs, suggested by the Inspector, may be effected as soon as possible, and a Teacher sent to take charge.

'He further desires me to say that important business will necessitate his leaving home soon and he may not be able to return home for a long time. I have the honor to be Sir, Your most obedient servant Humphrey James '

It had been a little over a week since James had resigned, yet he continued to work *pro bono publico,* as it were, showing that his interest lay with the children and their parents, before his own. It also shows that Joseph Brown and the other parents still held him in high regard. Despite this, he had resigned - fallen on his sword - for their good and to remove a possible impediment to their attempt to become a public school.

After this last communication with Wilkins on behalf of the school committee, James blended back into his community. He may have taught privately, but as the years stretched he withdrew into himself, not seeking or needing companionship. Perhaps he thought himself not good enough to mix with ordinary people, or was it that he felt that some had let him down? He met John Dick Smith at Pitt Town and was later to live on his property, which according to Croll, was 130 acres near the junction of Cattai Creek and O'Hara's Creek and which, at the time he prepared his manuscript, was still in the Dick Smith family.

Smith was involved in the community through the Presbyterian Church and was a great reader, particularly of poetry. He claimed in the *Windsor and Richmond Gazette*, that James had been well educated and widely read. This was one area of commonality between them. It is hard to know what else they shared. Smith was a trustee of the School of Arts, which was established by the Literary Institute and was elected Honorary Secretary in 1897, which reinforces an understanding of his sensibilities. His uncles and cousins were involved in schooling in Windsor as part of their committed public service. Education would have been comfortable common ground. Both men were seekers of enlightenment and the Victorian era was a wellspring for those seeking wisdom. Then there was religion. The devout Scottish Presbyterian would have been interested, even bemused by James' threshing of religious dogma in his search for truth. Their discussions would have been been invigorating for both of them. Their conversations pleased James and stimulated his thinking. He obviously offered considered personal reflections, which engaged Smith, for he returned for more over the years. He claimed that it was hard to draw information from James about his military experiences, something that generations of soldiers after him would also find hard to discuss. It was difficult for James to hide his service because of his battle scars, which were all too obvious, but he hid his Victoria Cross from the world and would not discuss it. He did disclose to Smith that he had been approached by a man in England who was compiling a book on Victoria Cross heroes and who had asked him for an account of his achievements, and a photograph. He simply ignored the request, which could have been from any one of a number of interested parties who wrote on the subject around that time. He had shunned attention for almost forty years and was not prepared to change his stance. His bodily wounds had been inflicted by the enemy, but his wounded psyche had come largely from his own side. He valued his cross and campaign medal enough to ensure their safekeeping at the Pensions Office in Sydney, but made no arrangements for them after his death.

There is no doubt that James was a troubled man, whose eccentric behaviour, though commented upon by his neighbours, was accepted as part of the ebb and flow of life in his small community. He was known to have been a teacher and a soldier to some and a shy reclusive man to others. In his own time and place, Humphrey James and his neighbours saw and understood each other more intimately than we do today; were more tolerant of idiosyncratic behaviour and more forgiving. He bothered no-one, and John Dick Smith, who sold liquor from his store and might well have supplied James with it, knew that he sometimes drank to excess.

He may have known that James had been arrested in 1870 for drunkenness in Windsor. It was on Tuesday 5 July and the Windsor Gaol Entrance and Description book entry shows that he remained incarcerated until the following Saturday, when Mr. McQuade JP, held his Court. The incarceration probably accounted for him, in mitigation, being discharged rather than being fined.[4] Again, he had time to reflect upon his situation, but luckily, he was far enough away from Pitt Town for most not to learn of his temporary fall.

He came under notice again three years later, on 26 April 1873. He appeared before Mr. McQuade again, but on the same day as his arrest, and was fined two shillings and sixpence in default of 6 hours imprisonment. His time in custody would already have amounted to six hours or more and he was discharged, without having to pay the small amount.[5]

Yet again, on 15 October 1881, he was arrested for being drunk and disorderly. He appeared before Mr. Dargin JP, at the Windsor Police Court, three days later and was fined five shillings and sixpence.[6] On each of the latter three occasions, July, April and October, his behaviour would have been precipitated by him being in Windsor to collect his pensions for the quarters, June, March and September of the relevant years. Cashed up and an exuding bonhomie he may have fallen into welcome company. He did, after all, admit in his letter to the School Board, following his dismissal from Lower McDonald River, that he was induced to taste, and sometimes more than taste, but very rarely, by meeting some enthusiastic friend.

His appearances, from the events in Wagga Wagga Court in 1863, Windsor in 1871 for the school incident, and for drunkenness in Windsor in 1870, 1873, and 1881, whilst not the hallmarks of civil behaviour, were nonetheless sporadic lapses during a period when intemperate behaviour was widespread. This was a man who maintained his home, fed and clothed himself, took pride in his appearance and refused charity. He maintained a bank account at the Bank of New South Wales in Windsor and his balance at the time of his death was said to be four times the average bank deposit in his day.[7] Judging his behaviour by the norms of the 21st century does not assist in properly understanding the failings of Humphrey James.

No medical condition had been diagnosed in his time, other than the broad 'neurasthenia', which had the benefit of sometimes preventing military executions. Overt reaction often led to charges of cowardice, and execution swiftly followed a hurried court martial. He was not to fall for that and in some respects, his wounds relieved him and gave him another focus, and a will to survive. His belief that he was 'damned and going to roast', did not make him any keener to hasten the event. He moulded a way to accommodate the nuances of his life, which worked for him most of the time, but his condition needed salving some of the time. The short term relief sometimes led him to a lesser grief. He had already seen his end many times throughout the latter years of his life. He believed that his death would not absolve him of his burden. He had yet, many deaths to die.

The purpose here has not been to sanitise the life of Humphrey James. He would be alarmed and disquieted by the attention, as we know, and the temptation has been ever present to honour his reserve and reticence, but his part in Australian, British and Indian history is important to illustrate. More than a century since his death it is time to tell his story, as much as can be told at this point, and I await his reproof at any moment. So be it. It is fortuitous that his family have played a large part in what has been able to be recounted about Humphrey James and Frederick Whirlpool VC. Their extant letters from 1899, still in the State Records Office of New South Wales, and his, from earlier times, in the same repository, have been revealing. Upon the settlement of James' estate, such as it was, equal parts were apportioned to his surviving siblings. His Indian Mutiny medal was distributed to his sister Deborah in Liverpool and his Victoria Cross to his brother Josiah in Southport, England. Receipts for both of them were duly received. Josiah wrote on 15 April 1901, acknowledging receipt of the Victoria Cross and thanking the Curator of Intestate Estates for sending it.[8] Josiah had been an army schoolteacher and it seems fitting that he should have held the medal. His brother Samuel had no memory of his brother, and Benjamin was confined to the asylum in America. Each of the siblings agreed with these distributions. As time passed and Josiah with it, the cross passed to his family. It appeared at Glendining's auction rooms in Argyll Street, London on 16 and 17 June 1927, where it sold for £46. It came into the possession of Captain G.W. Morris of Fish Hoek, Cape Province, South Africa, who was a collector of VC photographs and autographs. It next appeared at Baldwin's, London, in March 1962 for £450.[9] Denys Croll purchased the Whirlpool VC in the latter part of 1963 for £550. In a letter to Canon Lummis, of 29 January 1964, Croll informed him that he had held the VC for only about four months. 'I bought it from Baldwin's for £550, but to me it is worth a million.'[10]

It is indeed fortunate that it caught the attention of Denys Croll, Irish born teacher and medal collector, whose prescience saw the value of the cross to Australia. At the time it was thought to be the first Victoria Cross awarded in Australia. It seems a little pedantic to acknowledge that two Victoria Crosses were awarded in Sydney in March 1858. The award of the Victoria Cross to Frederick Whirlpool, who was wearing an Australia militia uniform, was certainly the first public presentation, but even then the public were generally not aware of the proceedings, knowledge of which was confined to the volunteer and military forces on parade. It has, by a rather circuitous route, found its way to the Hall of Valour at the Australian War Memorial in Canberra where it keeps excellent company with many others, some of which were won by battered and frail souls.

It is that this award may be presented across all ranks for valour in the presence of the enemy, and that it surpasses all other orders and awards, that makes it so very special. The late Denys Croll sought to get to the core of Frederick Whirlpool at a time when research was long, arduous and often unrewarded. He deserves to be remembered for what he has done to honour Frederick Whirlpool VC. Croll believed that James was not his real name, but lacked the easy access to digitised records we so readily take for granted in the half century or so since his research commenced. Though Croll was not afforded an opportunity to reveal the story of Humphrey James, his early achievements have certainly enabled all that has been gained since, from his purchase of the cross to his unpublished manuscript, which provided a launching pad for this endeavour.

A cursory glance at the roll of Victoria Cross recipients across the Commonwealth reveals many sad tales of neglect, deprivation and expunged memory. Too many recipients are buried in mass, unmarked graves - not on the battlefield, but in pauper's graves - many years after the conflicts in which they served. Some ended their days in the workhouse, others in abject poverty and despair. Humphrey James was not alone in combatting the demons of warfare.

Denys Croll was assisted in his search for detail of the life of Frederick Whirlpool by retired British colonel, Archie Cecil Thomas

White VC, MC who had an interest in army education. After active service he became a member of the Army Education Corps. The third member of this searching triumvirate was the Reverend Canon William Murrell Lummis, MC, who was a Victoria Cross and military historian, soldier, chaplain and collator of records, that became the catalyst for the work of others. The three corresponded and made inroads, which, while not revealing the body of fact now available, nevertheless cemented a record of considerable value, that has assisted in the telling of the Whirlpool story.

Croll was determined to find Frederick Whirlpool's Indian Mutiny medal with its 'Central India' clasp. It had gone to Deborah Manifold in Liverpool, a fact unknown to him, and there it remained. By the time of his death in 1979 he had not found the medal. In a tormenting twist it turned up in Ballarat, Victoria, in 1989, the town in which some proposed employing Whirlpool as a drill instructor in 1861. It was offered for sale by I.S. Wright Militaria[11] and presumably sold to a private collector. Its present whereabouts is unknown. It is to be hoped that one day it will be reunited with the Whirlpool VC in Canberra, safe in the Hall of Valour, positing his deeds and as secure for him as it had been in the pensions office in Sydney during his lifetime.

In another turn, James' last known incarceration in 1881, apparently not repeated, ensured that his path did not cross that of Arthur Berckleman, who had been appointed Windsor gaoler only months later, in 1882. Irish born and from Kerry, Berckleman was a Crimea Veteran. As a member of the 17th Lancers, he was one of the 'Noble Six Hundred' who had engaged an estimated 35,000 enemy at Balaclava in what was to become known as the 'Charge of the Light Brigade'. The action was immortalised by the Poet Laureate, Alfred, Lord Tennyson and is largely remembered because of it. Berckleman had joined the old New South Wales Mounted Police as a trooper in 1859, and had served in Armidale, a part of the Northern District. It was the closest these two men, both residents of the Hawkesbury, came to meeting. Their different paths could not have been more pronounced. Berckleman spoke publicly of the charge and his part in it and was widely recognised as one of the 'Noble Six Hundred.' He even named his property 'Balaclava'.

In 1904 Berckleman was buried at St. Matthews Church of England at Windsor with great ceremony. In a memorial service conducted shortly after his funeral, a huge crowd gathered with a half Squadron of the Australian Light Horse (NSW Lancers), 'A' Windsor Company, 3rd Infantry Regiment under Captain Paine and the Windsor massed bands. They had gathered to ensure that his heroism and life were recognised and honoured. Tennyson's 'Charge of the Light Brigade' was recited; the last verse ringing rather appropriately.

When can their glory fade?
O the wild charge they made!
All the world wondered.
Honour the charge they made,
Honour the Light Brigade,
Noble six hundred.

Tennyson ensured that this action at Balaclava in October 1854, which was an impetuous error, has never been forgotten.

Private Frederick Whirlpool VC, fought with great valour with his regiment, against all odds, without suffering a check against their success. His own reticence ensured no honours were accorded his final journey, just five years earlier.

CHAPTER THIRTEEN

———

REST

*'There must be very many Indian veterans ...
who have fought for the Empire during those
dark days which followed the Sepoy Mutiny,
and who are unknown heroes to their neighbours.
In most cases, I fear, the obituary column
will give the first intimation to the general public
of their whereabouts, or their past records...'*

'A Mining Engineer'
The Argus, Melbourne
Saturday 24 July 1897.

The Hawkesbury River showed signs of fresh as rains and thawing snow on the mountains sent torrents of ice cold water spilling into its brackish flow. An early morning chill left no doubt that Windsor was still in the grip of winter. The landscape appeared as limp and damp as a freshly worked watercolour, and a vapid sun struggled for relevance against the clinging vestiges of night. Exhalations from the great river and its tributaries forced amorphous mists into the folds of gullies and the slough of the lowlands, spilling unchallenged, over riparian barriers. This was winter in the Hawkesbury, confirmed by the shoe-leather rotting damp-cold that settles low and concentrates its worst effects to knee height, so that no amount of swaddling keeps it at bay. The townsfolk stirred and struggled towards their daily routines, slowly and deliberately, between their labours, to rub hands into life, light stoves and urge the sun's rays to work their wonder.

John Dick Smith had risen early, donned his mourning clothes and made his way to Linsley's Livery Stables in Macquarie Street, where he collected the horse and buggy he had hired. The single seat buggy cost five shillings for its morning's work, paid for from James' estate.[1] It was six days since James had died and in the prevailing weather there was little need of ice to preserve his mortal remains until burial. Richard Dunstan had finalised the details with Smith the previous day and it was readily agreed the funeral would be a quiet affair. Notwithstanding this, Smith ensured that he would depart in a fully mounted coffin, which would be driven to the Presbyterian cemetery in South Windsor, an area some of the older locals still called by its former name, *Nelson*, after another hero. A hearse drawn by a pair would also ensure that dignity would accompany his last journey. As if to signify James' total and earnest independence, though it was surely not his intention, his funeral, costing nine pounds, would also be paid from his estate, as were outstanding accounts for three months' supplies owing to Dick Bros., store.

Dunstan and his assistant Albert Butler, lifted the coffin into the hearse and made their way towards the cemetery, stopping at the Presbyterian Church where they collected the Reverend Mr. White and met John Dick Smith, to form a truncated cortege. They continued the short distance to the cemetery in silence, passing an occasional observer who may have wondered whose turn it had been. There had been no notice in the town of anyone of any importance having passed away, so it was only a fleeting curiosity. The horses snorted bursts of steam into the cold air and warm plumes rose from their flanks as the going got heavier; the haze trammelled by the sharp cold air it met. Turning into the cemetery, the steel tyres of the vehicles gnawed at the chilled gravel until the steady cadence of hooves drummed to a halt next to a freshly dug slot in the wet row that it would extend. Dunstan and Butler had prepared it two days before, knowing that once the inquest had been held it would be needed quickly. The four men unfastened the coffin, slid it from the hearse and carried it to the yawning grave. It hovered there while Reverend White recited the funeral rites, which, though sonorous, wafted across the graveyard on the light breeze, fading into the thin cold air. '... and the time has come for me to depart. I have fought the good fight to the end: I have run the race to the finish; I have kept the faith ...' When he was ready,

White gave a nod and the handsome coffin tightened the ropes on which it was slung and was lowered unceremoniously to its resting place. White completed his recitation in a murmur, and Dunstan and Butler began to fill the grave in their workmanlike manner, the clods of wet earth thudding home with each arcing swing of their shovels. There was little need for decorum in the absence of watchful eyes. Smith and the Reverend White had exchanged the pleasantries of those familiar with each other. There was no need to tarry in the dank, frosty field, so they took their leave of the toilers to resume their occupations and prepare for their day. Humphrey James had been laid to rest just as his family rejoiced in his return to their fold.

It had not been a satisfactory end as far as Smith was concerned. He was the only mourner. There was no forgathering of brethren, no military presence, no weeping loved one. A modicum of the trappings were there, some coming down from Roman times, like the black clothes, the procession and the *tumulus* mound that the undertakers would form once the grave was filled. This seemed fitting for an old warrior, but it was not enough. There was no muffled drum, no death march, no last post. Smith went to the *Gazette* newspaper office and gave information to the editor, resulting in a short notice.

'See what it is to be poor! The funeral of the late Mr. James (who will be recollected as an eccentric old gentleman who resided North Rocks way for a number of years) took place on Thursday, when Mr. J. D. Smith was the only follower. Had he been some local potentate, half the town would have been in the cortege.'[2]

This was true enough, but the reason there had not been a celebration of James' life was his own doing and he would not have wanted it any other way. His life was a disappointment to him. He probably never had a clear vision of what he wanted to achieve, as instanced by his first joining the army of the East India Company in ignorance of its fading star. Mismanagement had rendered this over privileged and rapacious child of a freak union of politics and capital, impotent, and its decision making dangerous and destructive. He could not have known this. He simply wanted to be his own man. It was in this service that he tasted the sweet flavour of imparting knowledge to those with a hunger to learn. Initially, he enlightened men of his own standing in the Indian Army in his animated and passionate way, for which he was later mildly criticised, but it had stemmed from his enjoyment of *the sharing*. His pupils came to him willingly, paying their tuppences for the privilege. He may have known of Samuel Johnson's truth, ' A man ought to read just as inclination leads him; for what he reads as a task will do him little good.'[3]

Circumstance led his army service to become active. He was well trained, although action was not envisaged, despite ample and clear warnings to his superiors. He excelled in the battles that followed, earning him the greatest acknowledgement his monarch and country could award. This double-edged sword would be the beginning of his flight from society. He valued his Victoria Cross and his campaign medal, but the limelight was not for him. It was as if the light shining on him revealed things about himself that he did not want to acknowledge and did not want others to see. Perhaps his Quaker leanings, which embraced pacification, were also outraged by his actions. He moved to the other side of the world when his army service was cut short, and again took up instruction, now teaching boys and girls for almost two years, and equipping them with skills and knowledge they would use and remember. However, action called and he attempted to join the Victoria Police, though once his fame was broadcast, he ran from the light again, further from the world and into frontier Tasmania, hiding so well that he left little trace. As if waiting for a storm to pass, he peered out and decided to try to join society again, travelling to New South Wales this time, in another active engagement, as a constable. But he had become a vassal after his time in the army and unable to work unsupervised. Or could he have become anomic? Once left to his own devices, he became embroiled in an incident in the Murray District of southern New South Wales, which resulted in him being placed on a bond to keep the peace. This he failed to do, ending his police career and landing him in gaol.

Again, he disappeared until it was safe to emerge, in Sydney this time, to take up teaching, leaving his assumed persona behind, hidden by the falsehood of a life at sea. Working alone, he failed again, with a little help from a waspish and aspirational supervisor. He hung on and rallied, taking up a similar position further up the valley that would be his home for the rest of his life. Here, despite his best efforts, his frailties were becoming more apparent and the Council of Education had not forgotten him, nor had it forgotten to shun him.

He withdrew more and more as rare public displays sometimes exposed his vulnerability, leading to his incarceration. It became easier to resign from the world. He stopped writing to his family in 1883. Perhaps they reminded him of happier times; or was it that he did not want them to know he had failed? He would not be the first person unable to face family due to a failed enterprise. Yet he softened and wrote to them with excruciating effort, for he must have felt them to be strangers. He was driven to do so, perhaps unconsciously, as his end was near. As it was, he left it too late to receive their replies. 'It was the last flare up of the expiring embers and he is gone,' his brother Samuel had exclaimed upon learning of his death.

And had he taken another course? Had he lived off his acknowledged valour, would he have been happier? Would he have served happily in a corrupt police force, pressed by a government which favoured him because of his valour, but which preferred Catholicism and a stint of policing in the old country? Would he have survived his transgressions in the police force of New South Wales, and if so, for how long? If the mood took him, he would drink again, and he did. And his teaching positions in the Hawkesbury may have been saved, as circumstances and his own principled stance had done on the first occasion he had run foul of his antagonist. He may have survived the second fall from grace, but the sword of Damocles still hung over him on a filament, leaving him susceptible to his failings or the machinations of a vigorous opponent. The Victoria Cross, though highly prized, would not take on its rich and highly esteemed place in the pantheon of public opinion until the Great War. It had its limits, had he wanted to test them, but it was definitely not within his proud nature to do so. His Victoria Cross would never be diminished by becoming his aegis.

Described as shy and retiring, as the valorous often are, he would never willingly draw attention to himself. That he felt his life a failure is beyond doubt and coupled with his proud and retiring character, it ensured that this man would never follow the path of the vainglorious. And he didn't. He quietly slipped towards oblivion and would have succeeded had not John Dick Smith softly touched him, engaged him and watched over him to the end. His releases to the press ensured that there was a thread for future generations to grasp, and grasp we have. Denys Croll took up that thread, returned the cross to Australia and wove the beginnings of a story. Others have played a part also. I trust that these efforts have woven more of the tapestry and shone the light solicitously upon his memory.

In the early days of the Victoria Cross, it could, and would be taken from a small number of recipients, for some breach of the Royal warrant in wholly discreditable circumstances, including treason, cowardice and felony. The warrant also allowed for the award to be restored. The provision remains, but no Victoria Cross has been cancelled since 1908. King George V, through his private secretary, Lord Stamfordham, on 26 July 1920, forcibly expressed his view: 'The King feels so strongly that, no matter the crime committed by anyone on whom the VC has been conferred, the decoration should not be forfeited. Even were a VC to be sentenced to be hanged for murder, he should be allowed to wear his VC on the scaffold.'[4]

Neither Humphrey James nor his alter ego, Frederick Whirlpool VC, committed any great crime. Nor was it a crime to drink and withdraw from society. His offence in Wagga Wagga would not have seen his decoration withdrawn. It would not have been of sufficient gravity to draw this censure and it is certain that he did not hide his VC to protect against this possibility. He had hidden it from his employers well before his fall from grace. He had earned his Victoria Cross twice over and deserves every accolade his actions have wrought. Valour cannot be undone.

John Dick Smith did not make arrangements for a headstone to be placed on James' grave. 'Who was there to read it anyway?' would have been his reasoning. His own memorial in the same cemetery is insignificant and shared with others. He is not buried there, but in the Gore Hill Cemetery in Sydney. James' final resting place is no longer identifiable within the confines of the small cemetery in South Windsor.

The poet, Charles Harpur, was born in Windsor in 1813, the son of the master of the Windsor District School. When he died in 1868, his proud friend, the poet Henry Kendall, wrote an elegy for him. It could just as easily apply to Humphrey James, son, brother and until now, a forgotten soldier in an unmarked grave who had 'passed out of the sight of men.'

> *'So let him sleep! The rugged hymns*
> *And broken lights of woods above him!*
> *And let me sing how sorrow dims*
> *The eyes of those who used to love him.'*
> 'Leaves from Australian Forests'
> 1869[5]

EPILOGUE

Though Private Frederick Whilpool's active service ended at Lohari, his fight for life continued as his wounds slowly healed. After his care at Jhansi, he was sent to Poona to continue his treatment, which extended over another five months. All through this period, his regiment continued to fight as part of the Central India Field Force, in increasingly appalling conditions. Whilst the action took place at Lohari, Rose had mounted others towards Mhow (Mau) and at a small fort, at Goormay, which surrendered to him. He sent Major Orr to the Betwa River to intercept the Rajahs of Banpur and Shahgarh who had split from their forces. Orr engaged the remainder, seizing their gun. After these actions, the 2nd Brigade, other than those left to defend Jhansi, joined Rose and the 1st Brigade to March against Kunch, where it was believed Tantia Tope and the Rani of Jhansi had assembled a force from Kalpi. At Kunch Rose was deeply affected by the sun, but rallied upon hearing firing and joined the fray, taking the fort. Shortly after, the retreating enemy were pursued and Rose was again felled by the sun. Recovering, he joined the pursuit. Seven men of the 71st Highlanders were reported to have died of sunstroke, but Rose was doused with water and revived. Three days later Rose reported to Lieutenant-General Somerset that he had pursued the retreating enemy for eight miles. Among the slain were sepoys of five regiments of the Gwalior Contingent and four of the Bengal Native Infantry and Mehidpur Artillery. European losses were slight with some soldiers killed and others, and their officers, felled by the sun, which measured 115°F in the shade. The action had taken 18 hours and the men were exhausted.

On 12 May, Rose marched on Kalpi, arriving on the 15th; the 2nd Brigade the following day. Sir Robert Hamilton reported that the Nawab of Banda and some 3,000 fighting men had joined the rebels at Kalpi. An attack had been mounted on the baggage train of the 2nd Brigade, but was repulsed with some loss to the rebels. He also reported that other ranking officials, including Rao Sahib and the Nawab of Banda, were in Kalpi. Rose claimed the fort also held 1,000 cavalry, adding to a force of 12 to 15,000 cavalry mutineers and several guns. He expressed concern for the health of his men, over three hundred of whom were hospitalised. A further 21 had died of sunstroke in a week. He feared a protracted operation. Supported by Colonel Maxwell who had been sent by the Commander in Chief, though instructed not to cross the Jumna River in aid of Rose, fire was opened on the town to good effect. On 22 May the rebels launched their well organised attack. Rose led his attack, which forced the rebels into retreat to Kalpi, but exhaustion prevented the infantry from pursuing them. Some rebels were cut up by cavalry led by Major Gall, but the main force managed to escape north. Kalpi was occupied the following day and for all intents and purposes, the campaign was over. Rose, declined an offer of command of the Gwalior and Kalpi troops as a divisional commander, wishing to return to Poona. He prepared to hand command to Brigadier-General Napier.

On 4 June 1858, he received news the rebels had regrouped and seized Gwalior, providing them with a base from which to again threaten southern and central India. Rose, without seeking permission, resumed command of the force, Napier graciously assumed the role of second in command. Troops from all available quarters were amassed and headed towards Gwalior. At Morar, which had been the cantonments of the Gwalior Contingent, Rose led an intense battle and retook them on 16 June. Gwalior was considered the strongest fort in India, incapable of being breached. Being short of numbers to properly invest it, the only option left to him was to take it by escalade. By the evening of the 20th, Gwalior was taken and it was discovered that most of the garrison had left. They were pursued by Napier and defeated.

Rose was called to account for his alleged breach of protocol by taking up his relinquished command without permission. He replied to Mansfield, arguing his case and it is clear that he had the support of the Governor General, the circumstances and the victory. It paid to have friends in high places.

Major-General Sir Hugh Henry Rose was appointed Commander-in-Chief of Indian forces upon the departure of Campbell, who was created Baron Clyde in 1859 and Field Marshall in 1862. Rose held the position from 1860 till 1865, during which time he reorganised the Indian Army after the dissolution of the East India Company. He was appointed Commander-in-Chief, Ireland in 1865 -1870. Promoted to General in 1867 and Field Marshall in 1877. To add to his Knight Commander of the Bath, he was made a Knight Grand Cross of the Bath, Knight Commander of the Star of India, Grand Commander of the Star of India (1866) and 1st Baron Strathnairn of Strathnairn and Jhansi (1866).

Lord Strathnairn retired from active service after his term in Ireland. He took an active part in military matters in the House of Lords, assisted by Sir Owen Tudor Burne in the preparation of his speeches. Burne's other role was to act as peacemaker between Strathnairn and the Duke of Cambridge, who often differed on military points.

In Versailles in 1885, to attend to a sheep farm he had purchased, he suffered a fainting attack and fell against a marble fireplace, wounding himself between the eyes. At his request, he was taken to the Hotel Rivoli in Paris, where his condition worsened. He earnestly requested his valet read him the service for the sick and telegraphed Burne, seeking his immediate presence. He died, however, in the presence of his valet and his cousin, Count de Gallatin, moments before Burne arrived on 16 October. He was 84 years of age. The French government ordered a guard of honour at the hotel and offered a public funeral. President Jules Grévy and Marshall Canrobert paid their respects, but it was his request he be laid to rest at the Priory Church at Christchurch, where his parents were buried. Present at his funeral were the Prince of Wales and the Duke of Cambridge. The Royal Horse Guards and the 92nd Gordon Highlanders, of which he was Colonel, bore him to his grave.

Arrangements were made for an equestrian statue to be made by Onslow Ford RA, which was cast from a canon seized by the Central India Field Force in 1858, provided by the Indian Government. It was erected in Knightsbridge, but in keeping with changing fashion and the ephemeral nature of fame, it was removed in 1931 and thirty years later was relocated to Griggs Green in Hampshire, where it now stands.

Lieutenant Frederick Clench Donne, whose life Frederick Whirlpool had saved at the taking of Lohari Fort, survived his wounds and continued to serve in the 3rd Bombay European Regiment. He was born in 1834 to Catharine Donne, nee Hewitt. His father was William Bodham Donne, a noted scholar. His grandparents were first cousins and said to be related to the English poet and clergyman John Donne and the poet William Cowper. Frederick Clench Donne was baptised on 16 November 1834, at Norwich, Norfolk, the location of the family home, South Green House, Mattishall.

In April 1860, Donne married in County Down, Ireland and is mentioned in the *Cork Examiner* of 28 May, with his new wife Annie, arriving at Finn's Royal Victoria Lake Hotel, Killarney, as Mr. & Mrs. Frederick Donne, H.M.'s 3rd Bombay Regiment. Their daughter, Annie Beatrice Donne was born in Ireland on 18 January 1865 and died exactly six months later. The following year, their son, Frederick Edward Mowbray Donne was born in Aden, but being in delicate health, he and his mother returned to England to live with the Donne's at Mattishall. On a visit to her relatives in Liverpool, she met the son of a wealthy brewer, Frank Walter Shepherd and formed a relationship with him. She left a note with her son's nurse and eloped to France with Shepherd and was not heard of for some years. In December 1870, she was discovered living with Shepherd in Dorset Square, London, and Donne, by now a Captain with the 109th Regiment,(formerly the 3rd Bombay European Regiment) sued for divorce. A decree nisi was granted in 1871. At this time Captain Donne was living with his father and family at Mattishall and his son was living with other family.

Promoted to major in October 1871, Donne retired on half pay. In early February 1875, he collapsed at Greenwich, apparently from a stroke, and died five days later on 7 February 1875, in the presence of his sister Valentia. He was just 40 years of age. By November 1877, the *Freeman's Journal* announced briefly, 'Major A. Bennett, 7th Foot, to be Lieutenant-Colonel, vice the late Major F.C. Donne, half-pay, late 109th Foot, whose promotion to Lieutenant-Colonel is cancelled.'

Ensign William Henry Newport was born in Bombay, the second son of Major Christopher Newport of the Bombay Army. He was educated at Cheltenham College and was gazetted into the 3rd Bombay European Regiment in 1855. He recovered from his wounds received at Lohari and fought on at Kunch, Muttra, Golaoli,

Kalpi and Gwalior. He also fought in Abyssinia in 1867. In 1868, he married Caroline Clark of Cheltenham. He rose through the ranks of Captain, Brevet Major, attaining his full majority in December 1875, and was made a Brevet Lieutenant-Colonel in December 1876. In April of the following year he was appointed wing commander of the 28th Bombay Native Infantry, of which he was the second in command. He was killed in action in Afghanistan, on 16 August 1880; shot in the chest ' ... whilst leading his men in the most forward manner'... during an attack on Deh Khoja, a village just east of Candaha (Kandahar).[1]

Richard Herbert Gall, was born at Fort William, Bengal, on 10 November 1815. His parents were George Herbert Gall and his wife Ann. He was a member of the 3rd (or East Kent) Regiment of Foot, (or Buffs) and on 21 October 1843, he married Mary Molesworth Barr in Bombay. He began his term during the mutiny, as a Captain of the H.M. 14th Dragoons (or Hussars) and took an active part in the Central Indian Field Force, displaying courage and leadership, which earned him promotion to Major. After further service, he returned to England where he entered the half pay list and was promoted to Colonel in 1878. In the same year he was made a Companion of the Bath and Aide-de-camp to the Queen. He was appointed Lieutenant Governor of the Royal Hospital Chelsea, a position he held until his death there on 21 February 1881, in his 66th year.

Lieutenant Joseph Bonus was born on 14 September 1836, to Elizabeth Bonus. His father, John Bonus, was a merchant and his large family lived in Blackheath. His early education at the school of Dr. Grieg at Walthamstow, prepared him for admission to the Addiscombe East India Company Military Seminary in 1853. Addiscombe had been established by the company to train officers for its army. After training he was commissioned as a Second Lieutenant of the Bombay Engineers and undertook further training at the School of Military Engineering at Chatham in Kent, qualifying as an engineer officer two years later. Attached to Headquarters of the Bombay Sappers and Miners at Poona, he arrived there some months before the outbreak of the mutiny and was assigned to its 2nd Company. It was in this capacity that he was to participate, firstly in the Nerbudda Field Force and eventually, the Central India Field Force under Sir Hugh Rose.

Lieutenant Bonus was engaged in the whole of the campaign, during which he was mentioned in despatches on six occasions and was promoted to Brevet Major. As a result of the upheaval in the aftermath of the mutiny, when the government took over all of the roles formerly held by the East India Company, Major Bonus became integral to the development of the railways across India. He held important positions, rising to Superintending Engineer, and was promoted to Lieutenant-Colonel At the outbreak of the 2nd Afghan War in 1878, he was commander of the Queens Own Sappers and Miners and served as a Field Engineer. He was promoted to Brevet Colonel for his service. In 1879, he was a Brigadier-General involved in survey work until the end of the campaign. He was mentioned in despatches and received the 2nd Afghan campaign medal. After the war, he resumed development of the railway and with it, senior positions. Just prior to his retirement in 1886 he was promoted to Major-General after 31 years service.

Upon his return to England he lived in Somerset. He married for a second time some years after the death of his first wife and both unions produced children. He died in his 90th year on 11 June 1926.[2]

Brigadier Charles Shepherd Stuart was born at Strathdon, Aberdeen, Scotland and baptised on 28 April 1804. His father was William Stuart of Invernaughty and his mother, Christian, nee Gordon of Strathdon. He entered the Honourable East India Company Army in 1820, and served with the 1st Bombay European Regiment in Arabia in 1820-21; in the Mahi Kantha (India), and at the capture of the Fort of Mahadeoghur in 1832. He served through the mutiny to the taking of Gwalior.

He was made a Knight Commander of the Bath in 1859, commanded a brigade at Bombay, and was commander of Morar — Gwalior when confronted with the 'White Mutiny' of his troops, who did not want to be transferred to the Queens Army. He was promoted to Major-General in 1863. As a Lieutenant-General in 1875, he was created a Knight Grand Cross of the Bath. Promotion to full General followed, in 1877. He died on 2nd April 1879 at his home 'Southlands', Exmouth, Devon. His wife, Adelaide, died in 1911 and her obituary noted that Sir Charles, ' ... was the last person to read the Riot Act in Exmouth. 'The occasion was one on which, in November,

1867, the windows of the bakers' and butchers' shops of the town were broken as a protest against the price of provisions.'³ It seems that the old soldier was hard to keep from the fray. Sir Charles and Lady Stuart were survived by a daughter and two sons.

Brigadier Charles Steuart, sometimes confusingly spelled by others, Stewart or Stuart - as if the fact of two Brigade leaders, named similarly, wasn't confusing enough, was born in 1807. He is probably identical to Charles Steuart who was baptised on 6 September 1807, in Dunfermline, Fife, Scotland. His father was also Charles, and his mother, Mary Wilkie. He joined the army as a Cornet on 10 December 1825 and became a lieutenant on 5 February 1829. Promoted to Captain, by purchase in 1838 and Major ten years later, he served with the 14th Light Dragoons in the Punjab campaign of 1848-49 and at the Battle of Chillianwallah, where he received a sabre wound. He also served at Goojerat and in the pursuit of Afghans over the Khyber Pass. Promoted to Lieutenant Colonel in 1850 and Colonel in 1854, he was commander of a cavalry brigade in the Persian expedition of 1857, and was made a Commander of the Bath. As commander of the 2nd Brigade of the Central India Field Force under Sir Hugh Rose, he campaigned up to and including the taking of Kunch. His actions at Kunch, though not elaborated upon by Sir Hugh Rose, led to him being relieved of active command. It is supposed that Rose thought him wanting in his actions at Kunch and on his approach to Kalpi. Rose wrote to Mansfield, Chief of Staff to the Commander in Chief, on 11 October 1858, 'I am sorry to have to write to you on a painful subject. Consideration for the service alone prevented me from enlarging in my despatches on the conduct of Brigadier Steuart C.B. Commanding 2nd Brigade (of the 14th Light Dragoons) at Koonch and subsequently, which retarded and acted very unfavourably on my operations, and the health of his Brigade.

'Putting the most charitable construction I can on that conduct, truth and duty compel me to say that it would not be right that Brigadier Steuart should ever again command troops on service, the reward to which under other circumstances he would probably have been entitled for the Special Mention and Mentions of his conduct at Rathghur and Jhansi. All this is the more regretted because I hear that he behaved gallantly at Ramnuggar. But like others he has been the victim of twenty years in India, too much smoking etc.'[4]

And again, on 23 December 1858, in a private communication to Lord Canning.

'There again nothing could be worse than the unfortunate Brigadier Steuart of the 14th Light Dragoons. It was necessary for the sake of the truth, and in justice to the troops to show in my report that they were not to blame for the delay and very unfavourable results of Brigadier Steuart's misconduct. But it was also necessary for the credit of the Army not to proclaim to the world that Brigadier Stewart (sic) has lost his name and his head. However, I thought it right to let the Duke of Cambridge know that the unfortunate Brigadier ought never again be placed at the head of Troops, and an answer which I received from Sir C. Yorke a few days ago tells me that that opinion is shared at the Horse Guards. The most singular part of the whole affair is that he was considered the best cavalry officer in India.'[5]

The detail of Steuart's offences are not clear, but whatever they may have been, Rose thought that he had been too long in India and his comment about too much smoking may have referred to hashish. The use of this drug at the time would not have been viewed seriously, but the effects impacting upon performance of duty certainly would have been.

Steuart prevailed however and was promoted to Major-General on 3 October 1864 and appointed Colonel of the 11th Hussars in February 1873. His fall from grace must not have been too severe as he attended a banquet for Lieutenant-General Sir Robert Napier, at the United Services Club, Pall Mall on 13 July 1868, in the presence of the Prince of Wales, the Duke of Cambridge, Lord Strathnairn and Sir Charles Stuart.

Charles Steuart died at the Queen's Hotel, Hastings on 22 May 1873, in his 65th year. He left an estate of something short of £70,000, to his brother Archibald, with smaller bequests to his sister Ann Pole and friends.

Robert Francis Bayley's venture at the Sydney Riding School ended in insolvency in June 1865, when the Supreme Court ordered a meeting with his creditors at the King Street Courtrooms on the 14th of that month, '...for the proof of debts against the said Estate, and for the collection, administration, and distribution of the same; that the Insolvent may account for his Insolvency; for directing the Official Assignee whether the Insolvent will be allowed to retain for his own use his household furniture, wearing apparel, beds, bedding, and tools of trade, or any part thereof respectively ...'[6]

Bankrupt and seeking relief from the Supreme Court, he apparently left for New Zealand, where he joined the police force. On 31 January 1881, he appeared as a witness in a prosecution for assault, where he was referred to as 'constable' and 'sergeant' by different witnesses.[7] As had occurred in the past, his fall back position was policing.

The *Sydney Morning Herald* of 15 January 1907, announced the retirement of Superintendent Creaghe, and he was quoted as making some disparaging remarks about the squad with which he had drilled upon joining the police force. He said, '... he had seen the service when it was but an armed rabble, composed of broken down swells and others, all utterly at a disadvantage in coping with the well-trained bushrangers who made things so unpleasant in those days. The first squad he drilled with was altogether a cosmopolitan one. There were soldiers, sailors and he could not say what else in it ... '. Robert Bayley could scarcely restrain himself, writing to the editor of the same paper of 1 February 1907; Sir, — In your issue of the 15th inst. appears an article, no doubt inspired by Mr. Superintendent Creaghe, of Bathurst. Amongst other things he gives a description of the squad he was drilled with. As I drilled that squad I ought to know something of the personnel of it. There were in it the present Superintendent Latimer, and, I think, Superintendent Cotter, and others who distinguished themselves in the service, who joined about the same time. There were the late esteemed Mr. Critchett Walker, C.M.G., Principal Under-Secretary, E. Fosbery. C.M.G., late Inspector-General, Mr. Henry Garvin, Sub-Inspector, father of the present Inspector General, the present Inspector-General himself. Superintendents Lydiard, T. B. Carne, Morrisett, Morrow, etc, Inspectors Davidson, Kerrigan, Johnston, Thorpe, Norton, Roberts, D. Byrne, Myles, Burns, Medley, and others, all of whom were a credit to the service, not forgetting the distinguished Superintendent M. Brennan, who, however, joined under the 1850 Act.

'The only swell I remember in the squad was Mr. Creaghe himself, who was far from being broken down, a fine, tall, good-looking young fellow, but rather awkward to drill with friends at court. There are conflicting accounts of the shooting of Pat Connell by members of the party, who were, it is said, nearer the front of the battle. When Mr. Creaghe was Sub inspector at Hay Mr. Inspector H. Davidson was in charge of the south-western district (headquarters Deniliquin), Mr. Creaghe, I think, was in charge for a month or so during Mr. Davidson's absence on leave the only bushrangers out in the district at that time were the "Bluecap Gang," with whom Mr. Creaghe had nothing to do; Mr. Davidson, a cool and courageous officer, of Ben Hall fame, being the man directing the operations that brought the gang to justice.

'I am, etc., ROBERT T BAYLEY Jan 29 Ex-Sergeant and Drill Instructor.'[8]

Still the policeman at heart, he was not letting an apparent braggart escape unchallenged. His recollections did not accord with those of Superintendent Martin Brennan,[9] who gave Creaghe a major part in the pursuit of the Connell gang. Whilst Constable Kelly shot and killed the bushranger Pat Connell, Creaghe and others pursued three members of the gang and were fired upon by them. Creaghe, then a Senior Sergeant, was rewarded with £100 and was promoted to sub-inspector. Kelly, however, was overlooked, receiving a small reward. He took to drink and retired from the police force. What the letter does show is Bayley's tenacity, even as he entered his seventies and his keen interest in the doings of the police force. It also shows that he had returned to Australia.

By 1918 Robert Bayley was living at 119 George Street West, in Sydney, when he was struck by an 'electric tram car' near his home on 15 June, and severely injured. He died in Sydney Hospital the following day. He was 81 years old. He was buried in the Church of England section of Rookwood Cemetery, on the outskirts of Sydney. The *Sydney Morning Herald* added to his death notice, 'New Zealand papers please copy' indicating that his family wished for his friends and colleagues in that country to be advised of his death.

Deborah Manifold continued her caring role, which extended beyond her family. She became a certified nurse and midwife, working into advanced age. Her loved ones fell away after her brothers William and Humphrey died. Benjamin, still a patient in the Patton Asylum, and still believing that he was more sane than his keepers, died there on 13 March 1907. His effects were $6.86 in cash and $42.00 in pension money held on his behalf. Josiah, who had joined the army as a schoolmaster in 1869, and now a pensioner, died in 1910. Dinah Prescott, their sister, died in Dublin in 1911. Deborah lost her husband, Samuel, in 1915 and she succumbed in June the following year, aged 73. Samuel Robert James, died in Pennsylvania, one day short of his 88th birthday on 19 January 1936, and with him passed a generation of the James family. The fruit not falling far from the tree, his son Stanley Livingstone James, who had liked shooting as a boy and who Samuel could not encourage to study, graduated from the U.S. Military Academy, West Point. He saw service in WWII and became a prisoner of the Japanese, becoming the most senior officer to survive the death marches. He achieved the rank of Colonel and died in 1949, from complications to injuries inflicted while a prisoner of war. His son, Stanley Livingstone 'Jimmy' James Jr., also attended the West Point Academy and attained the rank of Lieutenant Colonel. After retirement he taught mathematics at Middle School level in Texas. He died in 2009.

Both of the Stanley Livingstone James' lived long enough to have known their grandfather and father, Samuel. How much they learned from him about their uncle and great uncle, Humphrey, is not known. Yet it is to be wondered at; for how was it that these men of military persuasion, though springing from an Irish born book-keeper, followed their paths of service to their country with honour, in the same way that Humphrey James had done so long before them?

And so, the story of Humphrey James and Frederick Whirlpool VC, one and the same, has been untangled, threshed out and told, as much as can be at this time. Let him join ranks with his peers and remain honoured in the way that only those who have achieved the highest of distinctions deserve.

Endnotes

───────

Chapter 1

1 *Windsor and Richmond Gazette*, Saturday 24 June 1899, p.2

2 *Sydney Morning Herald*, Thursday 22 June 1899, p. 4

3 *Idem.*

4 *Windsor and Richmond Gazette*, Saturday 24 June 1899, p. 3

5 Croll, Denys, *Whirlpool V.C. A Fragment of Australian History*, unpublished, n.d., p. 41. Private Record PR84/008 Australian War Memorial, Canberra — recollection of Miss Bessie Dick Smith, daughter of John Dick Smith to Croll

6 Letterhead of R. W. Dunstan. Account to Curator of Intestate Estates, 29 June1899, for 'Burial of the late Humphrey James." State Records Office, NSW 229/99 — 10/27563

7 Register of Coroner's Inquests and Magisterial Inquiries, NSW 1895-01 p. 434, vide www.ancestry.com.au

8 Report of Constable Tate Intestate Estate Papers State Records Office NSW 229/99 — 10/27563

9 Intestate file op.cit.

10 *Windsor and Richmond Gazette*, Saturday 9 December 1899, p 6

11 Itntestate file op.cit.

12 Intestate file op.cit.

13 U.S. Army, Register of Enlistments, 1798 — 1914, vide www.ancestry.com.au accessed 4 July 2014

14 U.S. National Homes for Disabled Volunteer Soldiers, 1866 — 1938, vide www.ancestry.com.au accessed 4 July 2014.

15 U.S. Army, Register of Enlistments, 1798 — 1914, op. cit.

16 Samuel James letter to Humphrey James, 15 July 1899, Intestate file op.cit

17 Benjamin James letter to Samuel James, 7 May 1899. Intestate file op.cit.

Chapter 2

1 Deborah Manifold letter to Humphrey James 29 June 1899 Intestate papers SRO NSW 229/99 — 10/27563

2 Pigot & Co., *City of Dublin & Hibernian Provincial Directory*, (1824)

3 Thom, Alexander, *Thom's Irish Almanac and Official Directory, etc., for the year 1852,* Alexander Thom, London, 1852.

4 Titmarsh, M.A., (William Makepeace Thackeray) *The Irish Sketchbook 1842, p.277,* Chapman & Hall, London 1857.

5 Croll, op.cit. p. 1

6 Titmarsh, op.cit. pp. 286-298

7 Room, A., (ed.) *Brewers Dictionary of Phrase and Fable*, Cassell, 1999, p.359. Dotheboys Hall, a private boarding school in Dickens' 'Nicholas Nickleby' (1838-9) where boys were taken in and 'done for' (hence the name) by Mr. Wackford Squeers,a brutish, ignorant,overbearing fellow, who starved them and taught them nothing. The ruthless exposure of this kind of school led to the closing or reformation of many.

8 Woodham-Smith, op.cit., p. 35

9 Titmarsh, op.cit. pp. 349-350.

10 Hunter, Thomas, 1831-1915, The Autobiography of Dr. Thomas Hunter, founder and first president of Hunter college, 1870-1906, president emeritus till October 14, 1915; edited by his daughters. The Knickerbocker Press, New York, 1931, pp. 24-26.

11 Irish Petty Sessions Court Registers 1828-1912, 14 March 1854 & 24 March 1854, vide http://search.findmypast.co.uk accessed 10 July 2015

12 *Windsor and Richmond Gazette*, Saturday 1 July 1899, p. 4

13 Vere Foster Papers, NIPRO, D3618/D/10/14, cited by Ruth-Ann Harris, '*Where the poor man is not crushed down to exalt the aristocrat': Vere Foster's programmes of assisted emigration in the aftermath of the Irish Famine.' 'The Irish World Wide. History, Heritage, Identity. Vol. 6 'The Meaning of the Famine', (ed.) Patrick O'Sullivan. Leicester University Press, London, 1997.*

14 Stanley, Peter, *White Mutiny. British Military Culture in India 1825-1875, p.13*, C. Hurst & Company, London, 1998. Also citing *Northbrook India papers, School of Oriental & African Studies, University of London, 118332/14.*

15 Stanley op.cit. p. 15

16 Bodell, J., *A Soldier's View of Empire. The Reminiscences of James Bodell 1831-92, p.20*, K. Sinclair (Ed.), The Bodley Head, London, 1982.

17 Stanley, op.cit. p. 36 citing Brown, Private J., '*A Private journal*' , 1854-60, National Library of Scotland

18 Lord Byron, *Childe Harold's Pilgrimage,* Project Gutenberg, www.gutenberg.org accessed 3 January 2016.

Chapter 3

1 Marland, Hilary, University of Warwick; Cox, Catherine, University College, Dublin. 'Madness, Migration and the Irish in Lancashire — 1850-1921', www2.warwick.ac.uk/fac/arts/history/chm/research.

2 Marland et. al. op.cit.

3 *Liverpool Mail, Saturday* 17 April 1847, p.2

4 *Liverpool Mail, Saturday* 19 May 1849, p.3

5 *Liverpool Mail, Saturday* 15 June 1850, p.3

6 Peter Stanley, '*White Mutiny*', C Hurst & Company, London, 1998, p.16.

7 Burne, Owen Tudor, *Rulers of India, Clyde and Strathnairn*, pp. 128-129, The Clarendon Press, Oxford, 1895

8 Forrest, George W., (ed.) *Selections from the Letters, Despatches and Other State Papers preserved in the Military Department of the Government of India 1857-58 Vol. 4, p.226*, Superintendent Government Printing India, Calcutta, 1912.

9 Stanley, op.cit. p. 12

10 Butler, W. F., *An Autobiography*, pp. 41-42, Constable & Co. 1911,

11 Butler, op.cit. pp. 22-23

12 Standing Orders of the East India Company's Depot, 1844.

13 Holmes, Richard, Redcoat — *The British Soldier in the Age of Horse and Musket, p.4*, Harper Collins Publishers, London, 2001.

14 Curtis, Robert H., The History of the Royal Irish Constabulary, pp.102-104, McGlashen & Gill, Dublin, 1871.

15 Robson, Brian (Ed.) *Sir Hugh Rose and the Central India Campaign 1858*, pp. 104-105, Sutton Publishing Ltd., Gloucestershire, 2000.

16 Small, Hugh, *The Crimean War, p.139*, Tempus Publishing: Knowledge Leak, London 2007/2014.

17 Standing Orders, op. cit., p. 14

18 Standing Orders, op. cit. p. 9

19 Standing Orders, op. cit. p. 31

20 Stanley, op. cit. p. 44

21 Standing Orders, op. cit. p. 24

22 Standing Orders, op. cit. p. 30

23 Sutton, Jean, *Lords of the East. The East India Company and its Ships, p.105*, Conway Maritime Press, London, 1981.

Chapter 4

1 Stanley, White Mutiny, op. cit., p.38

2 Scene derived from a description by Mrs Leopold Paget, *Camp and Cantonment. A Journal of Life in India & etc.*, p.56, Longman, Green, Longman, Roberts & Green, London, 1865.

3 Paget, op. cit., p.72

4 Paget, op. cit., p. 85

5 *The Imperial Gazetteer of India*, Vol XX, Published Under the Authority of His Majesty's Secretary of State for India in Council, pp.181-183, Clarendon Press, Oxford, 1908,

6 Archie White VC, MC, in a letter to the Reverend Canon Lummis MC, 30 July 1964, National Army Museum, Victoria Cross Biography No. 43.

7 Paget, op.cit., p. 85

8 Holmes, Richard, *Sahib — The British Soldier in India, 1750-1914*, p. 480, Harper Collins, London, 2005.

9 Holmes, Richard, Redcoat — *The British Soldier in the Age of Horse and Musket*, p.300, Harper Collins, London, 2001.

10 Holmes, *Sahib*, op.cit., p. 480

11 Sutton, Jean, *Lords of the East — The East India Company and its Ships*, p. 9, Conway Maritime Press, London, 1981.

12 Sutton, op.cit., p. 16.

13 Holmes, *Sahib*, op.cit., p. 233

Chapter 5

1 Mabbert, Ian, *A Short History of India, p.187*, Cassell, Australia, n.d.

2 Mason, Philip, *The Men Who Ruled India*, pp.108-109, Jonathan Cape, London, 1985.

3 Mason, op.cit., p.337

4 Dubois, Abbé J.A., *Hindu Manners, Customs and Ceremonies*, p. 356, Dover Publications, New York, 2002. First published in French in 1809 and English, under the auspices of the East India Company, in 1815. Enlarged by its 3rd edition in 1905.

5 Holmes, *Sahib*, op.cit. p. 459

6 Dalrymple, William, *The Last Mughal*, p.62 , Bloomsbury, London, 2007,, quoting Christopher Hibbert, *The Great Mutiny: India* 1857, London, 2000 & Saul David, *The Indian Mutiny 1857*, London, 2002.

7 Mason, op. cit. p.143

8 Kaye, John & Malleson, G.B., '*History of the Indian Mutiny, 1857-8*', p.260 , London, W. H. Allen & Co., 1880, vol.3, ch.1,. http://www.ibiblio.org/britishraj/KayeMalleson1/index.html

9 Jerosch, Rainer, *The Rani of Jhansi — Rebel against Will*, p. 3, Aakar Books, Delhi, 2007,

translated from the original German edition of 2005 by James A. Turner.

10 Mason, op.cit., p. 143

11 Holmes, *Sahib*, op.cit., p. 72.

12 Mason, op.cit., p. 143

13 Jerosch, op.cit. p.9, quoting Lt. Hugh Gough of the 3rd Light Cavalry.

14 Chick, N.A., *Annals of the Indian Rebellion 1857-58*, p. 23, Charles Knight & Co. Ltd., London, 1974 (1859).

15 Chick, op.cit., p. 25

16 Chick, op.cit., p. 25

17 Burne, Owen Tudor, *Clyde and Strathnairn, Rulers of India*, p.19, Clarendon Press, London, 1895.

18 *Clyde and Strathnairn, Rulers of India,* p.19, Clarendon Press, London, 1895.

19 Burne, op. cit., p. 20

20 Jerosch, op. cit., p. 10

21 Jerosch, op. cit., p. 13

22 Mason, op. cit., p. 160

23 Lowe, Thomas, *Central India During the Rebellion of 1857 and 1858*, Longman, Green, Longman and Roberts, London, 1860

24 Lowe, op. cit., p. viii

25 Dalrymple, op.cit., p. 402, quoting, Michael Maclagan, Clemency Canning, London, 1962, p. 98.

26 Punch, October 24, 1857, p.170, "*THE SEPOY GOVERNOR-GENERAL*"

27 *Idem.*

28 Burne, op. cit., p. 33

29 Burne, op. cit., pp. 38-39

30 Chick, op. cit., p. 269, quoting from Lord Stanley's Statement in Parliament, providing figures as at January, 1857.

Chapter 6

1 Burne, op. cit., p. 22

2 Burne, op. cit., p. 24

3 Burne, op. cit., p. 48

4 Burne, op.cit., pp.94-95

5 Crook, Michael J., *The Evolution of the Victoria Cross, pp. 12-13*. Midas Books, Kent in association with The Ogilby Trusts, London, 1975.

6 Crook, op. cit., p. 280

7 Burne, op. cit., p. 96

8 Crook, op. cit., pp. 37-38

9 Burne, op. cit., p. 165

10 Crook, op.cit., p. 39

11 Crook, op. cit., pp. 39-40, citing D. H. Parry, The VC- Its Heroes and Their Valour, 1913, p.193

12 Robson, Brian (Ed.) *Sir Hugh Rose and the Central India Campaign 1858, p. xiii,* Sutton Publishing, Gloucestershire, for the Army Records Society, 2000.

13 Stanley, Peter, *White Mutiny*, pp..98-99, Hurst and Company, London, 1998.

14 Robson, op. cit., p. 19

15 Robson, op. cit., p. 17

16 Sylvester, John Henry, *Recollections of the Campaign in Malwa and Central India under Major General Sir Hugh Rose etc.*, Smith, Taylor and Co., Bombay, 1860, pp.11-12

17 Robson, op. cit., p. 24

18 Robson, op. cit., p. 25

19 Robson, op. cit., pp. 26-27

20 Robson, op. cit., p. 47

21 Lowe, op. cit., p. 166

22 *Leeds Intelligencer*, Saturday 20 February 1858, p.5.

23 Robson, op.cit., pp. 283-284

24 Robson, op. cit., p. 80

25 Lowe, op. cit., p. 166

26 *The Birmingham Daily Post*, p.1, Monday, 26 April 1858. Private Hugh Kenalty (Kennalty) was born in Birmingham and was attached to the 3rd Bombay European Regiment, Reg'd. No. 250. He had been a 'painter and gilder on glass' and left for India on the 'Vernon'. He enlisted for ten years, but died on 22 September 1858, at Lyher.(Lahar) He is buried at the cantonment cemetery in Jhansi. British Library, Asian and African Reading Room, L/MIL/9/44; L/MIL/9/102; L/MIL/12/113 & L/MIL/12/204

27 Francisco Goya, Los 'Desastres de la Guerra' , a series of etchings created between 1810 and 1820 depicting the horrors of various conflicts between 1808 — 1814, but not published until many years after the events.

28 Jacques Callot 'Les Miseres et les Mal-Heurs de la Guerre' 1633, depicting scenes of rape and plunder by mutinous soldiers and their eventual executions and torture, during the Thirty Years War.

29 *The Leicestershire Mercury*, Saturday, 17 April 1858, p 6

30 Robson, op. cit., p. 60

31 Robson, op. cit., p. 70

32 Robson, op. cit., pp. 64-65

33 Lowe, op. cit., p. 186

34 Lowe, op. cit., p.189

35 Lowe, op. cit., p. 190

36 Lowe, op. cit., pp. 194-195

37 Sylvester, op, cit., p. 72

38 *Birmingham Daily Post*, op. cit., p.1

Chapter 7

1 Lowe, op. cit., pp. 232-233

2 Lowe, op. cit., p. 20

3 Burne, op. cit., pp., 118-119

4 Robson, op. cit., p. 98

5 Dubois, Abbé J. A., *Hindu Manners, Customs and Ceremonies*, p.668, Dover Publications, New York, 2002

6 Lowe, op. cit., pp. 252-254

7 He, in all probability, was James Flude, the son of a stocking maker of Hinckley in Leicestershire, who was born in 1833 and followed the trade of a bricklayer. He seems to have enlisted as Thomas Few, Regimental Number 651 and gave his birth year as 1833 and his occupation as 'bricklayer'. He claimed to be a native of Walsall in Staffordshire. Flude is recorded as living temporarily in Walsall in 1851. A Thomas Few who married in Hinckley in 1845 may have been the inspiration for James Flude's adopted identity. James Flude's story did not end at the wall of Jhansi. Fragments of his letters to his parents between 1857 and 1859 give accounts

of his time in India during the whole of the Central India campaign and provide a glimpse of what the ordinary soldier experienced. He was part of the force, which engaged Tantia Tope at the battle of Betwa, meaning that Frederick Whirlpool undoubtedly accompanied him.

8   *The Leicestershire Mercury,* Saturday, August 7, 1858, p.8 See Annexure A for full text.

9   Burne , op.cit., notes pp120-121

10   Burne, ibid.

11   Steuart, Brigadier Charles, *The London Gazette, Page 3364,17th July, 1858, Issue 22163.*

12   Robson, op. cit. p.169

13   *Elgin Courier,* Friday, 18th June, 1858, p.2

14   *Ibid.*

15   Robson, op. cit., p. 156

16   Robson, op. cit., p. 156

17   Robson, op. cit., pp. 64-65

18   Sylvester, op. cit., pp. 114-115

19   Lowe, op. cit., pp. 259-263

20   Burne, op. cit., p.124

21   Robson, op. cit., pp. 7-9, from Sylvester's diary, Oriental and India Office Collections, British Library, MSS Eur C241, p. 31

22   Robson, op. cit., p. 172

23   Sylvester, op. cit., p. 75

24   Robson, op. cit., pp. 139-141, quoting Vishnu Godse, in retelling an eyewitness account.

25   Robson, op. cit., p. 139

26   Jerosch, op. cit., p.201

27   Jerosch, op. cit., p.202

28   Dalrymple, op.cit., pp. 462-463.

29   Dalrymple, op.cit., p. 364 quoting R. Montgomery Martin, *Indian Empire,* p. 449, London, 1860, vol. 11.

30   *Glasgow Sentinel,* 10 July 1858, p. 2., attributed to Sergeant A.G., Alexander of the 93rd Regiment, which was not present in the campaign. This man was more probably Corporal Adam Alexander of the 3rd Bombay European Regiment.

31   *Glasgow Herald,* 7 June, 1858, p.5., Letter of a private of the 3rd Bombay European Regiment, signed 'P.McP.' and certainly Peter McPherson, the only person with those initials in the regiment.

32   *Punch,* p.107, 5 September, 1857, Vol's 32-33 vide https://book.google.co.uk

33   Lowe, op. cit., p. 265

34   Holmes, *Redcoat,* op. cit., p. 208

35   Sylvester, op.cit., p. 122.

36   Edwardes, Michael, *Red Year — The Indian Rebellion of 1857,* p. 122, Hamish Hamilton, London, 1973., in which the author quotes from Vishnu Godse, 'Majha Pravas', Poona, 1948, translated from Marathi.

Chapter 8

1   Robson, op. cit., p. 175

2   Robson, op. cit., pp. 179-181. Gall letter to his brother c.11 May 1858

3   Sylvester, op.cit., pp. 122-123 See Annexure B for detail.

4   Robson, op. cit., pp. 173-174

5   Burne, op. cit., pp. 128-129

6   Gall, Major R. H., *The London Gazette,* pp. 3543-3545, 28 July 1858, Issue, 22167. See also

Annexure C.

7   Johnson, Catharine B. (ed.) *William Bodham Donne and his Friends*, pp. 221-222,London, Methuen & Co., 1905.

8   Johnson op.cit., p.222

9   *The London Gazette*, pp. 3792-3793, 21 October 1859.

10 Holmes, *Sahib*, op. cit., p. 406, Dr John Murray...during the First Sikh War wrote that: 'Some of the wounded lay two or three days on the field.....& I have heard — officers — say they would much rather be shot dead than than severely wounded under such conditions'

11 Johnson, op.cit., pp. 228-229.

12 Croll, Denys, *Whirlpool V.C. — A Fragment of Australian History*. n.d., Unpublished MSS, Private Record: PR84/008/Folder No. 1/1 DPI: 300. Croll had the advantage of interviewing Miss Bessie Dick Smith, daughter of John Dick Smith, who as a young girl remembered the elderly Humphrey James. She related this information as well as the description of his 'mutton chop' whiskers.

13 *The Bury and Norwich Post*, 29 June 1858, p. 2.

14 Thomas Few, (Pte.), (Corporal James Flude) Letter to his parents from Mhow, 1 June 1859. Leicestershire, Leicester and Rutland Record Office, op. cit.

15 Burne, op. cit., p. 150

16 Burne, op.cit., p. 90

17 Burne, op. cit., p. 98

18 Burne, op. cit., pp. 98-99t

Chapter 9

1   *Sydney Morning Herald*, 19 October 1857, p. 4, in a report taken from Allen's India Mail.

2   *Sydney Morning Herald*, Thursday, 10 January 1867, p. 4. Reporting from the Daily Southern Cross, December 1866.

3   Lord Clive Military Fund Pension Register and Payment Books, British India Office Army and Navy Pensions, L-AG-23-2-66 vide http://search.findmypast.com.au accessed 2 July 2014

4   Victoria Public Records Office, Whirlpool application to join Victoria Police VPRS 937/PO Unit 159

5   *Bendigo Advertiser*, 1 March 1860, p.3

6   *Fitzroy City Press*, Saturday, 20 August 1881, p.3. Obituary of James Conly

7   *South Bourke Standard*, Friday 20 September 1861, p. 2.

8   '*The Argus*' Melbourne, Saturday, 29 September 1860, p.4.

9   McWilliam, Gwen, *Hawthorn Peppercorns*, p. 77, Brian Atkins, Melbourne, 1978.

10 *The Argus*, Melbourne, 7 August 1897, letter of J.J. Bradley, p. 14.

11 *The Argus*, Melbourne, 24 July 1897, letter of M.H. Mortimer, p. 14.

12 Wilcox, Craig, *Red Coat Dreaming. How colonial Australia embraced the British Army*, pp.108-110, Cambridge University Press, Melbourne, 2009.

13 *The Age*, Melbourne, Friday, 25 July 1919, p.7, obituary of Mr. E. A. Atkyns.

14 *Bell's Life in Victoria*, 21 June 1861, pp. 5-6.

15 *The Age*, Melbourne, Friday 21 June 1861, p. 6.

16 *The Argus*, Melbourne, Friday 21 June 1861, p. 5.

17 *Bell's Life in Victoria*, op. cit., pp. 5-6.

18 Wilcox, op.cit., p.53, quoting Anthony Staunton, '*Victoria Cross sesquicentenary*', *Verbosity*, vol. 21, no. 1, 2005, p.2

19 Ibid., pp. 67-68

20 *Aldershot Military Gazette, Saturday, 17 August 1861, p. 2., column headed 'Australia', From the correspondent of the Times ...*

21 *The Argus*, Melbourne, Thursday, 27 June 1861, p. 5.

22 Croll, op. cit., p. 23.

23 Crook, op. cit., pp. 234-235.

24 Letter written by Frederic (?) H. Whirlpool, Melbourne, 6 October 1861, to The Honorable, The Military Secretary, Military Department, India Office, acknowledging receipt of the Mutiny Medal. He completes his letter, " Your most obedient, humble servant, Frederic H. Whirlpool" and in keeping with this tone and his 'singularly modest and retiring' nature, he did not use the post-nominal "V.C." to which he was entitled.

25 *The Star*, Ballarat, Friday, 28 June 1861, p. 2.

26 *South Bourke Standard,* 24 January 1862, pp. 2-3.

27 Haldane, Robert, *The People's Force — A History of the Victoria Police, p. 68*, Melbourne University Press, 1986.

28 Victoria Public Records Office, Application by Frederick Whirlpool of 15 October 1860 to join the Victoria Police , notations and accompanying letter by Chief Commissioner Standish. VPRS 937/PO., Unit 159

29 Ibid.

30 Ibid.

31 Haldane, op. cit., p. 67

32 Ibid., p.55

33 Wilcox, *op.cit.*, p. 154 and East India Company Pension Register, Returns of Payments of Army and Other Pensions 1842-1883, Series

Chapter 10

1   John Donne, 1572-1631, the great metaphysical poet, was claimed by his family, to be an ancestor of Lieutenant Frederick Clench Donne, whose life Whirlpool saved at Lohari Fort.

2   Burne, op. cit., p. 108

3   Haldane, op. cit., p. 82

4   Ibid., p. 87

5   Ibid., p. 85-86

6   Idem

7   NSW Police Register of Appointments, State Records Office, New South Wales, series No. 10943 Reel 3042.

8   Haydon, A. L., *The Trooper Police of Australia,* pp.206-207, London, Andrew Melrose, 1911.

9   Report from Inspector-General of Police on working of Police Regulation Act of 1862, presented to both Houses of Parliament, 4 June 1872. '*Documents on Police in New South Wales, 1789 — 1879*,' (Ed.) Richard Hammond, n.d. (c.1979) N.S.W. Police Department.

10 Gaol Entrance Book, Wagga Wagga, State Records Office of New South Wales, series No. 2569, July 1862 — December 1866 (4/8509 part) SR Reel 2377

11 Haldane, op. cit., p. 20

12 Leah, S., *Wagga Wagga Community Heritage Study, Vol. 2, 7.3*, citing A. Atkinson, and M. Aveling, (eds), 'Australians 1838', p. 275, Fairfax, Syme and Weldon, Broadway, 1987.

13 *The Wagga Wagga Express*, 23 May 1863, p.3

14 *The Empire,* Sydney, Saturday 23 May 1863, p. 2 and T*he Armidale Express and New England General Advertiser,*' Saturday, 13 June 1863, pp. 2-3, quoting from the *Yass Courier of May*, 1863.

15 *New South Wales Police Gazette*, 20 May 1863.

16 Copies of Letters Sent Wagga Wagga Gaol, State Record Office, NSW. Series No. 2565, date range 31/07/1862 to 17/07/1905 (6/5400-01 vol.)

17 Stanley, *White Mutiny, op. cit., pp.* 94-95

18 *Australian Dictionary of Biography*, vol. 5, Melbourne University Press, 1974, vide www.adb.anu.edu.au

Chapter 11

1 New South Wales Registers of Police Employment, 1847 — 1885. State Records Office NSW vide www.ancestry.com.au accessed 14 July 2015.

2 *Sydney Morning Herald*, Saturday, 11th February, 1865, p 12.

3 State Records Office NSW, Council of Education Miscellaneous In-letter books, Series 2621 container 1/745. Vol 11 Lismore-Macquarie Plains.

4 Ibid

5 Ibid

6 Ibid

7 Ibid

8 Ibid

9 Ibid

10 Ibid

11 Ibid

12 Ibid

13 Ibid

14 Ibid

15 www.sonsoftemperance.info/hst19-austalia-nsw.htm accessed 23 March 2015

Chapter 12

1 Croll, op. cit., p.71

2 State Records Office NSW, Council of Education container 1/874

3 State Records Office NSW, Gaol Description and Entrance Books, 1818-1930. Windsor 1864-1898 vide www.ancestry.com.au accessed 20 July 2014

4 State Records Office NSW, Gaol Description and Entrance Books, 1818-1930. Windsor 1864-1898 vide www.ancestry.com.au accessed 20 July 2014

5 State Records Office NSW, Gaol Description and Entrance Books, 1818-1930. Windsor 1864-1898 vide www.ancestry.com.au accessed 20 July 2014

6 State Records Office NSW, Gaol Description and Entrance Books, 1818-1930. Windsor 1864-1898 vide www.ancestry.com.au accessed 20 July 2014

7 Wilcox, *Red Coat Dreaming,* p.75.

8 State Records Office NSW, Intestate papers, container 10/27563, item 0229/1899

9 National Army Museum, London. Victoria Cross folio No. 43, Frederick Whirlpool, prepared by Rev. Canon Lummis, containing a letter from Archie White VC regarding the sale of the Whirlpool VC, dated April, 1964 n.d. NAM 1974-07-83

10 Letter of Denys Croll to Canon Lummis, 29 January 1964. NAM 1974-07-83

11 Lot 6, Postal Bids Sale, 97 Bridge Mall, Ballarat, Victoria, closing date, 19 May 1989. Indian Mutiny Medal 1857-58 with bar 'Central India', 3 prong buckle clip. Impressed to 'Fred. K. Whirlpool, 3rd Bombay Eurpn's' The estimate was $4,500. Copy of catalogue entry Whirlpool folio NAM 1974-07-83

Chapter 13

1   State Records Office NSW, Intestate file, op.cit.

2   *Windsor and Richmond Gazette*, 1 July 1899, p.3.

3   Boswell's Life, vol. 1, 14th July, 1763, p.428, (T*he Life of Samuel Johnson*), 1791, from G. B. Hill, (Ed.) 1934, revised by L. F. Powell, 1964, quoted in T*he Concise Oxford Dictionary of Quotations, p.184:10*, Oxford University Press, 1994.

4   Crook, op. cit. p. 64

5   Kendall, Henry, '*Charles Harpur*', *The Colonial Poets, G. A. Wilkes (Ed.) Sydney, Angus and Robertson, 1974*. Originally published in, Leaves from Australian Forests, George Robertson, Melbourne, 1869.

Epilogue

1   Casualty Roll, Afghanistan Campaign, www.britishmedals.us

2   De Santis, E., (ed.), F. Larimore, '*Major General Joseph Bonus — Royal Engineers and Bombay Sappers and Miners — 1836-1926*', Published to internet, 2002.

3   *Exeter and Plymouth Gazette*, Friday, 3rd February, 1911.

4   Robson, *op.cit., pp.*279-280

5   Ibid. p. 283

6   *New South Wales Government Gazette*, 1865, p1209.

7   *Marlborough Express*, Volume XVI, Issue 25, 31 January, 1881, p.2

8   *Sydney Morning Herald*, Friday, 1st February, 1907, p 8

9   Brennan, Martin, *History of Notorious Bushrangers*, unpublished, n.d., Mitchell Library, Sydney, A2030, published to the intertnet *via www.grafton.nsw.free.fr (ed.) Peter Mayberry (n.d.)*

BIBLIOGRAPHY

Bodell, James. Sinclair, Keith (ed.) *A Soldier's View of Empire. The Reminiscences of James Bodell, 1831-92,* The Bodely Head Ltd., London, 1982.

Boxall, George E., *History of the Australian Bushrangers,* T. Fisher Unwin, London, 1899. Via Project Gutenberg Australia.

Brennan, Martin, *History of Notorious Bushrangers,* unpublished, n.d., Mitchell Library, Sydney. Published to internet by Mayberry, Peter (ed.) n.d.

Butler, W.F., *An Autobiography,* Constalbe & Co., London, 1911.

Burne, Owen, *Clyde and Strathnairn,* The Clarendon Press, 1895.

Chick, N.A. (compiler), Hutchinson, David, (ed.) *Annals of the Indian Rebellion 1857-58,* Charles Knight & Co. Ltd., London 1974. (First published in Calcutta in 1859)

Croll, Denys J.F.A., *Whirlpool VC. A Fragment of Australian History,* unpublished typescript, n.d. Private Record PR84/008, Australian War Memorial, Canberra.

Crook, Michael, *The Evolution of the Victoria Cross,* Midas Books, Kent, 1975.

Curtis, Robert H., *The History of the Royal Irish Constabulary,* McGlashen & Gill, Dublin, 1871.

Dalrymple, William, *The Last Mughal. The Fall of a Dynasty, Delhi, 1857,* Bloomsbury Publishing, London, 2007.

Dubois, J.A., *Hindu Manners, Customs and Ceremonies,* Dover Publications, New York, 2002. Republication of 1905 edition in English. Written in 1806 and first published in 1897.

Edwardes, Michael, *Red Year. The Indian Rebellion of 1857,* Hamish Hamilton Ltd., London, 1973.

Edwardes, Michael, *Battles of the Indian Mutiny,* B. T. Batsford Ltd., London, 1963.

Edwardes, Michael, *Everyday Life in Early India, B.T. Batsford Ltd., London, 1969.*

Forrest, G.W., *(Ed.) Selections from the Letters, Despatches and Other State Papers presented in the Military Department of the Government of India 1857-58, Superintendent Government Printing India, Calcutta, 1912.*

Foster, Roy F., *Modern Ireland 1600-1972,* Penguin Group, London, 1989.

Haldane, Robert, *The People's Force. A history of the Victoria Police,* Melbourne University Press, Carlton, Victoria, 1986.

Haydon, A.L., *The Trooper Police of Australia,* Andrew Melrose, London, 1911.

Holmes, Richard, *Redcoat. The British Soldier in the Age of Horse and Musket,* HarperCollins*Publishers,* London, 2001.

Holmes, Richard, *Sahib. The British Soldier in India.* HarperCollins*Publishers, London, 2005.*

Hunter, Thomas, *The autobiography of Dr. Thomas Hunter, founder and first president of Hunter college, 1870-1906, president emeritus till October 14, 1915; edited by his daughters. The Knickerbocker Press, New York, 1931.*

Jerosch, Rainer, *The Rani of Jhansi. Rebel against Will,* Aakar Books, Delhi, 2007.

Johnson, Catharine B., (ed.) *William Bodham Donne and his Friends, Methuen & Co., London, 1905.*

Kaye, John & Malleson, G.B., *History of the Indian Mutiny, 1857-8,* W.H. Allen & Co., London, 1880.

Kohl, Johann G., *Travels in Ireland,* Bruce and Wyld, London, 1844.

Lowe, Thomas, Central India During the Rebellion of 1857 and 1858., Longman, Green, Longman, and Roberts, 1860 (facsimile edition.)

Mabbert, Ian W., *A Short History of India*, Cassell Asian Histories, Legge, J.D. (ed.) Cassell Australia (n.d.)

Mason, Philip, *The Men Who Ruled India*, Jonathan Cape Ltd., London, 1985.

Macfie, J.M., *Myths and Legends of India. An Introduction to the Study of Hinduism*, Rupa & Co., Calcutta, 1996.

McWilliam, Gwen., *Hawthorn Peppercorns*, Brian Atkins, Melbourne, 1978.

Murphy, James, *Liverpool VCs*, Pen & Sword Military, Barnsley, South Yorkshire, 2008.

O'Sullivan, John, *Mounted Police in N.S.W. A history of heroism and duty since 1821*, Rigby, Sydney, 1979.

O'Sullivan, Patrick (ed.) *The Irish World Wide, History, Heritage, Identity, Vol. 6 The Meaning of the Famine.* Leicester University Press, London, 1997.

Paget, Mrs. Leopold, *Camp and Cantonment. A Journal of Life in India & etc.*, Longman, Green, Longman, Roberts & Green, London, 1865.

Peel, V., Zion, D., Yule, J., *A History of Hawthorn*, Melbourne University Press, 1993.

Robson, Brian, (ed.) *Sir Hugh Rose and the Central India Campaign 1858*, Sutton Publishing Ltd., Gloucestershire, 2000.

Room, A., (ed.) *Brewer's Dictionary of Phrase and Fable*, Cassell, London, 1999.

Small, Hugh., *The Crimean War. Queen Victoria's War with the Russian Tsars, Tempus Publishing, reprinted by Knowledge Leak, London , 2014.*

Stanley, Peter, *White Mutiny. British Military Culture in India 1825 — 1875*, C. Hurst & Co. (Publishers) Ltd., London, 1998.

Streets, Heather, *Martial races. The military, race and masculinity in British imperial culture, 1857-1914*, Manchester University Press,

Manchester, 2004.

Sutton, Jean, *Lords of the East. The East India Company and its Ships,* Conway Maritime Press Ltd., London, 1981.

Sylvester, John H., *Recollections of the Campaign in Malwa and Central India under Major General Sir Hugh Rose etc.,* Smith, Taylor & Co., Bombay, 1860.

Titmarsh, M.A., (William Makepeace Thackeray) *The Irish Sketchbook 1842,* Chapman and Hall, London, 1857.

Wilcox, Craig, *Red Coat Dreaming. How colonial Australia embraced the British Army,* Cambridge University Press, Port Melbourne, 2009.

Wilkes, G.A., (ed.) *The Colonial Poets,* Angus and Robertson, Sydney, 1974. Originally published in, *Leaves from Australian Forests,* George Robertson, Melbourne, 1869.

Woodham-Smith, Cecil, *The Great Hunger. Ireland 1845-1849, Penguin Books, London, 1962.*

Yule, Henry & Burnell, A.C., *Hobson-Jobson. The Anglo-Indian Dictionary,* Wordsworth Editions Ltd., Hertfordshire, 1996 (First published 1886)

NEWSPAPERS & JOURNALS

Age (The), Melbourne

Aldershot Military Gazette.

Argus (The), Melbourne.

Armidale Express and New England General Advertiser (The)

Bell's Life in Victoria.

Bendigo Advertiser.

Birmingham Daily Post.

City of Dublin & Hibernian Provincial Directory, Pigot & Co, Dublin, 1824.

BIBLIOGRAPHY

Bury and Norwich Post (The)

Documents on Police in New South Wales 1789-1879, Hammond, Richard (ed.) n.d. NSW Police Department publication, c. 1979.

Elgin Courier.

Empire (The),Sydney.

Exeter and Plymouth Gazette.

Fitzroy City Press.

Glasgow Herald.

Glasgow Sentinel.

Imperial Gazetteer of India (The), Clarendon Press, Oxford, 1908.

Leeds Intelligencer.

Leicestershire Mercury (The)

Liverpool Mail.

London Gazette (The)

Maitland Mercury and Hunter River General Advertiser (The)

Marlborough Express. New Zealand.

New South Wales Government Gazette.

New South Wales Police Gazette.

Otago Witness, New Zealand.

South Bourke Standard

Standing Orders of the East India Company's Depot, Warley, 1844.

Star (The), Ballarat.

Sydney Morning Herald (The).

Thom's Irish Almanac and Official Directory, etc., for the year 1852, Alexander Thom, London, 1852.

Topographical Dictionary of Ireland etc.(A), Lewis, S., London, 1837.

Victoria Government Gazette, 1 December, 1859.

Wagga Wagga Community Heritage Study, Vol 2., Leah, Samantha, Wagga Wagga City Council, 2013.

Wagga Wagga Express (The)

Windsor and Richmond Gazette.

Yass Courier.

INTERNET REFERENCES

Internet references may be located in the endnotes to each chapter.

Australian newspaper references from www.trove.nla.gov.au/newspaper

British newspaper references from www.britishnewspaperarchive.co.uk

ANNEXURE A

———

Letter from James Flude (Few) to his parents in 1858 describing the Battle of Betwa and the taking of Jhansi.

'Camp Jhansi 24th June. We marched into Jhansi on the 21st March. All that day and the next, was spent by the General in reconnoitering and taking up positions; nothing extraordinary occurring except that the cavalry cut up a party of the enemy, about 50 in number, carrying in provisions and ammunition. On the 23rd, our guns began to play upon the city in fine style. Our regiment being pushed out within 300 yards of the wall to cover the guns and to cut off any that should be so daring as to show themselves. Up to the 30th we still kept the same position, our General received news that a large force was coming to assist the rebels, and to cut off our rear. On the 30th, the General took every available man, leaving only the investing party behind, and marched out 9 miles to meet them, but finding them taking up too strong a position on the banks of the river Betwa, made a feint retreat, so as to draw them across. We bivouacked all night on the plain, returning next morning to camp. The same evening we marched out again, and again made a retreat. This time the fish took the bait, and at daybreak, we found them drawn out in fine order on a nice level plain. This was what we wanted, we went into them in fine style. The enemy now found out their mistake. They forgot it was all fools day. They fought desperately. The 14th Dragoons charged the guns twice, and were driven back , but the third time they captured six of them; which struck such a terror into them that they all turned and fled, leaving almost 2000 dead, 19 guns, 4 elephants, 9 camels, a great many bullocks, and a great amount of treasure. During the fight the people of the city tried to come out and attack us, but were driven back with great slaughter. On the 2nd of April, a breach was made in the city wall, and at daybreak of the 3rd, we stormed the place in four different places. The first brigade went over the breach, consequently they lost very few men. The second brigade were told off to escalade the walls in three places. We had to advance under a murderous fire, and when we got to the wall we were

saluted with a shower of stones. Rockets, powder-bags, and great pieces of timber were thrown over the walls upon us, but in spite of all obstacles we placed the ladders, but oh horror! as we were rushing up, the ladders broke! and down came the men, leaving two poor fellows on the top. It is needless to say they were cut to pieces. We retired and got a fresh supply of ladders and we were over the walls in no time. We met with great resistance till we took the Queen's Palace, which was done in about three hours. All that day and the next we were fighting from house to house, not a house but there were 10 to 20 killed. On the night of the 4th the Queen escaped in the disguise of a cavalry man, and it is thought she has gone to Calpee. On the 5th the fort was taken, with very little resistance, and the British flag was hoisted by an officer of our regiment whilst the air was rent with cheers. It is estimated that during the three days we were taking the city the enemy lost 4000, and at the battle of Betwa 2000, making in all 6000 since we came into Jhansi. The loss on our side is about 350 killed and wounded. Our regiment has had 25 killed and 45 wounded. I am sorry to say our men are dying fast of sickness, the heat is terrible being 120 degrees in the shade. On the 27th the force marched for Calpee leaving the right wing of our regiment, the 24th regiment of natives and some cavalry to garrison Jhansi with our Colonel in command the whole. The forces have had four fights since they marched for Calpee, but I cannot give you any particulars, except that Calpee is taken by the force with tremendous loss. We expect they will come back soon, and then we all think the mutiny will soon end, for Calpee is their last stronghold. I can assure you we shall not be sorry for it, for we have had great knocking about, having marched close upon 3000 miles. You will be glad to hear that I am promoted to full Corporal for rescuing the body of Lieutenant Dicks from the city walls while under a heavy fire.'

ANNEXURE B

———

Account provided by John Henry Sylvester, after the confrontation with Monohur Singh,

'Major Gall now placed a couple of guns and two howitzers in position, outside a ditch and second line of works which surrounded the fort. Lieutenant Armstrong, with two companied of his corps, the 3rd Europeans, took advantage of a sort of guard house near the ditch, and from thence advanced to the gateway of the fort, and without difficulty forced open two doors guarding the entrance; but the enemy were behind the third, and stopped all further progress until Lieutenant Bonus, of the Engineers, repaired to the village, and found an old pair of bellows, which he charged with sixty pounds of gunpowder and hung on the door, and fired it. This opened the way for the stormers, and in they went, the 3rd Europeans led by Donne and Newport, and the 25th men by Rose, while Fenwick made a false attack on the south side. It was a bloody hand-to-hand fight. Fifty seven mutineers were killed in the gateway, and thirty three in the interior, making a total of ninety. One hundred and fifty small arms were taken, and one brass gun, together with drums, bugles and plates bearing the number of the 12th Bengal Infantry. It was a most successful affair, attended with the small loss of one killed and twelve wounded: of these Lieutenants Donne and Newport of the 3rd Europeans.'

ANNEXURE C

'Major R. H. Gall, Commanding Field Force Detachment, to the Chief of the Staff, Central India Field Force.
SIR, Camp, Poorh,
5 May 1858

I HAVE the honor to report, for the information of the Major-General, commanding Central India Field Force, that, in pursuance of his instructions, I marched with the force, as per margin ‡, at 2 A.M. on the 2nd instant, upon the fort of Loharee, about nine miles distant from, and to the north-west of, Poorh.

My cavalry rapidly pushed forward, had completed the investment of the place soon after daybreak, and my main body was halted on the plain to the east of the fort, and within cannon-shot of it, at half past 6 o'clock.

As I passed Girsa, I sent a party of the 3rd Regiment Hyderabad Cavalry, under a Duffedar, to Khullea, a fort reported to be occupied by the enemy, and to my right, as I advanced, with orders to watch any hostile movement that might be made from that quarter.

When the force halted, I rode, accompanied by Captain Baigill [Baigrie?], Deputy Assistant Quartermaster-General, Central India Field Force, and Guneshee Lall, a native official in the service of the Governor-General's agent for Central India, through the village of Loharee, up to the walls of the fort, and sent Guneshee Lall to the main gateway with directions to summon the killedar of the place to surrender at discretion. A man soon after made his appearance, whom I supposed to be the killedar, but he was not, though he did by my orders summon the garrison to surrender; they paid no attention to him.

Discovering, however, that Munshur Singh was himself in the fort, I sent Guneshee Lall to summon him.

Munshur Singh delayed obeying my summons for a long time, but at last he came out with a small retinue and gave up his sword, and his retinue laid down their arms.

To Munshur Singh I returned his sword at his own urgent request; at

212

the same time I called upon him to order out his garrison and direct them to lay down their arms. To the best of my belief he endeavoured to induce them to do so, but they refused. Munshur Singh clearly had no control over them whatever.

All my own efforts failing to induce the garrison to give themselves up, I proceeded to make my disposition for attack, my skirmishers advancing through the village until they had reached some low mud enclosures, beyond which was an open space between it and the fort, about 150 yards in extent. I placed two guns on the Khullea road, and a howitzer and one gun opposite a guard-house that stands outside of, and on the eastern side of, the fort.

The fort and village of Loharee are situated in an extensive level plain; the village being separated from the fort by the clear space of ground above alluded to.

The little fort itself is square, and built of mud and sun-burnt bricks. The square is flanked by round towers at the corners; it has a ditch and a second line of works outside the ditch, and the length of the interior side is about 100 yards.

A company of the 3rd Europeans crossed the open space between the village and fort without opposition, and established themselves in the guard-house close to the ditch.

Two of the fort gates were opened for us by Lieutenant Armstrong, commanding the left wing of the Europeans. They were undefended, the garrison having retired within a third which was closed, the enemy taking post behind it.

The last of several summonses, accompanied by a threat that, if not obeyed, I would destroy the fort and the garrison too, having failed to cause a single man to come out and lay down his arms, I directed Captain Field, Royal Artillery, to open fire with two 9-pounders and a 24-pounder howitzer on a building at the summit, whence the men of the 3rd Bombay Europeans might have been seriously annoyed by the sepoys, who were collecting there.

Captain Field continued firing on various parts of the work, wherever the enemy showed themselves in any numbers; and the enemy replied to my fire with matchlocks, and with a 9-pounder brass gun, that fired grape and round shot alternately upon the dragoons in the plain and all who came near a well, commanded by the bastion on which it stood.

Lieutenant Bonus of the Bombay Engineers, after a very close reconnaissance, had reported to me the extreme difficulty of taking the place by escalade. Nothing then remained, in my opinion, but to blow open the third gate with a bag of gunpowder, and carry the fort by storm. By good luck a gunsmith's shop had been discovered in the village, and in it an old pair of forge. Lieutenant Bonus borrowing fifty pounds of powder from the artillery, soon converted this into a very efficient powder-bag.

The distribution for the assault was as follows.

Twenty five files of the 3rd Europeans, under Lieutenants Armstrong and Dunn and Ensign Newport, were told off as a storming party; an equal number of the 25th Bombay Native Infantry under Lieutenant Rose of that regiment, was formed in support.

The storming party and support occupied the gateways that were already in our possession; twenty five files of the Bombay Europeans and 50 files of the 25th were in reserve behind the guard-house.

The remainder of both detachments were so disposed as to afford support to the guns, and also to meet any attempt at escape from the fort into the village.

A false attack with three scaling ladders, under the superintendence of Lieutenant Fenwick, drew off the attention of a few of the garrison for a short time to the south side, and was not without its use.

When the powder-bag was filled, Lieutenant Bonus, under the cover of a sharp fire from the 3rd Europeans, placed it in front of the closed gate — a strong wooden one with iron spikes, — the small piece of port-fire was lighted, and the firing party withdrew. After about a minute and a half the explosion took place. The gate was demolished, and the stormers under Lieutenants Armstrong and Donne and Ensign Newport, whom I accompanied, rushed in through the smoke, and almost immediately met the enemy face to face at a fourth gateway at right angles to the third, and from which a very narrow curved passage with a wall of seven feet in height on either side led to where the garrison was assembled, and whence they rushed, getting down sword in hand and firing matchlocks.

A desperate combat commenced, and as the stormers, so well led, advanced, they were assailed by a shower of stones and brickbats from above, as well as by men who cut, and stabbed, and shot at them from the walls on either side as they went by; the enemy were giving way when a cloth full of loose powder, and burning, was dropped from above into the midst of the crowded stormers who, thrown into some confusion, fell back to avoid the explosion, which not taking place immediately, was harmless; the enemy following their advantage, came close up to the bayonets of the Europeans and dealt sword-cuts at them, but were repulsed.

A third time Lieutenant Donne and Ensign Newport led on their men with daring valour into the very midst of the enemy, from whom, I regret to say , these noble young men received some very severe wounds whilst fighting hand to hand, yet, wounded as they were, they beat off their assailants, and their retreat was protected by the bayonets of their men. Lieutenant Armstrong could give them no assistance, as he had just been knocked down by a blow on the head from a brickbat, which stunned him for a time. Matters were becoming serious, as the enemy pressed boldly down to the fourth gateway, in which, however, they were not permitted to gain a footing.

Lieutenant Rose now came opportunely to the front, and the fight was continued in the narrow lane, with a final shout and charge, the Europeans with some of the 25th Native Infantry, fairly broke and drove their foe before them to our right, along what I can only describe as an uncovered way passing round the walls of the fort, but, at less than fifty yards beyond the first corner, turned the fugitives, rallied behind two trees, and firing off their matchlocks actually advanced again; beneath the trees a bloody melée took place, and in this spot ten of the garrison were cut, or shot down; the regiment, now reduced to five and twenty, fled.

Some vainly sought refuge in a mud guard-house below the south wall, some in the interior of the place itself; they were followed up and slain.

A last stand was made by a few desperate men to the immediate left of the gateway near which the conflict had commenced, and here the last man of the garrison of Loharee fell.

Fifty seven bodies were counted by an officer within the gate-way of the fort.

Previous to forming the columns of the assault, I had made over the command of the cavalry on the plain to Captain Thompson, 14th Dragoons; he reports that several of the enemy, being observed letting themselves down from the bastion at the north-west angle of the fort, he moved forward a division of his Dragoons, intercepted and cut them down.

All who endeavoured to escape on the south side into the village were met and shot by a company of the 25th under Lieutenant Fenwick.

I can safely assert that none of the garrison (which must have numbered, including Munsheet Singh and his retinue, at least ninety men) escaped.

During the assault Captain Blyth, of the 14th Dragoons, rode within a very short distance of Khuleea and observed a great many men assembling on the bastions of that fort, and some in the "topes" that surround it, but seeing our cavalry drawn upon the plain between them and Loharee, they did not attempt to make a forward movement.

I would here observe that many indications of the presence of the mutineers sepoys amongst the garrison met my eye; for instance, an European drum and bugle were found in the fort; also many brass cap plates, belonging to the 12th Regiment Bengal Native Infantry, which garrisoned Jhansie at the period of the mutiny there, and several red dooties with yellow facings. Many of the slain had the appearance of sepoys of the Bengal army, — tall, broad shouldered, narrow waisted men.

In conclusion, I trust I may be permitted to bring to the notice of the Major-General the gallantry and steadiness displayed by the officers and men of all arms composing the field force, which I had the honor and the pleasure of commanding on this occasion. I feel much indebted to Captain Little, commanding the left wing of the 25th Bombay Native Infantry, for the manner in which he brought up a support consisting of 25 files of his detachment which followed close upon the heels of the storming party, when the place was carried, and subsequently aided them in several combats with the remnant of the garrison before it was completely destroyed. Captain Field, commanding the battery, I have to thank for rendering untenable by his fire the strongest position the enemy could have occupied to annoy me, and Captain Thompson, 14th Light Dragoons, for his dispositions outside the fort during the assault, and for the vigilance with which he intercepted the fugitives.

Captain Baigrie, Deputy-Assistant Quartermaster-General deserves my best acknowledgements for making himself generally useful to me throughout the day.

I beg also to thank Assistant-Surgeon O'Brien attached to the 3rd Europeans, and Assistant-Surgeon Skipton 78th Highlanders, attached to the 14th Light Dragoons for their prompt attention to the wounded; but the following officers and men I beg especially to recommend to the protection of the Major-General, as having under my own eyes greatly distinguished themselves in the conflict at the gates — one of unusual severity :-

Lieutenant Armstrong, 3rd Bombay Europeans, who commanded the storming party.

Lieutenant Donne, 3rd Bombay Europeans;

Ensign Newport of the same regiment; who both fell severely wounded.

Lieutenant Rose, of the 25th Bombay Native Infantry, who joined me from the rear, and when the two former officers were struck down ably supplied their place.

Also:-

Regimental No. 1031#, Private Frederick Whirlpool*, No. 5 Company, 3rd Bombay Europeans.

Regimental No. 223, Private Robert Howard, No. 8 Company, 3rd Bombay Europeans.

Regimental No. 153, Private Patrick Fitzgerald, 3rd Bombay Europeans.

Private Bhola Gudurya, 9th Company, 25th Regiment Bombay Native Infantry.

The readiness of resources evinced by Lieutenant Bonus will I feel be appreciated by the Major-General. I can further bear witness to the coolness with which, under fire, Lieutenant Bonus adjusted the powder-bag to the gate, and enabled us to effect an entrance into the fort.

I subjoin a list of casualties in the F. Detachment under command.

On the wall of the fort a brass 9-pounder gun was captured and brought into camp. I had the carriage, which was perfectly new, destroyed.

Upwards of 150 stand of arms were taken from the enemy — swords, matchlocks, and spears, which I caused to be broken up. One of the garrison used a double-barrelled gun.

I have, &c

R. H. GALL, Major,

Commanding Field Force Detachment'

* This gallant man fell covered with wounds at the final charge, in which he was one of the very foremost.

‡ 1 squadron 14th Light Dragoons, 120; Hyderabad Cavalry, 100; 4 guns Royal Artillery, under Captain Field; left wing 3rd Europeans; left

wing 25th Bombay Native Infantry; 20 Sappers, Bombay.

\# The Regimental number shown belonged to Private Charles White who followed Whirlpool alphabetically on the muster list. It seems it was incorrectly transcribed. His number remained 2200.

ACKNOWLEDGEMENTS

Writers, like visual artists, often work in solitude, save for the thing they seek to create, which becomes all consuming. There comes a time however, when the opinion of others is garnered to gain a perspective that might be clouded by isolation. The input of others, skilled or expert in their field, is sought to make the path easier. I have been blessed with many willing contributors, friends and professionals, whose candid advice and encouragement must be acknowledged.

Not a stone throw from Frederick Whirlpool's resting place, the indomitable Diana Lee-Gobbitt, has been there from the beginning, encouraging, proofreading, advising, as only a fine artist experienced in the ups and downs of a creative life, can do. For her assistance I am eternally grateful. Similarly, a friend since childhood, Marion Anderson of Bellingen, took my calls, offered advice and read my drafts, when time was very precious to her. Her encouragement has been invaluable. My cousin, Norman Leek, another indomitable soul who has not only stayed the course, reading my drafts and offering advice, but acted as mentor and motivator. It seems to be a role made for him as I am not the first writer he has successfully encouraged. Dr John Hoskin, Psychiatrist, of Orange shared his wealth of knowledge of the alcohol addicted, providing me with some insight into the mind of those who abuse alcohol. Peter Bessant of Bathurst, who pored over the drafts, offering me commas where there were none and taking them from where they shouldn't be. I remember this puzzling process more clearly than his other suggestions, which were insightful and, of course, correct. And all this while he laboured over his own work.

Mike Trenchard of The Trenchard Partnerships, UK, a professional researcher who is familiar with the labyrinthine East India Company Records held by the British Library, saved me the many days I would have wasted searching in a fog of ignorance. The fruits of his labour were a joy to behold. Mary McConnon of MC Research (Genealogy and History), of Dundalk, uncovered the wealth of information on the James family. Her efficient and friendly assistance was a gift that kept giving.

Lucille Andel B.A (Hons) History, researcher of Victoria, unearthed Frederick Whirlpool's handwritten application to join the Victoria Police and Chief Commissioner Standish's memo on Whirlpool's suitability as a police force candidate, held by the Victoria Public Records Office.

The very generous David Humphries, friend and sometimes neighbour, gave many hours to a complete edit of the manuscript. He honed the text as only a trained and experienced journalist could. Assisted by the Honourable Diane Beamer, they returned to their home and bunkered down for months combing through the work in fine detail.

Robin James of California, great grand-daughter of Samuel James of Pennsylvania provided me with the interesting accounts of Stanley Livingstone James, snr, nephew of Humphrey James and of her father Stanley Livingstone 'Jimmy' James, jnr, and their distinguished military careers.

The staff of New South Wales State Archives and Records were unflagging in their support and professional assistance. Special mention of Janette Pelosi is needed. Her enthusiasm, personal interest and desire to help, coupled with her professional expertise at the records office, made my work so much easier.

Leanne Diessel, Research Officer, Wagga Wagga & district Family History Society Inc., and Jenny Mountford, Deputy Registrar of the Wagga Wagga Local Court for their friendly, and encouraging assistance. So too, members of the Hawthorn Historical Society Inc.

The helpful staff at the Australian War Memorial Museum, Canberra, who provided me access to the Croll manuscript, which proved an invaluable aid. And of course, to the late Denys Croll whose early efforts, untiring research and purchase of the Whirlpool Victoria Cross, made my efforts possible.

To my friends who grinned and bore my imposed discourse on the progress of the work and my discoveries. To my wife who has lived with the work for six years and has no need to read it, I offer my thanks and appreciation for standing firm, where a lesser person would be excused for running, screaming from the room. My sincere thanks are due also to Mr. Cyril Drury, Headmaster of the Dundalk Grammar School 2005 - 2016, who led me to former Chairperson of the Dundalk Grammar School Board of Governors, Dr. Laurence Swan who has assisted this endeavour greatly. His copy of Dr. Thomas Hunter's autobiography was invaluable in providing a window into the boy, Humphrey James and his early development. He is justly proud of the Dundalk Grammar School in its current form as a leading, innovative, interdenominational modern seat of learning in the Republic of Ireland.

GLOSSARY

---

abatis - A collection of felled trees with the smaller branches removed and laid side by side with the branch ends towards assailants, forming an obstruction to their progress.

bagh - Pers. large garden or orchard.

bakhshi / bakshi - Pers. *'bakhshi', paymaster of Muslim armies.*

bat - soldier's argot or slang.

batta - an extra allowance made to officer, soldiers, or other public servants, when in the field.

bodger - from 'tree bodger', crafters of green timber to make chair parts.

bugeechas / bagicha - garden or orchard. See *bagh*.

bund - any artificial embankment, dam, dyke or causeway.

Bundeelahs / bundela - lawless, marauding tribesmen.

charpoy - bed. From the Persian chihār-pāī, meaning, four feet.

compearance - Scots law. To present one's self in a court in person, or by counsel.

cotwal - A police officer; superintendent of police; native town magistrate.

Deccan - the South. The Southern part of India, the Peninsula, and especially the Tableland between the Eastern and Western Ghauts.

dhooli / doolie - a covered stretcher or litter carried by two or more bearers. A palanquin or covered conveyance carried by poles.

dragoon - a cavalry soldier.

Drum-head court martial - - a court martial called suddenly in the field.

duffadar - Hind. (from Arabo-Pers.) *daf'adar,* a non-commissioned officer corresponding in rank to a corporal or sergeant in Indian irregular cavalry.

Durbar - *Pers.* 'darbar'. A Court or Levee , also the Executive Government of a Native State *escalade* - (F. from L. *scala*, a ladder) A furious attack made by troops on a fortified place, in which ladders are used to pass a ditch or mount a rampart. To scale.

firinghee - This term for a European is very old in Asia. Applied especially in the south to Indian born Portugese, or when used more generally, for European, applies something of hostility or disparagement.

forlorn hope - (D. *verloren hoop* - 'lost troop') (F. equivalent enfants perdus - 'lost children'. Refers to a body of men chosen for some desperate task attended with some uncommon peril.

Gehenna - A term used in the New Testament as typical of the place of future punishment and translated hell, hell-fire.

gharry / garry - Hind. *gari*, a cart or carriage.

ghat / ghaut - passes over the range of mountains. Sometimes used for mountain ranges.

ghurree / gurry - a little fort. Hind. *garhi*. Also *gurr*, i.e. *garh*, 'a fort'.

hateh / haat - Hin. *haat* market, stall, shop.

infernal machine - a machine or apparatus of an explosive nature, contrived for the purpose os assassination or other mischief.

investment - the act of besieging by an armed force.

Jain - The non-Brahmanical sect, believed to be represent the earliest heretics of Buddhism, chiefly found in the Bombay Presidency.

juhar - Rajput practice of suicide by women and children by immolation, or their murder by husbands and fathers before entering a forlorn battle, to prevent them falling into the hands of the enemy.

killadar - The commandant of a fort, castle or garrison.

khaki / khakee / kharki / kharkee - Hind. *khaki* for dusty or dust coloured. Pers. *khak*, earth or dust.

lotah / lota - Hind. *lota* The small spheroidal brass pot Hindus use for drinking and sometimes for cooking.

mamelon - A small hill or mound with a rounded top (F. a nipple; L. mamma, a breast.)

matchlock - a musket fired by the engagement of a slow match to the firing pan, which ignited the priming powder to discharge the weapon. It obviated the need to ignite the charge with a hand held match, leaving both hands free to hold and aim the weapon..

Memsahib - A hybrid term used as a respectful designation for a married European lady. From 'ma'am' and 'sahib.'

Nawab / Nabob / Naib - Port. *'Nabado'*, and Fr. *'Nabab'* Hin. *'Nœwab'* which is the Ar. pl. of sing. *'Nayab* - a deputy, a delegate of the supreme chief, e.g. the Nawab of....

ordnance - same as ordinance. Fr. *ordounance*, arrangement, equipment, originally referring to guns of a particular size or equipment. Cannon or great guns, mortars and howitzers collectively; artillery.

pandal - Hind. A temporary, open sided structure for meetings etc.

Parsee - A descendent of emigrants of Persian stock, who left their native country, and retaining their Zoroastrian religion, settled in India to avoid Mahommedan persecution, is the old form of the word for Persian, viz, *Parsi*. which Arabic influences have in more modern times converted into *Farsi*.

Pathan - generic term applied to the Muslim tribes of Afghanistan and the North-West Frontier. A person of Afghan race settled in Hindustan; an Afghan.

picket / piquet - a detachment of troops in a camp kept fully equipped to protect the camp from surprise.

port-fire - a strong paper or cloth case, firmly packed with a composition of nitre, (saltpetre) sulphur and mealed powder, used as a match for igniting mines, guns, etc.

puggaree / puggry / puggerie - From Hindi *'pagri'* meaning 'a turban'. Used colloquially for a scarf of cotton or silk wound round a hat in turban form, to protect the head from the sun.

Raj - Hindu *'rule'*. British rule in India.

Rani / Ranee - A Hindu Queen, fem. of *raja*.

Sadr / Sudder - The chief station of a district.

Sahib - A respectful title for a European man. Used as a suffix to the name or office of the bearer.

sapper /sap - Fr. saper; L.L. sapa, a mattock. to cause to fall or render unstable by digging. To proceed by secretly undermining. A ditch or trench by which approach is made to a fortress or besieged place within range of fire. Sapper, one who saps, a soldier of an engineer corps, or who is trained in fortification or siege works.

sepoy - A native soldier. Pers. *'sipahi'*, soldier/army.

shako - a military cap resembling a truncated cone with a peak at the front.

shako plate - a cap badge.

simoon - a hot, dusty wind - suffocating, especially in Arabia and India. From Ar. *Semum*, from *samm* - to poison.

sowar - Pers. *'sawdr'*, 'a horseman' A native cavalry soldier.

squattocracy - the long established and wealthy landowners who regard themselves as an aristocracy with political and social influence.

stink-pot - a pyrotechnical preparation of pitch, rosin, nitre, gunpowder, colophony,(black resin or turpentine boiled in water and dried), assafœtida (sap from a large Central Asian plant) and other offensive and suffocating ingredients in earthen jars.

talwar / tulwaur - Hind. *talwar* and *tarwar*, a sabre.

thakur / thakore - a term of respect applied usually to a feudal landlord or petty chieftan.

twopenny standup or **tuppenny standup** - furtive sexual intercourse, whilst standing. Still used today in the coarse expression, 'Couldn't give a tuppenny fuck,' meaning 'couldn't care less.'

twopenny hangover - an arrangement where for two pence, customers would be seated leaning over a rope whilst they slept. In the morning the 'valet' would release the rope thereby letting the sleepers fall, in a non too gentle hint that it was time to check out.

Walayati / Vilyati / Valaitis - a mercenary soldier of Pathan, Afghan, Baluchi or Arab descent, common in Central India in 1858.

INDEX

About the Author

Alan Leek left school at 15 and became a wool store rouseabout. He joined the NSW Police Cadet Corps two years later and is a 34 year veteran of the police. He served as a detective, before taking up command positions, including the tough Cabramatta patrol, then the centre of heroin trafficking in Australia and the site of Australia's first political assassination. He retired with the rank of superintendent. He holds an Associate Diploma in Justice Administration (Distinction); Post Graduate Diploma in Police Management and is a graduate of the FBI National Academy, USA.

He also holds the prestigious Peter Mitchell Award for outstanding performance of police duty, after leading a murder investigation. Co-founder and director of an exhibiting fine art gallery between 1983 – 2012, gave vent to his interest in art, art history and history generally.

www.alanleek.com.au